THE
RETURN
OF
GREAT POWERS

ALSO BY JIM SCIUTTO

The Madman Theory

The Shadow War

Against Us

THE
RETURN
OF
GREAT POWERS

———

RUSSIA, CHINA, AND
THE NEXT WORLD WAR

———

JIM SCIUTTO

DUTTON

DUTTON

An imprint of Penguin Random House LLC

penguinrandomhouse.com

LIBRARY OF CONGRESS CATALOGING-IN-PUBLICATION DATA

Names: Sciutto, Jim, author.
Title: The return of great powers : Russia, China, and the next
world war / Jim Sciutto.
Description: New York : Dutton, [2024] | Includes index.
Identifiers: LCCN 2023050387 (print) | LCCN 2023050388 (ebook) |
ISBN 9780593474136 (hardcover) | ISBN 9780593474150 (ebook)
Subjects: LCSH: Russia (Federation)—Foreign relations—Western countries. |
Russia (Federation)—Foreign relations—China. |
Western countries—Foreign relations—Russia (Federation). |
Western countries—Foreign relations—China. | Russia (Federation)—Foreign
relations—21st century. | Western countries—Foreign relations—21st century. |
China—Foreign relations—21st century.
Classification: LCC DK510.764 .S35 2024 (print) |
LCC DK510.764 (ebook) | DDC 327.47—dc23/eng/20231109
LC record available at https://lccn.loc.gov/2023050387
LC ebook record available at https://lccn.loc.gov/2023050388

Printed in the United States of America
1st Printing

To Tristan, Caden, and Sinclair,

who bring their mom and dad

more joy and inspiration

than they know every day

CONTENTS

Preface   xi

PART ONE

PROLOGUE: The Gathering Storm   3

CHAPTER ONE: Great Power Warfare   21

CHAPTER TWO: Dividing Lines   55

PART TWO

CHAPTER THREE: Flashpoint Baltic Sea   99

CHAPTER FOUR: Russia's Next Targets   125

CHAPTER FIVE: Target Taiwan   147

CHAPTER SIX: Taiwan's Existential Questions   169

PART THREE

CHAPTER SEVEN: "No Longer Unthinkable"   197

CHAPTER EIGHT: A Multifront War   225

CONTENTS

CHAPTER NINE: Trump Wild Card   256

CHAPTER TEN: Paths to Peace   276

EPILOGUE: The Long War   316

Acknowledgments   325

Notes   329

Index   339

PREFACE

The Return of Great Powers documents the end of a world order built up over decades, dealt a deathblow by the largest war in Europe since World War II. This reversal represents strategic shifts by Russia, the United States, and now China—with each side reappraising the others' objectives and remaking their own.

The new order of three great powers is lengthening and hardening dividing lines among the powers while breaking diplomatic and economic ties among them. It is sparking military expansions while reducing military-to-military communication. It is inflating nuclear arsenals and new categories of weapons while dissolving the treaties that regulate such weapons. It is drawing in middle powers and regional interests in unexpected, inconsistent ways. The return of great powers has upended the post–Cold War global order and replaced it with a new, less stable one.

As we shared coffee in his office at CIA headquarters in Langley, Virginia, CIA Director Bill Burns lamented the world's entry into a new and tenuous geopolitical reality. I had visited this same office—wood-paneled, with panoramic windows overlooking northern Virginia—and sat on the same couch with his predecessors Gina

Haspel and Mike Pompeo. In those visits, before war had engulfed Europe, terrorism, election interference, and counterinsurgency in Iraq and Afghanistan were often at the top of the agenda. Now, however, the chief of the world's largest intelligence agency was contemplating the challenges and perils of a growing great power conflict—as he searched for ways that the great powers can manage the conflict to avoid the worst outcomes, including great power war.

Burns lamented the diminution of guardrails and diplomatic and military channels that had been developed during the last Cold War. Following the Cuban Missile Crisis, when the US and Soviet Union very nearly descended into nuclear war, the great powers built a system of hotlines, treaties, and multilateral organizations precisely to avoid another close call. Unfortunately, these guardrails did not survive the interim. An avid basketball player, including during his studies at Oxford, Burns told me that today "we're playing without a net."

Burns carries the demeanor of a diplomat more than that of a spook. And, in fact, he spent most of his career in the State Department as ambassador to Jordan and later Russia, before rising to deputy secretary of state. During my service in the State Department in Beijing, I watched him deftly navigate some of the most difficult encounters with senior Chinese officials. Burns is a firm yet calm communicator of US interests, and as we discussed the return of great powers, he took care to highlight the deep importance of communication in times of potential conflict.

"Having those kinds of channels, especially military to military, are not a favor to us or to China. It's in both of our interests," Burns told me. "That, I think, doesn't really exist today, and that's what people need to be very mindful of."

I pressed him on what potential flashpoints among the great powers worried him most. The classic question for a senior intelligence official is, of course, "What keeps you up at night?" In Burns's view, the greatest risk in this new era of great power competition is not necessarily a deliberate decision to go to war, but a small encounter among the great powers spiraling into something far bigger.

"Any day you could have two military aircraft flying too close. Somebody clips another one. You could be off to the races, especially without a reliable mechanism to communicate with one another," Burns said. "So that's why I'm a huge believer in intelligence channels. If you're not talking to them, it's very hard to be able to manage crises, which inevitably are going to come up."

"Off to the races"—a consistent fear I heard from senior leaders I interviewed is of *momentum* toward conflict.

Even where there is disagreement on the danger of potential broader conflict, there is unanimity on this: the relative peace of the last thirty years is past. It is a sad moment for those—myself included—who celebrated the end of the last Cold War.

"My generation, we grew up during the Cold War," NATO Secretary General Jens Stoltenberg told me. "Then we saw the end of the Cold War. We saw the Berlin Wall come down. We saw democracy, freedom spreading throughout Europe. We saw all these former Warsaw Pact countries joining NATO and become countries like us, with democratic institutions, with freedom. . . . That was, of course, extremely encouraging. And for many years we thought it just would continue."

For the US and its allies, this is a 1939 moment. The US still celebrates standing up to an expansionist Nazi Germany and Imperial Japan. After World War II, the world descended into a new Cold War between the US and an expansionist USSR. When the Soviet Union collapsed, many celebrated the "end of history." Now, Russia intends to bring the international order down, and China to create an entirely new one. The US has difficult decisions ahead in both spaces, and many others.

PREFACE

Ahead, I will take you to the many fronts of this emerging conflict—from Ukraine to the Baltic Sea to Estonia and Taiwan—and to new battlefields among the great powers in near space, cyberspace, and outer space, where we find both the potential flashpoints and the paths to peace.

PART ONE

PROLOGUE

THE GATHERING STORM

November 2021
The Pentagon

The mood among senior leadership in the Pentagon was apprehensive. It was early November 2021, and alarm bells were going off in eastern Europe to a degree that seasoned officers had not witnessed in decades. I called one of my most reliable military sources to check in, and like a doctor about to deliver a troubling medical diagnosis, he told me to sit down before he delivered his warning: pay attention to Russia and Ukraine.

In the next several minutes, he delivered an eye-opening assessment of a Russian plan to invade and take control of Ukraine: a plan to invade Europe's largest nation, unprovoked and with an enormous and devastating invasion force. He told me this was, in the view of senior Pentagon leadership, the "number one threat to the US right now," outdistancing in urgency even China and the Biden administration's stated desire to redirect the bulk of US military and diplomatic power to Asia.

Russia's plan, my source told me, was to assemble a force greater than one hundred thousand troops drawn from military districts across Russia. The Kremlin's goal was not to further establish control over the parts of Eastern Ukraine that Russian-backed separatists had already occupied, but to invade the entire country, destroy the Ukrainian military, and remove the Ukrainian government—that is, to absorb Ukraine into a new Russian empire. To do so, Moscow had developed both a military plan and a political plan involving operatives from the FSB (the successor intelligence service to the KGB) to remove and replace Ukraine's elected leaders from the presidency and the parliament down to local officials in every Ukrainian city and town. A lawmaker briefed on the intelligence described the Russian plans as a "blitzkrieg"-style attack—a "lightning war" of missiles and air strikes, followed quickly by a rapid ground assault. This was going to be a devastatingly fast assault, in the view of western intelligence, with Ukraine almost certain to be quickly overwhelmed.

I was intrigued but skeptical. Russia had already successfully invaded parts of Ukraine in 2014 with a far more subtle strategy, deploying Russian forces—the "little green men," as they would come to be known—to Crimea without firing a shot. Years later, Russia still controlled Crimea as well as large parts of Eastern Ukraine while facing a manageable collection of economic sanctions and maintaining an energy stranglehold over Europe. Why would Russian president Vladimir Putin want to start a hot war now and risk all that? No, my source said, "The Russians are absolutely ready to move." And soon: the US assessed that Russia would have preparations complete for a full invasion in mid-February, just a few months away.

The US was evaluating the threat with deep seriousness. To convey US concerns directly to Moscow, the White House turned to someone who knew Russia and Putin perhaps as well as anyone in the US government. Bill Burns, current CIA director and previous US ambassador to Russia, had met Putin numerous times in his long career as a diplomat. With US assessments growing increasingly urgent, President Joe Biden dispatched Burns to Moscow to confront

Putin with what the US was seeing and demand clarification of Russian intentions.

In Moscow, Burns met face-to-face with his counterpart, FSB director Alexander Bortnikov, and other senior Russian intelligence officials. An in-person meeting with Putin, however, was impossible. US intelligence agencies believed Putin was deathly afraid of not only potential infection with Covid-19 but also assassination. There was a grim reciprocity to his fears: it is the US government view that Putin himself had likely ordered the death by poisoning and other means of many of his own opponents. His personal paranoia was by now an essential part of the US intelligence community's profile of the Russian leader. So, on November 4, Burns met Putin by video conference—the Russian president's required format for meetings with any foreign leader.

Burns's message was direct: the US could see the Russian buildup. What was Putin's intention? The scale of the Russian invasion force was staggering. By early 2022, according to US intelligence assessments, Russia would have close to 75 percent of its conventional forces postured against Ukraine. This included some 120 of Russia's total estimated 160 battalion tactical groups, or BTGs—Russia's primary combat units, encompassing seven hundred to nine hundred personnel, each with infantry, armor, artillery, and intelligence-gathering capabilities—all deployed about forty miles from Ukraine. Thirty-five of fifty known air defense battalions, fifty of its eighty medium and heavy bombers, and some five hundred fighter and fighter-bomber aircraft were deployed against Ukraine too. Russia was moving the bulk of its entire conventional military force to Ukraine.

Putin's message was unwavering. The force was necessary to protect Russia. Ukraine and NATO were the real threats to peace.

Burns left Moscow even more convinced that the first large-scale land war since the 1990s was coming to Europe.

LOOMING WAR ON TWO FRONTS?

As the US measured up Russian preparations and planning for invading Ukraine, another threat loomed on the other side of the globe. US officials had become increasingly concerned about China's plans to take Taiwan by force. Just as Russia viewed Ukraine as part of Russia, China viewed Taiwan as a rightful part of China. "Reunification," as China referred to it, was a long-expressed ambition for Chinese president Xi Jinping. The nightmare scenario, in the view of the Pentagon, was that both Russia and China might decide to move at the same time. This was not just a nervous hunch. Intelligence assessments posited exactly this scenario: China taking advantage of Russia's "blitzkrieg" invasion of Ukraine with a blitz-like invasion of its own against Taiwan. The two-front assault would not necessarily have to be coordinated between Moscow and Beijing. It could simply be opportunistic, with Xi seeing an opportunity he had long been looking for to seize Taiwan while the world was preoccupied elsewhere.

This fear of massive simultaneous invasions was clearly making the rounds beyond the hallways of the Pentagon. Over the next several days, I spoke with multiple lawmakers who had been briefed on the latest intelligence on the Russian buildup around Ukraine. They shared the Pentagon's alarm. And they echoed its nightmare scenario: What if Russia and China—increasingly aligned in international affairs and each with a stated desire to regain territory lost by what they viewed as historical injustice—acted at the same time? How would the US and its allies effectively respond? *Could* they respond effectively?

I drafted an email to then president of CNN Jeff Zucker to lay out the situation as I understood it. My immediate goal was not to report the US intelligence assessment of Russia's invasion plan, but to warn

CNN to prepare for what would become—if the intelligence bore out—a monumental and dangerous news story for our times. Most of my colleagues, myself included, had been in news only after the collapse of the Soviet Union. We had done our work after the fall of the Berlin Wall, after the dissolution of the USSR and Warsaw Pact, and as many former Soviet republics gained independence and even joined NATO. The stories we had covered were particular to a post–Cold War world: regional wars, not global ones. There were severe global threats, from terrorism to North Korea's and Iran's nuclear programs, but these threats involved smaller states or non-state actors. The signs of Russia's growing aggressiveness had been there. Russia's occupation of parts of Georgia was nearly a decade and a half old. Crimea had been formally annexed by Russia since March 2014. But a hot war in Europe and the potential resurrection of a conflict between global, nuclear-armed superpowers would be a new and very different reality on an entirely different scale. We needed to be prepared.

Zucker was receptive but wanted more. What can we report and when? Other media colleagues were far more skeptical. When I shared that Russia and Ukraine had become the number one threat in the eyes of not just my source but also then chairman of the Joint Chiefs of Staff, General Mark Milley, one fellow beat reporter said he knew for a fact that was not the case.

My own approach was tempered as well by the need to take intelligence for what it was: informed guesses, not a crystal ball. Years earlier, I'd had the highest-level security clearance during my service at the State Department in China. I'd read dozens of classified intelligence assessments—some remarkably accurate, others widely off the mark, and most falling somewhere in between. Intel, as I would come to learn, is imperfect information compiled and analyzed by imperfect people.

US intelligence was still reeling from its failure to foresee Russia's invasion of Crimea in 2014. More markedly, the cloud of the CIA's mistaken 2003 assessment of Saddam Hussein's weapons of mass destruction (WMD) program still hung over the agency nearly two decades later. But the US intelligence community did have a major, unmistakable source for assessing Russia's military preparations now: it could *see* them. Satellite imagery revealed virtually every tank, artillery piece, and supply column. And on top of that, US penetration of Russian communications was proving better than had been known. According to US intelligence assessments, the US had intercepted multiple conversations describing preparations, planning, and intent. The Russian military may have been on its way to becoming a "denied area," a blind spot for the US intelligence community, but it was a remarkably leaky one.

The US had gained a clear view into Russia's alarming plans. And the confident assessment of the US intelligence community was that the Russian military was ready to invade Ukraine, and Putin was ready to order it to do just that.

November 2021
Whitehall, London

In the secure rooms of the UK Ministry of Defence and British Foreign Office, intelligence and military leaders were reading the same intel as their American and NATO partners—and reacting with a combination of alarm and disbelief. They were also observing Russian units mobilize and deploy to areas around Ukraine's borders—and reading intercepted communications showing Russian commanders discussing preparations for an invasion. Despite all this, multiple western officials told me, a state of denial persisted as to whether the invasion threat was real.

"Many hoped that's where it would end—that tanks rolling would be unimaginable," one western official said, adding that he and his colleagues kept asking, "Is this really happening?"

Even with tens of thousands of Russian troops massed inside Russian territory on Ukraine's border, no longer hiding their names and flags, and thousands of Russian tanks and armored vehicles, and Russian fighter and bomber aircraft, and Russian ammunition depots and field hospitals, that "state of denial" persisted. Many still wondered if this could all be Putin's bluff. "It was a boiling-frog scenario," another western official said. Before the world's eyes, the temperature around Ukraine was reaching boiling point, and many officials refused to recognize how hot the water was getting, as doubts and disbelief reigned.

December 2021
Helsinki, Finland

Few countries had been watching Russia's military buildup in Ukraine with more concern and urgency than Finland, Russia's neighbor to the northwest. Finland was not yet a member of NATO. It had studiously steered clear of the alliance since its founding, maintaining a delicate balancing act between western Europe and Russia. To Finnish officials, their country's position was not quite neutrality—it was a full-fledged member of the European Union— but since World War II, Finland had in fact engineered a unique path to remain independent of an expansionist Soviet Union, in part by recognizing what it could do and couldn't do. It could not defeat the

USSR in a war, but it could maintain sovereignty by proving, one, the difficulty and costs of a Russian invasion; and, two, its usefulness to Moscow, particularly in providing a window to trade with the West, which it had maintained since World War II. Now Russia's vast buildup around Ukraine had the potential to deal a deathblow to that approach.

Putin's mounting threat to Ukraine was not a complete surprise to Helsinki. Finnish officials had seen warning signs from Putin and the Kremlin for more than a decade.

"The people grew more and more disillusioned about Russians. And that started, I would say, at the latest in 2008 with the attack on Georgia," said Mikko Hautala, ambassador of Finland to the United States. "There was a discussion in Finland that Russia is actually becoming something that it was not before: a threat."

The threat became eminently clear for many Finns when Putin released his demands for avoiding war on December 17, 2021. The Russian leader's list was so blunt and expansive that Finnish leaders knew Europe had a problem.

"When we saw the demands, I was more or less sure that there's going to be a conflict," Hautala told me. "Because you knew that he [Putin] is not going to back off."

Putin's demands—an eight-point plan released by the Foreign Ministry—were simply nonstarters for Europe. The Russian leader demanded that NATO remove all weapons and forces deployed to all countries admitted to the alliance since 1997. That list encompassed much of eastern Europe, including eastern-flank NATO members Poland and the Baltic states of Estonia, Latvia, and Lithuania. Those countries had something else in common: they all feared they might be the next target of Russian military action.

Putin also demanded that NATO halt any further expansion,

unacceptable for members that, as a matter of principle, view decisions on membership as the prerogative of the nations themselves. Though Finland had so far avoided membership, its leaders viewed joining as solely a decision for Finland.

"He tried to define Finland permanently outside the alliance," said Hautala. "And usually historically, if a great power with which you have a common border tries to block you and put you in a cage, then it's not a good idea to stay in the cage—at least you have to try to make sure that nobody locks the cage."

Russia's message necessitated immediate outreach to Moscow. One month after CIA Director Burns traveled to Moscow to speak with Bortnikov and Putin about his intentions in Ukraine, it was time for a phone call from the Finnish president, Sauli Niinistö, to Putin. Finnish officials up to and including the president have close to a hundred meetings with Russian officials every year. This routine contact has been part of a decades-long Finnish policy of engagement with Russia. This phone call would be different. The Finnish president's message was clear and simple: that Russia's apparent plans to invade Ukraine were in direct conflict with Finland's policies and interests.

"Then, everybody was still trying to find a way out without a war," said Hautala. "But we explained our policies, and the key part of our policies was that every country must have a sovereign right to choose, because if you don't have a right to choose, then you are no longer fully sovereign."

It was not an easy discussion. Finland's position was frank and so was Putin's. "You could easily see that there's no chance of bridging these two positions," said Hautala.

The military buildup was one thing. Officials worldwide were alarmed by what they were seeing on the Ukrainian border. Finnish officials, though, with a deep knowledge of Putin himself, had been watching other, very different signals from Moscow for some time—obscure ones to outsiders, but telling ones to Finnish leaders.

PUTIN'S MANUFACTURED HISTORY

In the years preceding the military buildup, Vladimir Putin had been quietly building a historical pretext for war. He based his claims on dusty maps and manuscripts in agencies and institutions charged with caretaking the history of the Russian state going back centuries. Quietly, Putin was aligning Russian academia and bureaucracy behind his plans. He transferred control of agencies and institutions few had ever heard of—the Federal Archival Agency, the Russian War History Association, the Russian Historical Society, the Russian Geographical Society—under the Kremlin and therefore under his personal control.

"There was this mushrooming of these historical associations," said Ambassador Hautala. "That was the time when we did realize that Russia actually has a fully fledged, state-led history program in order to explain things according to their politics and political needs," he explained. "Up until that point, history was an open field of study, and you had different voices, and the mainstream was still academically serious. But then, we realized that this country has adopted the Soviet way of top-down historical definition and history is part of the state policy."

In short, Putin had been rewriting the history of Russia and—crucially—Ukraine to create a justification for war, bending what even his own fellow Russians knew and believed of history to suit his view and ambitions in the present. The new history stated that Ukraine was and always had been part of Russia and the Ukrainian people were and always had been part of the Russian people. And so, Ukraine's sovereignty was the aberration, not a Russian invasion.

As Russian intelligence agencies were confidently reporting up the chain that Ukrainian forces would quickly fold, that Russian forces would dominate, and that the Ukrainian people would welcome them, Russian history professors and archivists were echoing Putin's version of history, with the message that Ukraine is and always has been part of Russia.

In his conversations with the Finnish president, first in December, then in February as the day of the invasion approached, Putin was proving indefatigable on his version of history and therefore his justification for war. No amount of pushback or contradiction would move him. Putin dismissed the doubters, including a Finnish leader he had known closely for years, as being ignorant of history.

"He feels that he's in the possession of truth at the higher level of aggregation," said Hautala.

The prevailing view among Finnish officials was that Putin was not simply manufacturing this historical justification for war. He was a true believer. For Putin, his manufactured history was the truth. The doubters were ignorant.

"'I know the deeper forces when you know only the surface,'" Hautala told me, describing Putin's point of view as expressed to Finnish leaders. "'You can have this or that argument, but I know the deeper currents of history. And if I look at the deeper currents of history, then I conclude that Ukrainians and Russians are the same people. You are just messed up with some recent ideas.'"

Hautala buys the "true believer" theory, because it gives Putin a convenient, historical rationale for carrying out an invasion so bold and dangerous. "How can you explain this idea of taking such a big risk, of illegally launching a major attack to try to occupy all of Ukraine, if you don't believe?" he said.

And so, while many in the West, the US, and even Ukraine continued to downplay the risk of invasion, Finland had concluded war was now a fait accompli.

"Military buildups had been seen before," Hautala said. "I think people understood this is now something for which Putin has decided 'I will see where I can get.'"

February 2022
Bucha, Ukraine

Three weeks before the war, Yana's mother told her, "The war will start soon." Now it was February 2022, and while capitals from Washington to Helsinki were awash in talk of an imminent Russian invasion, the streets of Bucha, Ukraine, a quiet, middle-class suburb of the capital, Kyiv, were full of skeptics, Yana among them.

"I frowned," Yana told me. "I was used to the fact that my mom was always making mountains out of molehills.

"I didn't want to listen," she continued. "I rolled my eyes and answered curtly: 'Mom, what war? We live in 2022!'"

Yana, like most of her friends and neighbors at the time, was focused on day-to-day routines, on balancing work and raising her three young children. School was in session. Local parks and playgrounds were open. Yana was taking driving lessons. Her neighbor was remodeling her kitchen. Another friend was busy planning her family's summer vacation, deciding where to fly.

"None of my friends believed this was possible," Yana remembered. "People were doing business as usual."

Many Ukrainians had grown used to—even numb to—different kinds of war. It had been eight years since Russian forces quietly invaded Crimea, capturing the area without firing a shot. A hotter war had been underway in Eastern Ukraine since then, with some four-teen thousand people killed, but the eastern front lines seemed far away from the quiet streets of Bucha. A full-on Russian invasion of the entire country? To Yana, the whole proposition sounded alarmist.

At the hospital where Yana's mother worked as a nurse, however, she and her colleagues took note of increased government deliveries of essential medical supplies—supplies one would use to treat the wounds of war.

"My mom told me that she had brought lots of gauze and cotton bandages to the hospital, more than usual," Yana remembered. "They told everyone not to use them for now."

The stockpiling was deliberate and the reason, her mother assured her, was real: "They are getting ready for the war." Unable to let go of the thought that her mother might be right—that war might really come to Ukraine—Yana started taking steps, but quietly.

"I stocked up on groceries. We have a basement in our apartment building. This would help us a lot later," she noted. "And there's plenty of room. So I bought ten kilograms of flour. I bought porridge—three-to-four-kilo bags of it—and tea, canned food, and sugar. I told my husband I was just buying all of it so I wouldn't have to run to the store so often," she added. "I was avoiding conversations about the war."

Yana also was quietly making more disturbing preparations. In searches on YouTube, she found a long list of instructional videos on how to survive a war. As it turns out, the internet is a busy place for war preppers.

Some of the tips were simple and expected, like sealing windows with tape to protect them from explosions. Others were more alarm-ing. Posts advised against keeping weapons or camouflaged clothing at home because invading forces will assume you're military.

And then she saw this: "Women were advised to look as

unattractive as possible," she recounted. "No jewelry. No makeup. Old clothes, even menswear. This way, you can protect yourself from rape."

Two weeks before the war, Yana began to plan a party for her middle daughter's birthday. On April 20, she would be turning seven years old.

"I wanted to surprise her," Yana said. "She'll wake up in the morning. We'll light the candles on the cake, give her the presents, and then I'll say, 'And now we're going to pack our backpacks and go on a trip—a surprise.'"

Yana bought train tickets and booked a hotel for a family trip to Uzhgorod, in Western Ukraine, home to a famous medieval castle.

"It's very reassuring," she said. "Planning for the future, even if it may not be possible, because then there is hope. A thread to hold on to."

At the time, US officials were increasingly warning the Ukrainian government about the danger of a Russian invasion.

"But they're just panicking, I decided, like most of my acquaintances," Yana told me. "Really? A war? It just can't happen."

In public comments, Ukrainian officials, including President Volodymyr Zelensky, were sounding a similar note. Zelensky repeatedly batted down talk of war, chastising western leaders for their warnings of an "imminent" invasion.

"There are signals even from respected leaders of states. They just say that tomorrow there will be war. This is panic. How much does it cost for our state?" he told reporters at a press conference in Kyiv in late January.[1]

In the same forum, Zelensky portrayed "destabilization of the situation inside the country" as a greater threat to Ukraine than the massing Russian invasion force. Zelensky said he was worried that the fears of a Russian invasion would lead Ukrainians to flee and hamstring his nation's economy. He put a dollar figure on the cost of panic: $7 billion per month in lost trade and income.

There was a defiant, even plaintive tone to the Ukrainian leader's pushback. "I'm the president of Ukraine," he told reporters in February, "and I'm based here, and I think I know the details better here."[2]

In a January phone call, Zelensky communicated the same concern to the US president, even as Biden again shared the US intelligence assessment that Russian forces were set to invade. And he had even sharper criticism for the US as it and other western nations began to evacuate their diplomats from Ukraine. "Diplomats are like captains," Zelensky said. "They should be the last to leave a sinking ship. And Ukraine is not the *Titanic*."[3]

Some European leaders and commentators echoed Zelensky's public skepticism, portraying US warnings as deliberately inflammatory and dubious, considering the US intelligence community's track record on issues such as Iraq's nonexistent WMD program before the US invasion nearly twenty years before. Right-wing commentators in the US accused the White House of a "wag the dog" strategy to distract from Biden's domestic troubles.

I heard similar doubts from some colleagues, who accused me of, at best, swallowing US intelligence assessments without sufficient skepticism and of, at worst, unwittingly taking part in a US government information campaign.

One week before the war, Yana and her family were growing beans on their windowsills and experimenting with growing vegetables in the backyard. Like Londoners during the Blitz, they were cultivating their own little "victory gardens." But Yana was making these out as just games.

They read books together. Yana learned to make medivnyk, a honey cake. "It is delicious," she said.

"The office of the president of Ukraine assured us that there was nothing to be afraid of—that there will be no war," she said. "People believed it, but I felt scared."

On February 19, five days before the invasion, Yana got together with her mother and her friends for what she feared could be the last time.

"It was so strange," she said. "I never take a picture with my mother. But on that day, I came to her hospital and suddenly I wanted to take a picture."

Fact is, Yana, who was living at what would become the epicenter of the Russian invasion, was similarly doubtful, right up until the very last moment. Her own president remained so as well. On February 22, less than forty-eight hours before Russian forces would cross the Ukrainian border, and after Putin had officially recognized two regions of Eastern Ukraine occupied by Russian-backed separatists, Zelensky urged his fellow Ukrainian citizens not to panic.

"We are committed to the peaceful and diplomatic path, we will follow it and only it," Zelensky said in a televised address to the nation. "But we are on our own land, we are not afraid of anything and anybody, we owe nothing to no one, and we will give nothing to no one," he added.[4]

In the early morning hours of February 24, Yana's sister called to wake her up with the news: "The war has begun."

"Huh? What do you mean?" Yana replied, still disbelieving, until she heard a helicopter fly right over the roof of her home.

"My husband and I usually went to drink coffee in a coffee shop. A five-minute walk from our home, and you're in Hostomel—the same place where Russian paratroopers landed on that fatal February 24," she told me. "The war did begin." She and her family would spend the next eight days in their basement, holding one another, hoping the next blast wouldn't land on top of them.

February 24, 2022
Penghu Islands, Taiwan Strait

On board the Taiwanese frigate *Feng-Chia* (PFG-1115), stationed on the Penghu Islands in the Taiwan Strait, Captain Peng Chung-Hsiao could barely believe the news of the Russian invasion.

"When the Russo-Ukrainian war erupted, I, like many others, found it hard to believe," Captain Peng told me. And yet, with his duty in mind as commander of a ship then training to defend the island against an invasion by China, he immediately went to work.

"I promptly returned to my unit to analyze the combat tactics and methods used by both sides and assess the overall impact of the conflict on the Asia-Pacific region," Peng said. "At the same time, I reinforced my commitment to my primary duties, ensuring I am fully prepared to confront any threats and challenges."

Lieutenant Colonel Pi Shih-Chuan, commander of a squadron of Taiwanese fighter jets also based on the Penghus, recalled a Song dynasty poem as news of the Russian invasion reached him: "Unless you have personally felt the sorrow of parting," Lieutenant Colonel Pi said, quoting the poem, "you won't believe that grief can turn hair white."

The "parting" he was thinking of in those first days of the Ukraine war was among Ukrainian soldiers and civilians now losing their loved ones in battle.

"Seeing the helpless faces of these people amidst the ruins that used to be their homes, I can only hope that this suffering will come to an end soon and that no one will have to endure such suffering again," Pi told me.

Lessons from history were on the minds of several commanders of Taiwan's Republic of China Armed Forces.

"We adhered to the spirit of *The Art of War*: 'Rely not on the likelihood of the enemy's not coming, but on our own readiness to receive him,'" said Colonel Chang Chi-Ming the commander of Taiwanese ground forces stationed on the Penghu Islands, quoting Sun Tzu's famous work.

He, like many others in Taiwan, immediately saw a direct connection between the war then engulfing Ukraine and the one they were now training for. In one moment, on opposite ends of the globe, Russia's invasion of Ukraine fanned fears of not one but two wars for national survival.

"We harbor no unrealistic fantasies about peace," Chang said. "Based on the conviction that defending the homeland is our duty, our national military strives to serve as the strongest line of defense for the country."

He added, "When the Russo-Ukrainian war broke out, I realized that it was a battle for *our* survival."

It was conflict being wrought by great powers, engaging the rest of the world, erupting out of a period of relative postwar calm into what could now be seen as nothing short of a crisis.

CHAPTER ONE

GREAT POWER WARFARE

3:00 A.M. PHONE CALL

Close to 3:00 A.M., on Monday, February 21, 2022, a member of Congress I know well woke me up in Kyiv with a call from Washington and a question. "Has the State Department or White House warned you guys at all about what's coming in Kyiv?" he asked me. I knew that Russia had surrounded Ukraine with a massive force and was in the final stages of preparations for an invasion—and I knew that I was then lying in a bed in a hotel at the center of Russia's prime target. But I wondered if I was missing something. Was the attack going to be even larger than feared? So I pressed him: "Warned us about what specifically?"

"For the hell Putin is going to unleash on the capital," he said. "Are your people aware? Are you ready?"

By then, CNN and several other US and European networks had stationed our teams at the InterContinental Hotel in downtown Kyiv. It was an ideal though precarious location for witnessing the launch of a modern war. Situated on the eastern edge of the capital, where the city is perched on high ground over the Dnipro River, the hotel provides clear views of the eastern and northern approaches to Kyiv—the most likely paths of a Russian invasion. But the hotel was also right across the street from not one but two juicy targets for Russian air and missile strikes: the Ukrainian Ministry of Foreign Affairs and the headquarters of the national police. News agencies, including CNN, had made sure to communicate the location of their staffs to the Russian authorities. But as a very good friend of mine in the Pentagon had warned me a few days earlier, "The Russians don't have very good aim."

Now wide-awake, I thanked the congressman and called one of my bosses in the US to share the congressman's warning. Had we had any communication with Biden administration officials about a particular threat to this location? I asked him. By then, I had a pretty good idea of what the first wave of the invasion would look like. According to US intelligence assessments, Russia planned a "shock-and-awe" barrage of missile and air strikes on the Ukrainian capital, modeled to some degree on the shock-and-awe campaign that had prefaced the US invasion of Iraq, nearly nineteen years earlier. On March 20, 2003, as the US assault on the Iraqi capital began, I'd been sitting at a Romanian airfield, surrounded by a battalion of US Green Berets, ready to board a night flight into Iraq. The accounts we heard over the radio were awe-inspiring and frightening. Two decades later, as committed as I was to be on the ground in Ukraine to cover the coming war, I was not entirely prepared to be engulfed in the shock and awe myself this time around.

The prospect of a punishing air assault on Kyiv was not a surprise. I had been warning CNN since the previous November that US intelligence agencies were forecasting a wave of air and missile strikes as the first salvos of the Russian invasion. We had staffed up in the capital with those threats in mind. But the call merited a discussion.

Were we truly ready? My boss said he'd reach out to the White House and hung up the line.

PERSISTING DOUBTS

Still in bare feet and with my hair standing on end, I walked down the hall from my room to the suite turned CNN workspace to share the news with our staff and security team. Skepticism reigned. One colleague told me the congressman could be just looking to get in good with a TV reporter. Others wondered if I'd allowed myself to become a conduit for US disinformation. The doubters were not outliers. Despite repeated public warnings from US and NATO officials, many European and American commentators were not convinced. The word "imminent," as US officials had been describing the invasion for a handful of weeks now, had become a punch line. What does "imminent" mean? people asked. Tomorrow? Next week? Next year? The doubts didn't come from nowhere. US intelligence had missed Russia's 2014 invasion of Crimea—and memories of Iraq's nonexistent WMD endured. "Why should we believe them this time?" they asked me.

I understood the doubts from years covering the intelligence agencies and holding a top secret security clearance myself. Over decades, the US had built the most comprehensive and capable intelligence-gathering apparatus in history, but its products required reading with a critical eye. However, the assessments of Russia's invasion plans were different, because the invading force was visible, laid out right before the watchful eyes of US surveillance satellites and aircraft. And what they saw was alarming. Russia was readying for war.

"Iraq's weapons of mass destruction were phantoms," I told them.

"The Russian invasion force is right along the border in 3D. They're not guessing this time."

US agencies had collected other revealing intelligence as well. In a triumph of signals collection, the intel community had penetrated Russian communications networks. They now had direct access to Russian battlefield communications. They were listening in real time as Russian commanders discussed in detail preparing and positioning their units for attack.

Yet the doubts extended far beyond our newsroom, with some NATO leaders downplaying or even dismissing the more ominous warnings of an impending Russian invasion. Tensions broke out into the public discussion even between US and Ukrainian officials. On January 28, Ukrainian president Zelensky told reporters in Kyiv, "There is a feeling abroad that there is war here. That's not the case." Ukrainian officials were fearful in part that the more dire warnings might cause panic among the Ukrainian population, with the economic costs of fleeing businesses and a panicked end to travel in and out of Ukraine. But more broadly, Ukrainian officials told CNN privately, they feared that Ukraine was becoming a pawn in a game of geopolitical chess between the US and Russia.

With detectable pique, Zelensky said, "I can't be like other politicians who are grateful to the United States just for being the United States."

Russian officials were of course eager to dismiss the fears of war as well. On February 10, two weeks before Russian forces stormed into Ukraine, Russian foreign minister Sergey Lavrov stood beside then UK foreign secretary Liz Truss and derided the West's warnings as purely emotional.

"The deployment of Russian troops on our own territory causes incomprehensible anxiety and very strong emotions among our British colleagues and other Western representatives," Lavrov said.

"Unlike the hundreds and thousands of British troops stationed in the Baltics."[1]

Beyond the public differences over just how real or imminent the Russian invasion threat was, there was disagreement within the alliance over the possibility of finding a so-called diplomatic off-ramp for Vladimir Putin. President Emmanuel Macron of France's dialogue with Putin continued into the week of the invasion.

Few begrudged Macron's attempts at peace. However, at the core of those efforts appeared to be a misreading of Russian intentions. Macron told *Le Journal du Dimanche* on February 6, eighteen days before the invasion, that Moscow's goal was "not Ukraine, but a clarification of the rules . . . with NATO and the EU." Here was the French leader saying that Putin had no territorial ambitions in Ukraine, only a desire to establish, among other things, that Ukraine would not be joining NATO anytime soon.

"We must protect our European brothers by proposing a new balance capable of preserving their sovereignty and peace," Macron said. "This must be done while respecting Russia and understanding the contemporary traumas of this great people and great nation."[2]

The fiction that Russian ambitions were limited to preventing Ukraine from entering the NATO alliance would endure even after the invasion, on both sides of the Atlantic, as some conservative commentators and lawmakers in the US shifted blame for the invasion from Moscow to western leaders. Their argument was that those leaders goaded Russia into war by pushing NATO's borders too far east.

Macron's dialogue with Putin continued until days before the war. Even on Sunday, February 20, the French president's office released a statement saying that the two leaders had agreed on "the need to favor a diplomatic solution to the ongoing crisis and to do everything to achieve one." The Élysée Palace added that French foreign minister

Jean-Yves Le Drian and Russian foreign minister Lavrov would meet "in the coming days."[3]

Then, on Thursday, February 24, around 4:00 A.M., I was woken with a call from the CNN News Desk that the war had begun. "I thought you'd like to know," my colleague told me, with understatement. It was grim news; the warnings had been right.

KYIV SURPRISE

The Russian invasion of Ukraine marked the cleanest break between the post–Cold War period and the new world disorder. With echoes of 1939, one great power had marshaled the bulk of its conventional military might and attempted to redraw the map of Europe.

But while western intelligence had gotten the Russian invasion right, it got Ukraine's defense wrong. From my first conversations in November 2021 with US military sources about Putin's invasion plans, I'd been told the war would be over almost as soon as it began. Western intelligence expected Russian forces to take the capital city of Kyiv within seventy-two hours, via a combination of punishing air and missile strikes, electronic warfare crippling communication networks, and then a rapid ground invasion from the east and north.

The air strikes did come. The electronic warfare did not. And Russian forces were quickly bogged down, their advance on the capital stalled, and they were eventually forced into retreat.

As I witnessed and reported on the war unfolding inside Ukraine, there were many moments that surprised me—and that pointed to an outcome far different from that forecast by western intelligence. One such moment played out live on air the very first day of the invasion. My colleague Matthew Chance and a CNN team were reporting on Russian military activity around the Antonov Airport, in Hostomel, just outside Kyiv. As they arrived, they came across a small group of soldiers engaged in a firefight.

"Where are the Russians?" Chance asked.

"We're the Russians," they answered.

Not just any Russians. They were Russian special forces, which had been dropped into Hostomel in the early hours of the invasion. And in that moment, one of the most crucial operations of the Kremlin's invasion plan, assigned to one of its most elite units, was being broadcast to the world on live television. Russia needed to control the Antonov Airport in order to ferry in more forces to march on the capital. But Ukrainian forces would prevent that, ultimately repelling the Russian assault and helping foil Putin's plan to take Kyiv within seventy-two hours. It was an early-round victory for Ukraine in a long bout, but ultimately a telling one.

Within a few days, US military officials pointed me to another warning sign for Russian forces. One week into the invasion, a forty-mile-long convoy of Russian tanks, armored vehicles, and towed artillery was stalled on a highway outside Kyiv—easy targets for Ukrainian ambushes. UK intelligence reports indicated "little discernible progress" by the Russian forces.[4] Inside the Pentagon, US officials were assessing something more significant than a short-term obstacle to Russia's war plans. Ukrainian forces were proving themselves surprisingly capable of meeting a far larger Russian invasion force, with smaller but more mobile and highly trained units, armed with what was proving to be the "star" weapon of the war so far: the shoulder-fired Javelin anti-tank missile.

In two key battles, at Hostomel and on the highway to Kyiv, Ukrainian forces were not just getting lucky. They were demonstrating the capability, perhaps, to win the war. Ukraine's small, mobile, highly trained units were the Davids; Russia's large, plodding, poorly commanded units were the Goliaths.

TEMPLATE FOR GREAT POWER WAR

The war in Ukraine has proved to be a bloody laboratory of modern warfare. Ukraine and Russia have deployed old and new weapons and tactics, adapting along the way. All three great powers have participated to some degree and learned as well. As Ukrainian and Russian forces have fought and died, they have also inadvertently become subjects of a real-world experiment in great power warfare.

The battlefields of Ukraine—from Ukraine's early surprising defense of Kyiv, to its rapid counteroffensive in Kherson and Kharkiv in late 2022, to its more plodding counteroffensive in the east and south in 2023—have showcased a remarkable combination of modern warfare, featuring new tactics and weapons systems, and antiquated warfare—becoming, quite literally, bogged down in the trenches.

"What you've seen is this paradox that we have a combination of twentieth-century warfare combined with twenty-first-century warfare," NATO Secretary General Jens Stoltenberg told me. "We have trench warfare, which resembles the First World War, and then we have autonomous weapons systems and unmanned drones. We have infantry or artillery duels, resembling the First and the Second World Wars, but then we also have advanced electronic warfare."

What lessons have Ukraine, Russia, and NATO taken away? Farther afield, what have China and Taiwan learned from the fighting and the world's response? And does the war in Ukraine hint at what a war between the great powers would look like? Some answers become apparent from examining the war in a series of distinct phases: Ukraine's early defense of Kyiv, its first counteroffensives in the south and northeast in 2022, and the long, slow ground war in the east, including Ukraine's more recent offensive push in 2023. The battlefields of Ukraine provide lessons for potential future conflicts and flashpoints among the great powers.

PHASE ONE: DEFENSE OF KYIV

Early on, the key for Ukrainian forces in the north was that David-versus-Goliath strategy of small, mobile units, ambushing Russia's slow-moving armored columns, which were visible to the world via civilian satellites as they made their way down Ukrainian highways. The Russian advance stalled. And Russian losses mounted.

On the battlefield, Javelin missiles became the conflict's early social media stars. Ukrainian soldiers posted videos of themselves firing them. An Instagram account titled Saint Javelin, with an avatar showing a saintly icon cradling a missile, helped popularize the posts, quickly gaining more than one hundred thousand followers.

By late March, barely a month into the war, Russia halted its advance and began to withdraw some of its forces around Kyiv in what senior US military officials told me at the time was a "major" strategy shift by Moscow.[5] The US observed Russia repositioning its forces from the north to the south and east. At the time, the Russian Ministry of Defense described the movements as an effort to "drastically reduce hostilities" in the north.[6] In reality, it was an ignominious retreat.

The US view, as military sources told me, was that this was not a short-term adjustment but a longer-term transformation as Russia came to grips with its failure to advance in the north. Already, US commanders in the region worried about European allies staying unified in their support of Ukraine, expecting some to press Kyiv to capitalize on its early surprise success by pursuing a peace deal to end the fighting.

Ukrainian officials themselves suspected a feint. Lieutenant General Kyrylo Budanov, head of the Defense Intelligence of Ukraine, said Putin could be looking to cut Ukraine into two countries or regions.

"There is reason to believe that he is considering a 'Korean' scenario for Ukraine. That is, [Russian forces] will try to impose a dividing line between the unoccupied and occupied regions of our country," Budanov said. "In fact, it is an attempt to create North and South Korea in Ukraine."[7]

US military officials saw something else. Costs to Russian forces were exceedingly high, and in large part due to Ukraine's punishing mobile assaults, Russia had lost more soldiers in Ukraine in a few weeks than it had lost in Afghanistan in ten years. Russia's supposedly modernized military hardware, recipient of billions of dollars in new investments under Putin, had ground to a halt.

Just weeks into the invasion, the US had assessed that Ukraine had effectively neutered Russia's conventional ground forces.

PHASE TWO: UKRAINE'S FIRST COUNTEROFFENSIVE

In late summer 2022, Ukraine unleashed its boldest attack since the successful defense of Kyiv—spanning from Kherson in the south to Kharkiv in the northeast. And once again, it outperformed even the most optimistic US intelligence assessments. Ukraine was attempting to change the face of the war.

In August 2022, I was among the first to report signs Ukraine was transitioning from defending territory to reclaiming territory lost since the Russian invasion. Ukrainian forces had begun "shaping" operations to prepare the battlefield for what US military officials told me would be the first significant Ukrainian counteroffensive. Ukrainian forces were showing themselves highly capable of combined forces operations, joining air and ground forces and benefiting from the arrival of US- and NATO-supplied high-mobility artillery rocket system (HIMARS) launchers, which allowed Ukraine to strike and destroy targets in Russian-held territory.

The offensive was beginning at the same time US intelligence agencies assessed that Russia had been able to deploy fewer units to the front lines than initially thought, a senior US official told me at the time. The official said many of the existing units—which Russia organizes into battlefield tactical groups comprising infantry, tanks, artillery, and air defense—were deploying below strength, some even at half their normal manpower.

Just one week into the forward push, Ukrainian forces were gaining back territory in the south. And now Ukrainian leaders had the ambitious goal of taking back most of the Russian-occupied region of Kherson by the end of the year, senior US officials and Ukrainian officials told me and my CNN colleagues. These were the most ambitious ground assaults by Ukraine since the Russian invasion began.

Ukrainian forces simultaneously stepped up attacks in Eastern Ukraine in order to prevent Russia from shifting forces to the south and defending territory it had seized there, US officials told me and my colleagues. The offensive was broad-based, to prevent Russian units from concentrating on any one point. At the same time, Ukrainian forces expanded sabotage operations and attacks on pro-Russian officials in occupied areas. And even before Ukrainian forces began increasing their artillery rocket and missile fire on the front lines in southern Ukraine, Kyiv had been actively disrupting Russian resupply efforts and command and control across the region.[8]

US officials tried to temper their ambitions. As my colleagues Katie Bo Lillis and Natasha Bertrand reported at the time, the US urged Kyiv to limit the operation in both objectives and geography to avoid overextending itself. Those discussions involved war-gaming with

Kyiv to help Ukraine understand what force levels it would need to be successful in different scenarios.[9] The message was clear: don't get ahead of yourselves.

"They Ran"

Undeterred, Ukrainian commanders delivered another surprise. With attention focused on fronts in the south and east, Ukrainian forces launched a third point of attack from the northeast, near Kharkiv. Advancing Ukrainian columns appeared to catch Russian forces by surprise, forcing a swift Russian retreat. And the Ukrainian president quickly delivered "good news" from the region to the Ukrainian public.[10]

Images geolocated by CNN showed Ukrainian forces quickly advancing town by town.[11] The combination of the element of surprise with previous Russian redeployments to defend against the anticipated offensive in the south appeared to deliver a triumphant and unexpected victory for Ukraine, and a debilitating failure for Russia.

In the weeks before the Ukrainian push, Russia had been digging into defensive positions situated close to the Russian border. And yet, as Ukrainian forces advanced, Russian forces executed a rapid retreat. "They ran," CNN's Nick Paton Walsh reported from the front. And they ran without many of their most valuable weapons. As CNN noted at the time, the intelligence website Oryx estimated that in just a five-day span, Russian forces left behind at least 338 fighter jets, tanks, and trucks.[12]

Ukraine's first significant counteroffensive of the war—and its first effort to take back Russian-occupied territory—had been a broad-based success.

PHASE THREE: SECOND COUNTEROFFENSIVE

Ukraine's second counteroffensive in the summer of 2023 was long anticipated, and now was burdened with much higher expectations. But it proved far less swift and effective. Signs of difficulty emerged early. As I reported in June 2023, based on conversations with multiple US and western officials, the counteroffensive was "not meeting expectations on any front," with Ukrainian forces having less success and Russian forces showing more competence than expected.[13]

Russian lines of defense were proving multilayered, well fortified, and devastatingly mined, making them difficult for Ukrainian forces to breach. Crucially, Russia's much-maligned military was showing signs it was learning and adjusting, bogging down Ukrainian armor with missile attacks and mines as well as deploying airpower more effectively to attack Ukrainian forces from above. While Ukrainian forces were proving "vulnerable" to Russian attacks, Russian forces were becoming more "competent" in their defense, one western official told me.

Ukrainian forces were also showing an ability to adapt to opposing tactics and defenses, including carrying out more dismounted operations and achieving some success shooting down Russian aircraft. Still, the counteroffensive was proving a "tough drive" for both Ukraine and Russia, with each incurring heavy losses, and Ukraine failing to make significant territorial gains.

President Zelensky conceded that progress had been "slower than desired." "We would definitely like to make bigger steps," Zelensky told the BBC. "But nevertheless, those who fight shall win and to those that knock, the door shall be opened."[14]

Retired Lieutenant General Mark Hertling, former commanding general of US Army Europe and former commander of the First

Armored Division in Iraq, told me that Russian defenses were "more difficult than anyone can imagine," riddled with tens of thousands of land mines. A rule of thumb for warfare, he said, is that attacking forces need a three-to-one advantage over defending forces in order to overrun their positions. The depth and complexity of Russian defenses in Eastern Ukraine might require a ten-to-one advantage. However, even with advantages in modern weapons systems and morale, Ukraine launched its counteroffensive with a ratio closer to one-to-one. Hertling has watched the most highly trained US combat brigades fail repeatedly in training to breach similar defenses.

"Russians have a number of defensive lines, and they [Ukrainian forces] haven't really gone through the first line," a senior western diplomat told me at the time. "Even if they would keep on fighting for the next several weeks, if they haven't been able to make more break-throughs throughout these last seven, eight weeks, what is the likeli-hood that they will suddenly, with more depleted forces, make them? Because the conditions are so hard."[15]

In addition, unlike Russia, Ukraine was hesitant to throw its forces into a meat grinder in the east. Zelensky told my colleague Fareed Zakaria at the Aspen Security Forum in July 2023, "We didn't want to lose our people, our personnel and our servicemen, we didn't want to lose equipment and because of that, they were quite careful about the offensive actions."[16]

Time was a factor too. The fall was rapidly approaching, when weather and fighting conditions were expected to worsen. And some US officials began to express concerns about the overall strategy. The slow progress, they said, exposed the difficulty of transforming Ukrainian forces into combined mechanized fighting units, with as few as eight weeks of training on new weapons systems. Preparations for the counteroffensive had been insufficient from the start.

In late summer 2023, Ukraine began to devote more of its most highly trained and well-armed units to the push. US officials identified the addition of the Ukrainian Army's Tenth Corps as a positive step, giving Ukraine's forces the ability to breach the first of three formidable Russian defensive lines. A senior US official told me at the time that the US saw a chance for Ukrainian forces to "gain momentum." One of the key questions related not to Ukrainian attackers but to Russian defenders. "How brittle are the Russians?" this senior US official asked. The US knew the Russians had poor morale and training. Would that translate into an opportunity for Ukrainian forces to advance?

As the summer ground on, the hoped-for breakthrough did not materialize. In August, multiple US and western officials told me they were seeing increasingly "sobering" assessments about Ukrainian forces' ability to retake significant territory.

"They're still going to see, for the next couple of weeks, if there is a chance of making some progress. But for them to really make progress that would change the balance of this conflict, I think it's extremely, highly unlikely," a senior western diplomat told me.[17]

"Our briefings are sobering. We're reminded of the challenges they face," said Representative Mike Quigley, an Illinois Democrat who had recently returned from meetings in Europe with US commanders training Ukrainian armored forces. "This is the most difficult time of the war."[18]

My story ruffled feathers among Ukrainian officials and Ukraine's supporters in the West. Americans had grown used to accounts of Ukraine exceeding expectations, not falling short of them. There was growing concern the Ukraine war was devolving into a "frozen conflict," which Putin had been hoping for as an outcome short of victory.

BLAME GAME

As disappointment—public and private—set in, a blame game began to emerge. Addressing the Aspen Security Forum in July, President Zelensky offered another explanation for the counteroffensive's slow progress: the slow arrival of more advanced weapons systems from the West.

"We did plan to start [the counteroffensive] in spring, but we didn't," Zelensky told my colleague Fareed Zakaria. "Because frankly, we had not enough munitions, and armaments, and not enough properly trained brigades, I mean properly trained in these weapons."[19]

Zelensky noted that each new system—such as German Leopard tanks—required new training for Ukrainian forces outside the country, further delaying their deployment. These delays, he complained, allowed Russia to dig its forces into defensive positions more deeply and more effectively.

"It provided Russia with time to mine all our lands and build several lines of defense," Zelensky said. "So, definitely, they had a bit more time than they needed; because of that, they built more of those lines. . . . Because of that, a slower pace of our counteroffensive actions."

"The problem, of course, here is the prospect of the blame game that the Ukrainians would then blame it on us," a western diplomat told me, by saying the West hadn't provided enough support and early enough. "I hope Zelensky doesn't do that. . . . His own people may be looking for scapegoats, but this will also have an impact on the morale of the society."

Just as Ukrainian success helped breed unity, failure was feeding division, and fear grew that a blame game would sow division among Ukraine and its allies.

"Putin is waiting for this," Representative Quigley told me. "He can sacrifice bodies and buy time."

The negative turn in outlook marked a change from the optimism that had reigned since the initial, successful defense of Kyiv. Officials conceded the expectations that Ukraine could rapidly take back Russian-occupied territory in the east were now "unrealistic."

And, in fact, it was not the first time US officials had expressed concerns about the possibility of a frozen conflict in the east. Testifying before Congress in early March, Director of National Intelligence Avril Haines said that the Ukraine conflict had by then become a "grinding attritional war in which neither side has a definitive military advantage," but warned that Putin was likely to carry on, possibly for years.

"We do not foresee the Russian military recovering enough this year to make major territorial gains, but Putin most likely calculates the time works in his favor, and that prolonging the war, including with potential pauses in the fighting, may be his best remaining pathway to eventually securing Russia's strategic interests in Ukraine, even if it takes years," Haines testified.

At the Pentagon in September 2023, assessments of Ukraine's progress were improving slightly. However, pressure was building. The approach of winter would soon limit Ukrainian forces' room for maneuvering. War plans—as they often do—were running into the reality of war. As the saying goes, "No plan survives contact with the enemy."

"The plans and the war games anticipated a certain timeline, but then you get real war, real people are really dying, real vehicles getting blown up. And that tends to slow things down," General Milley told me. "So, what we've seen is a counteroffensive that has been slow but very deliberate. And it is achieving steady but incremental and slow progress."

LESSONS IN GREAT POWER WARFARE

As the first hot war of this new great power conflict, the war in Ukraine was already providing lessons about what might raise up great powers and what might threaten them. In strategic terms, the war had exacerbated Putin's stated justifications for the invasion.

"[Putin] wanted . . . no further NATO enlargement, the removal of military infrastructure from allies that had joined after 1997, and, of course, no membership for Ukraine. He's getting the exact opposite," NATO Secretary General Stoltenberg told me. "He's getting more NATO troops. We have increased the number of NATO troops deployed in eastern part of the alliance. And Finland is also a member. Sweden will be a member soon, and Ukraine is closer to NATO membership than [it] ever has been before.

"So, this demonstrates that President Putin made a huge strategic mistake. [He] not only underestimated the Ukrainians, but also the political effects on NATO and partners like Finland and Sweden."

For now, perhaps, but for the long term? If Russia had no clear off-ramp, would it ultimately win simply by not losing?

RUSSIA FALLING, UKRAINE RISING

One clear, counter result of the war's length is that Russia's conventional forces—and therefore its conventional threat to Europe—have been deeply damaged. Feared by Europe and, supposedly, modernized by Putin, they have grossly underperformed. In the understated language of a British diplomat, one senior UK official summed up the performance of the Russian military this way: "It hasn't gone well for them."

In short, western officials told me, Russia's ground capability has been "almost negated." Russia lost the capability to carry out significant ground operations anywhere in the world for the foreseeable future.

Then there are the devastating losses in pure human terms. In July 2023, two Russian independent news outlets, Mediazona and Meduza, released a comprehensive study based on inheritance data in Russia that calculated that by May 2023, just over a year into the war, Russia had lost between 40,000 and 55,000 soldiers, which was consistent with a US intelligence estimate of 50,000. The same study found that some 78,000 Russian soldiers had been wounded so badly, they had left military service. With total casualties between 118,000 and 133,000, Russia had lost combatants equivalent to the size of its entire original invading force.[20]

By August 2023, the US assessment of Russian war casualties had soared. *The New York Times* reported the US estimate now approached some 300,000. "The number includes as many as 120,000 deaths and 170,000 to 180,000 injured troops," the *Times* said, more than double Ukraine's still devastating losses, estimated at between 170,000 and 190,000 killed and wounded.[21]

"It's got to be a generation before the Russian military can rebuild itself," CIA Director Bill Burns told me. "They have some smart state economists, they've weathered some of the worst of the storm on sanctions and export controls. But they still suffered a fair amount of long-term damage. They are going to end up being an economic colony of China if they're not careful."

This was a devastating loss for Russia and a resounding victory for Ukraine, the US, and their allies: by expending only single-digit portions of their total defense budgets, the West had perhaps irreparably degraded the Russian military.

Simultaneously, Russia's invasions in 2014 and 2022 had transformed the Ukrainian military into one of the largest armed forces on the continent. It was now bigger than the British Army and—with the brutal experience of war—the most battle-tested as well. In a stark irony, as NATO allies debated Ukraine's membership in the alliance, it had built perhaps the most capable armed forces in all of Europe.

Still, as the war approached the end of its second bloody year, Ukrainian advances stalled, and Russian defenses held. The implications, like so many aspects of the Ukraine war, were not entirely black-and-white. Ukrainian forces hadn't lost, but could they win? Similarly, Russian forces hadn't won, but could they just wait the whole thing out?

"The strength of the Russian army was not that it could end the war in three days but that it can go on fighting perpetually," Representative Quigley told me after returning from a delegation to visit NATO forces in eastern Europe.

"I'm convinced personally that he is of the opinion that despite the original setbacks, the big wheel is turning in the right direction," Finnish ambassador to the US Mikko Hautala said of Putin. "And probably, he sees this as a multiyear, almost permanent war."

"Permanent war." This was the essence of the "Gerasimov Doctrine"—the Russian military strategy for great power conflict, as laid out by the chief of the general staff of the Russian Armed Forces, General Valery Gerasimov. This means—to Russian leaders—neverending conflict on multiple fronts.

I spoke to current and former military leaders in the US, Europe, and Asia to ask for their list of lessons about great power war, as this one ground on. Consistently, they spoke of the remarkable combination of old and new on the battlefield: small, highly trained, mobile units employing high-technology weapons systems—such as attack and surveillance drones and shoulder-fired missiles—along with old-school deployments of enormous ground forces, backed by massive artillery barrages and often locked into trench warfare and house-to-house fighting reminiscent of the First and Second World Wars.

"What's old is new," former NATO Supreme Allied Commander Admiral James Stavridis told me. "Alongside everything that's advanced, we've got trench warfare. We've got tanks rolling."

"We need to realize that there is this combination: quality and quantity. Mass matters, but of course quality also matters," said NATO's Stoltenberg. "So, it is a combination of old and new types of warfare. And in the war in Ukraine, both are used at the same time, in parallel."

Each aspect—quality and quantity, old weapons and new ones—gives hints at what conflicts big and small among the great powers may look like in the future. In many ways, it was already a proxy war among the great powers.

"It's a hybrid proxy war," said Stavridis. "One great power is fully engaged with troops and firepower, and on our side, we don't have troops in there, but we do have money and ammunition."

Quality and quantity have proved more or less effective. Small, mobile units gave Ukrainian forces the advantage during Russia's plodding assault on Kyiv. Those small Ukrainian units were able to assault miles-long Russian armored convoys almost with impunity, in the end repelling what was intended to be the decisive force of the Russian invasion within days of the start of the war.

"As a Marine infantryman—stalkers and hunters—clearly, the Ukrainians have done that in spades," John Kelly, retired US Marine Corps general and former chief of staff in the Trump White House, told me. "The beauty of what the Ukrainians are doing—small units—they're out there hunting."

Later, Russia's dependence on massive, artillery-driven ground warfare helped it defend occupied territory in Eastern Ukraine from repeated Ukrainian attempts to claw it back as well as break the crucial "land bridge" between Russian-occupied Eastern Ukraine and Crimea.

"Russians are not very well trained," Kelly added. "In World War I, World War II, Afghanistan, they have always been short on tactical skill. They win by massive firepower and not caring who they kill. They're intentionally hitting civilian targets."

Russia's artillery-driven defense of territory it occupied in Eastern Ukraine exhibited this dependency on massive firepower but also its effectiveness. It has been—quite literally—a scorched-earth campaign in the east.

The war in Ukraine has showcased the effectiveness of a range of old and new military technology as well—what still works but also what's new that works now. Military experts have long discussed when unpiloted aircraft and naval craft would begin to play a significant role in warfare and perhaps someday replace human operators. Ukraine has propelled them into action. Military leaders consistently identify drones as one of the most impactful new technologies. "We all underestimated how important drones would be," said Representative Quigley.

"The biggest is unmanned technology," said Stavridis. "We are not quite at the level of swarm technology yet, but we're at the edge of that. What's really cool is the command and control—information instantly passed to a targeting system. I'll paraphrase Carville here and say, It's the command and control, stupid, not the hardware."

Ukrainian forces proved adept at using drones both to track Russian forces and to attack them with ordnance attached even to commercially available quadcopter drones. Larger, Iranian-supplied attack drones helped Russian forces lay waste to Ukrainian cities. However, experienced military commanders caution that no new weapon is invulnerable.

"Drones have been around for a while, but Ukraine is using smaller, cheaper, off-the-shelf drones in unique ways," said Lieutenant General Hertling.

Another star of the Ukraine war is shoulder-fired missile systems, including the Javelin anti-tank missile and Stinger and other versions of shoulder-fired anti-aircraft missiles. Each has given small mobile units of Ukrainian fighters the ability to take on much larger Russian units equipped with tanks and armored personnel carriers. These missiles proved so successful, especially in the early stages of the war, that they rose to the top of the list of weapons systems many believe the US should prioritize providing to Taiwan.

Still, military officials caution against being too quick to eulogize older weapons systems, including tanks and armored personnel carriers. Early in the war, Russian armor looked like far too easy a target for Ukraine's modern, mobile weapons systems. But in the fighting in the east, armor has proved useful, especially to advancing Ukrainian forces.

"Tanks were dinosaurs," Quigley noted. "Now they're critical."

"There were many at the start of the war that said the tank was dead," said Hertling. "Perhaps the Russian tanks are, but mobile armored platforms of some types are not."

And then there is real-time video and photography. Even before Russian forces crossed the border, the world had an unprecedented, real-time view of what used to be tightly held intelligence: the location, size, and movements of military forces. The public saw the Russian military buildup in great detail, due both to the ubiquity and capability of commercial satellites and to the decision of western intelligence agencies to declassify their own images of the mobilization to corroborate their warnings of the Kremlin's invasion plans.

Stavridis and others highlighted "the extraordinary level of information warfare." Once the war started, drones proliferated on the battlefield, and commercial satellite imagery was available daily, now giving not only a view of military movements but also combat, again in real-time. Today, the battlefield is virtually transparent to the warring armies and to the world.

"The battlefield is transparent," said Stoltenberg. "There is nowhere to hide, in a way, because drones, satellites, different sensors, electronic means, make it very hard to hide. So you have to move. You have to protect yourself to be able to operate on the battlefield."

On a rapidly evolving battlefield, the side that adjusts most quickly and effectively maintains the advantage. This has often been true in warfare, only more so in a conflict characterized by rapid changes in weapons and tactics. As the war has evolved through its different phases, Ukrainian forces in particular have shown the immense value of adaptation in the moment.

Military observers have repeatedly pointed to the Ukrainian forces' ability to innovate in real time. One notable example is how they adapted to fire their artillery for far longer and with greater frequency than had been assumed possible. Dire necessity, said Representative Quigley, was the mother of adaptation.

"They learned how to adjust on the fly," Quigley said. "You'd be surprised how fast you learn when your ass is on the line and you don't want your spouse to be raped."

Many commanders credit training by NATO forces, which accelerated following Russia's first invasion of Ukraine in 2014. In particular, under western instruction, Ukrainians invested their officers and NCOs with the ability and agency to make their own decisions on the battlefield—to take the initiative and adapt on their own.

"The US is typically like that," said General Kelly. "Our troops are very well trained. Our troops are the best at it: 'Take the hill,' commanders say, 'and I'm not going to tell you how to do it.'"

Russian forces, on the other hand, reserve decision-making to only the highest ranks. "The Russians are very top-down, very controlling," said Kelly. "One thing Stalin would never buy is too many people taking the initiative. Communist regimes didn't want their people thinking. Warfare is so chaotic. If you haven't developed your people so that they're very good on their own, I think you will always lose to someone who is doing that."

As attention increasingly focuses on China's potential invasion of Taiwan, many see similar orthodoxy in the Chinese military. "One of China's great weaknesses," Kelly said, "is that when things get crazy, you don't have time to call up for 'Mother, may I?'"

These tendencies are not monolithic; Russian forces did prove adaptable in certain circumstances as the war raged on. Learning from their failed assault on Kyiv in the early days of the invasion, Russian forces no longer attempted long, highly visible armored convoys but moved in smaller groups that were harder to target.

They also proved more capable of using airpower, including drones and aircraft, and long-range artillery to strike Ukrainian targets at a distance. Russian forces scored successful strikes on Ukraine's highly prized, NATO-supplied HIMARS via air and artillery. They have also deployed electronic warfare to defeat Ukrainian drones and other weapons systems.

"Electronic warfare and jamming have proven to be a real player in countering GPS guidance for weapons systems and maneuvering forces," said Lieutenant General Hertling.

According to Hertling, unexpected failures have forced both sides to adapt. "Russia believed they were ten feet tall at the beginning of the war and they were humbled," said Hertling. "Now Ukraine feels that way because they initially beat the Russians and they're now being humbled since they're on the offense and the defensive mission is easier for Russia."

However, Hertling, like many others, believes Ukraine retains the advantage because of a more open system that rewards initiative. "Each side has adapted," he said. "Ukraine better than the Russians, in my view, due to the culture and character of government leaders allowing it."

EXPOSING THE "AMAZON MODEL"

Children of the last Cold War will remember the brief period of hope following the imagined "end of history" that the age of large armed forces was over. Many in the West downsized their militaries and military budgets and gradually dismantled the military supply chain behind them. America's long wars in Iraq and Afghanistan kept US military budgets enormous but favored weapons systems for counterinsurgency over great power conflict and de-emphasized the need for massive military production of what were seen as relics of another age of warfare, such as tanks and artillery ammunition.

The largest war in Europe since World War II has now exposed deep shortcomings in that supply chain. The US and its allies, officials and commanders in the US, Europe, and Asia told me, have been lulled into a false security. Today's NATO leaders lament their predecessors' focus on extracting a "peace dividend" following the end of the last Cold War. Now, there is a growing awareness of the need to reinvigorate the supply chain.

"We have developed armies based on an Amazon model: just enough, just-in-time delivery," said Lieutenant General Hertling. "No excess that corresponds to potential needs in a large-scale conventional war."

"I think that the one lesson, just overarching what we have learned, is that we need to invest more in defense," said Secretary General Stoltenberg. "There's an enormous need for weapons, but also ammunition, spare parts, the ability to sustain a war with a peer adversary. And that's also the reason why we now see additional increased defense planning across the alliance."

Ammunition has been a story of its own in Ukraine as the world's largest military alliance has struggled to meet Ukraine's need for ammunition, particularly as it and Russia pummeled each other in a months-long artillery war in Eastern Ukraine throughout 2023.

The pace of the Ukrainian artillery's use of 155-millimeter shells far outstripped supply, even from the world's largest military.

"The United States produces fourteen thousand 155-millimeter artillery rounds a month, and we are providing much of those to Zelensky and Ukraine," General Kelly noted to me. "They're firing about six thousand a day, and in some cases, if we went to war against an adversary like Russia, like Iran, we'd be firing six thousand an hour."

US military planners are aware of the shortfall and are gradually increasing capacity. But those changes appear out of pace not only with the current war but with any potential war to come.

"The United States is going to up its industrial capacity from fourteen thousand a month to twenty-five thousand a month but won't be able to do that till 2025. Our industrial base is hurting, and we don't really have a merchant marine to speak of anymore," said Kelly.

In reality, Representative Quigley explained, the US needs to increase production not by less than 100 percent but by some 500 percent—by five times—to meet the demands of Ukrainian forces and the need to maintain US supplies. The math is simple and alarming: Ukraine fires in two to three days what the US produces in an entire month.

Some see this as a continuing legacy of the US long wars in Iraq and Afghanistan. "Of the many problems that were created by the distraction of the Iraq and Afghanistan wars, the dismantling of our ability to build weapons and munitions in a rapid and scalable manner is now turning out to be a pretty significant problem," said Matthew Pottinger, deputy national security advisor under President Donald Trump.

"We have been in a counterinsurgency, counterterrorism environment for too long, because many declared the large-scale conventional war 'dead,'" Lieutenant General Hertling agreed. "We've wished away the need for excess storage or the ability to generate an industrial base in armaments."

At the Aspen Security Forum in July 2023, National Security Advisor Jake Sullivan acknowledged the difficulty of keeping up.

"Several months ago, we began the process of ramping up 155 production quite dramatically so that we could reach a point where monthly production would meet all the needs necessary for Ukraine, for us, and for everybody, for all of our allies and partners. But that takes time," Sullivan said. "You'd be surprised by how much time. I think a lot of us think about the World War II concept of Rosie the Riveter and rolling tanks and planes off to production lines that were converted from being car factories, and we did that in a matter of months. The sheer sophistication of these rounds, the supply chains, the workforce, the contracts, the time it takes to get from x1000 rounds a day to triple x1000 rounds, is not a matter of weeks. It's a matter of months."

That gaping shortfall helps explain the disturbing US decision in July 2023 to supply Ukraine with cluster munitions, banned by most countries, including many US allies.

"We have a gap. And we need to fill that gap so that Ukraine is not defenseless, because we are not going to leave them defenseless,"

Sullivan said. "So that is why the president decided to bridge that gap, we would provide cluster munitions because the alternative to providing cluster munitions was them not having enough bullets."

The reinvigoration of the military supply chain has already proved necessary for Ukraine's defense. Today, NATO leaders believe it will prove even more crucial for the defense of Europe. "We need high-end capabilities," added Stoltenberg. "We need the battle tanks. We need planes. We need modern ships, and we need all the different heavy high-end capabilities. For many years, NATO was very focused on more light expeditionary crisis management in Afghanistan, Iraq, and so on. Now we are back to the heavy collective defense of Europe."

A FOURTH PHASE?

More and more, "heavy collective defense" described the approach to the war in Ukraine as well. As the invasion approached its second year, Ukraine and its allies began to realize they were headed for a war of attrition. During a visit to Washington, DC, in September 2023, President Zelensky told *The Economist*, "I have to be ready for the long war."[22] This was a surprisingly blunt appraisal from the Ukrainian leader. Since Russian forces first stormed into his country, he had projected an air of defiant optimism. Now he and US and European leaders were acknowledging that the knockout punch they had hoped for from the second counteroffensive had so far failed to materialize.

Heavy collective defense for Ukraine meant a greater emphasis on defensive weapons systems and a defensive strategy. Ukrainian forces did not need to give up their attempts to claw back Ukrainian territory now occupied by Russia. And Ukraine was proving itself more and more capable of effectively striking Russian forces behind enemy lines. Missile and drone attacks on Russia's Black Sea Fleet were particularly impactful. But given the relatively slow pace of the counteroffensive, Ukraine and its allies would need to step up preparations for the long haul. Among the most crucial were air defense systems to better defend against Russian missile and drone strikes, which were now devastating the Ukrainian population and civilian infrastructure.

As I sat down with US and European officials in the fall of 2023, it was clear to me they were increasingly resigned to this new reality. They said Ukraine could still win a long war, but Ukraine and its supporters abroad needed to prepare for the possibility of victory delayed.

THE GENERALS' VIEW

What does a proxy war between the great powers—and one looking longer and longer by the month—mean for the possibility of direct conflict between those powers? The weight of history looms over world leaders steering their nations amid the return of great powers. Every politician, diplomat, and military commander I spoke with for this book—from the US to Europe to Asia—marked his and her comments with references and deference to historical events that either averted or precipitated war.

General Mark Milley, who was chairman of the Joint Chiefs of Staff under Presidents Trump and Biden, infused virtually every answer in our interview with history, ranging from the recent past of the last Cold War to World Wars I and II, the European wars of the seventeenth and eighteenth centuries, and all the way back to ancient conflict in the Peloponnesian War—basis of the now famous

"Thucydides Trap." And those lessons, he notes, are soberingly consistent.

"The historical record is not optimistic," Milley told me. "The historical record tells us that when that condition obtains, when a revisionist power and a status quo power meet and they have irreconcilable core vital national security interests, historically, most of the time that ended up in armed conflict."

In his vast office in the Pentagon, Milley and I sat for three and a half hours as he described the many challenges of this new world order. His office itself is infused with history—his own and his nation's. Milley still has the build and bearing of an ice hockey player, and pictures of his high school and college teams adorn the shelves. However, he took care to point out two black-and-white photos side by side, showing soldiers taking cover in trenches. The soldiers on the left and right looked indistinguishable. In fact, he said, one was in France in the First World War, the other in Ukraine just last year. "History may not repeat itself," Milley said, paraphrasing Mark Twain, "but it does rhyme.

"Great power war can happen. Bad things do happen," he said. "In the hundred-plus years since World War I, have we evolved as a human species that we make better decisions today? Maybe, maybe not. So we have to be careful. So you need sets of rules. You need guardrails to prevent great power war."

General Milley then walked me through several hundred years of great power war and subsequent efforts to prevent the next one. This took us from the Thirty Years' War to the Treaty of Westphalia, from the Seven Years' War and American and French Revolutions to the Concert of Europe, and, later, to World War I and World War II, and the Bretton Woods agreements that followed. His point was not to inundate me with history but to make clear that the postwar order put in place after 1945 had helped keep the peace among the great powers and was now falling apart. In brief, Milley argues that the choice for world leaders today is between a system of albeit imperfect rules, or no rules at all and what he describes as a "Hobbesian . . . dog-eat-dog world."

"My concern today is that the international system is weakening that potentially could make great power war more likely rather than less likely," he continued. "And we have to guard that system very jealously, or you'll have problems in the future."

To add to the danger, this dissolution of the old order is happening, as the great powers have far greater weapons at their disposal and far fewer agreements to limit them.

"Great power war today is exponentially more dangerous than it was in World War I or World War II because of the advent of nuclear weapons, but not just nuclear weapons," said Milley. "The conventional weapons—they are unbelievably more powerful than they were back in those days."

Are the great powers at risk of repeating history and tumbling into another world war? Retired general John Kelly is, like Milley and most senior US military officers I meet these days, a student of history as well. And over several conversations, he shared his concern that the new focus on Russia and China and great power competition could harden the conflict—that by focusing so much attention and energy and rhetoric on the stand-off, conflict can become a self-fulfilling prophecy. For context, he says, we need to look back only as far as the Korean War.

"So we get involved in the Korean War," he said. "And there was nothing more critical than fighting the Korean War. And then when that was over, we said, 'Well, we're not going to do that again. We're not going to fight on the Asian mainland again.' And then we ended up going to the Vietnam War.

"We forgot about the European Soviet threat," Kelly continued.

"And then at the end of the Vietnam War, we rediscover the Soviet Union and the army . . . Everyone starts to bulk up again so they can take on the Soviet Union."

"We, as the United States of America, as a war power, we have to absolutely remember that there are many, many threats out there," he said, citing terrorism and what he sees as by far the most significant threat to the US today: opioid trafficking and the opioid epidemic.

Kelly's point is not that the US should not contest an increasingly aggressive Russia and China, but that there are dangers in the world's new focus on great power competition and its drift toward military response to the standoff—a drift he says he witnessed during his service under both President Trump and President Barack Obama.

"When there are problems out there, there's a tendency, for a lot of different reasons, I think, to look to the military first for the solution," he said. "There are some very powerful tools in the kit bag that Congress has, Treasury has, State Department has, or sanctions and those kinds of things. But there's this tendency to immediately look at the Department of Defense and the military and say, 'Okay, what can we do?'"

The West's forceful response to Russia's invasion of Ukraine was helping to defend a sovereign nation. But western involvement also expanded the conflict into a proxy war among the great powers. The war has played out with constant concern about both vertical and horizontal escalation—vertical, as in escalating to weapons of mass destruction, including nuclear weapons (which I address in detail in Chapter 7)—and horizontal escalation, meaning expansion to include NATO member states.

The war has brought the return of great power proxy wars, with powers on each side of a new global divide "picking a side" and then backing that side diplomatically, economically, and, to varying degrees, militarily. What do those dividing lines look like for the world? And where are the next potential flashpoints for great power conflict?

CHAPTER TWO

DIVIDING LINES

AT NATO SUMMIT, WAR IN THE AIR

At the June 2022 NATO summit in Madrid, the first meeting of alliance members since the Russian invasion of Ukraine, the threat of broader war was in the air. As I spoke to leaders, foreign ministers, and defense officials of multiple NATO allies, I was struck by the unity of members' rhetoric and actions. Together, they described a clear and present danger to Europe from a revanchist Russia. That threat now required defense, not just deterrence, and concrete, measurable increases in troop and weapons deployments, rather than merely moving units in and out of various locations, to send a message to the Kremlin. Those signals and words weren't working. It was time for broader action.

I sensed another disturbing change as well. Just four months earlier, even as the US was counting Russian soldiers, tanks, artillery pieces, and jets arrayed in formation on Ukraine's border, doubts as to Russia's actual intentions permeated NATO leadership as well as US media and political circles. They could see it—the satellite images were now public—but they didn't believe it. The invasion of course did come. And now there was open discussion of something far bigger: the prospect of a broader war between Russia and the alliance itself.

"Is war in Europe beyond Ukraine a genuine possibility?" I asked Foreign Minister Pekka Haavisto of Finland.

Without hesitation, he answered me clearly: "Of course it's a possibility, and that's why it's so important to support Ukraine at the moment. Because if Ukraine is losing, then [Russia's] sphere of interests can spread from Ukraine to other countries."

The repercussions of the Russian invasion of Ukraine had radiated out from eastern Europe like the shock waves of a missile strike, lengthening and hardening the dividing lines among the great powers through both Europe and Asia, and solidifying spheres of influence reminiscent of the last Cold War. Only this time, there were three spheres: one each for the West, Russia, and China.

Take a map and draw one vertical line between Russia and NATO countries, extending from Finland in the north to Turkey in the south. Turn your attention east and draw another vertical line separating China and Russia on one side from the US and its allies, extending from the Arctic in the north through the Bering Strait, down between China and Japan, North and South Korea, and China and Taiwan, and south to the South China Sea. These two lines, a virtual V-shaped barrier between East and West, are the new dividing lines of great power competition. The great powers are hardening, fortifying these new lines by deploying more forces and weapons systems and, at the same time, testing each other's limits and reactions with incursions closer and closer to—and sometimes over—those lines.

As a result, these frontiers are marked by multiple potential flashpoints along them, from the most present threats in Ukraine and Taiwan to Russian aspirations in the Baltics; China's land claims in the South China Sea; North Korea's missile threats to South Korea and US bases in Asia; the East China Sea, where China and Russia are conducting more joint exercises; the coast of Alaska, where Russia regularly tests US defenses and where China sent its spy balloon; and the Arctic, where all the great powers are now battling for control.

◼

Russia's invasion of Ukraine did the most to solidify and lengthen the dividing line—a new Iron Curtain—in Europe. Putin had expected a weak and disunified western response to his invasion. Many in the West had done the same. If Europe could live with a Russian invasion of Crimea and Eastern Ukraine in 2014—as well as a partial invasion of Georgia in 2008—and if the US had demonstrated its exhaustion with foreign entanglements by its recent withdrawal from Afghanistan, wouldn't the US and its allies reconcile themselves to a full-scale Russian invasion of Ukraine? In a long list of misguided predictions around the war, expectations of a muted western response proved off target.

Quite to the contrary, the West united to support Ukraine militarily and to punish Russia economically. The allies rushed military assistance to Ukraine, with an immediate impact on the battlefield: first with highly mobile weapons systems, which helped extinguish Russia's "blitzkrieg" plans for the initial invasion, and later, as the battle transitioned to a long Ukrainian fight to reclaim Russian-occupied territory, with a series of increasingly powerful weapons systems, from HIMARS to Storm Shadow cruise missiles, Leopard tanks and Bradley fighting vehicles, and eventually even F-16 fighter jets. Each was considered too incendiary until it wasn't, and each helped Ukrainian forces slowly claw back parts of their country from Russian occupying forces.

In the economic space, the US and Europe mobilized to virtually end Russia's trade with the West, restrict Russian access to the global banking and financial systems, and end Europe's dependence on Russian energy. Even its "no limits" partner China hesitated to send significant lethal military assistance, as Russia had hoped, leaving Russian forces to depend on North Korean and Iranian help.

Most impactfully of all, NATO found a new unity and mission. After a yearslong identity crisis, lurching from counterterrorism and counternarcotics to relief missions and peacekeeping, the alliance reoriented itself to its original mission: defending Europe against Russia and, now, a second strategic adversary in China. For better or worse, the world's largest and oldest military alliance was back in business and eager to grow.

At the Madrid summit, NATO members—which the Russian president had increasingly described as a direct threat to Russia—decided unanimously, as the terms of the alliance require, to admit both Finland and Sweden.

"The accession of Finland and Sweden will make them safer, NATO stronger, and the Euro-Atlantic area more secure. The security of Finland and Sweden is of direct importance to the Alliance, including during the accession process," read a joint statement from NATO members.

The decision to admit Finland and Sweden to NATO ended decades of deliberate neutrality for Helsinki and Stockholm, a position they had maintained for generations as a matter of both independence and national security. Their admission would more than double the length of the frontier between Russia and the alliance—requiring each country to expand its military commitments and deployments. And economically, the countries effectively decoupled from Russia, with Finland paying the highest price given its policy, dating from World War II, of furthering deep economic interdependence between the two countries. These are strategic, not tactical, decisions necessitating lasting change.

In Madrid, NATO allies had appeared to overcome political division at home and within the alliance itself, including opposition to Sweden's accession from member state Turkey.

"Overall, [we see] very wide support from other NATO members," the Finnish foreign minister Haavisto told me in Madrid, noting that strengthening and expanding the alliance bridged divides not only in Europe but also within US political parties. "You can see the [US] Senate is really pushing the thing. It is one of the bipartisan issues in the US and in many countries."

In the span of weeks, then, Putin had effectively eliminated fissures in the alliance. Before the invasion, disagreements as to the seriousness of the Russian threat and how best to respond to it had repeatedly spilled into the public conversation. Both Finland and Sweden had cultivated a middle path in relations with Russia, calculating that their security required avoiding open confrontation with Moscow, even as Putin steadily became more aggressive in words and deeds.

But Finnish leaders told me that the Russian invasion of Ukraine shook their country as never before.

And the NATO summit in Vilnius, Lithuania, in July 2023 made progress toward completing the expansion begun in Madrid a year earlier, with Turkey taking a step toward rescinding its opposition to Sweden's accession to the alliance. In less than two years since Russia's invasion of Ukraine, NATO's total membership appeared set to grow by two, to thirty-two, including fourteen countries that had previously been part of the former USSR and Warsaw Pact.

NATO's expansion had a significant military impact. Finland

alone, with one of the largest and best-trained armed forces in Europe, vastly expanded the alliance's military capabilities. And Finnish forces garner deep respect among NATO commanders I've encountered.

"[Finland] adds a very high-, well-trained set of armed forces, with regard to air force, navy, and army," Rear Admiral Thorsten Marx, commanding officer of the NATO Very High Readiness Joint Task Force in the Baltic Sea, told me. "They're a society with a high degree of resilience."

Finland's eastern border is long—more than eight hundred miles— the longest shared with Russian among the European Union's twenty-seven members.[1] The altered geography of the Russia-NATO divide necessitates a strategic shift from both sides. "It can be a threat to Finland having such a long borderline, but also it requires some effort on the Russian side to protect the borderline from their side," said Marx. "So that means the effort required, if they really feel threatened by NATO to defend themselves, is now severely increasing. From a military political point of view, they force Russia to adapt and to rethink."

Border walls torn down three decades ago are literally rising up once again. For years, the only fences marking Finland's border with Russia were wooden barriers to stop livestock. But in early 2022, Finland began construction of a taller, ten-feet-high barrier topped with barbed wire. The work would soon extend up to 161 miles. At the time, Finland was experiencing a Russian invasion of a different sort: military-age men fleeing conscription following Putin's partial mobilization to compensate for mounting losses in Ukraine.[2] But the project was part of a broader effort to boost security along the entire length of the border.

A longer frontier between the great powers with larger deployments and hardened defenses—the new "Berlin Wall"—now extended many hundreds of miles through Europe. And, like rival predators, NATO and Russian forces were increasingly coming into contact along that frontier, with new dangers of confrontation and escalation.

"For us, NATO membership support started from the twenty-fourth of February, when we saw that the security architecture of Europe is broken," Haavisto said. "This security architecture cannot prevent war in Europe. All that was gone in one day."

"War in Europe"—again, Europe's leaders were speaking openly of the prospect of a broader war. And again, NATO allies were united against Russia as they had not been since 1991 and the fall of the Soviet Union.

Targeting China

In Madrid, NATO made clear it was no longer confining its attention to its old adversary. In its updated "Strategic Concept" document, which outlines primary threats to the alliance, NATO for the first time identified China as a direct challenge to its security.

"The People's Republic of China's (PRC) stated ambitions and coercive policies challenge our interests, security and values. The PRC employs a broad range of political, economic and military tools to increase its global footprint and project power, while remaining opaque about its strategy, intentions and military buildup," read the document.[3]

NATO identified China's overall goal as overturning the world order on every front, saying, "It [China] strives to subvert the rules-based international order, including in the space, cyber and maritime domains." And it noted that Beijing and Moscow shared the very same ambition: "The deepening strategic partnership between the People's Republic of China and the Russian Federation and their mutually reinforcing attempts to undercut the rules-based international order run counter to our values and interests."[4]

An alliance formed at the dawn of the Cold War to defend Europe against one rival great power in Europe had now expanded its mission to defend against two great powers, virtually spanning the globe.

In Vilnius, beyond its expansion in Europe, NATO reaffirmed its turn eastward, stating, "We are working together responsibly, as Allies, to address the systemic challenges posed by the PRC to Euro-Atlantic security and ensure NATO's enduring ability to guarantee the defense and security of Allies."[5]

In our conversations, NATO Secretary General Jens Stoltenberg has made clear to me that NATO has two great power adversaries in its sights: "You see, Europe, like the US, sees China as a global threat, so it will respond together as an alliance to a threat it sees as potentially existential."

China as a "global threat" and the threat as "existential"—these are the new calculations of the world's largest military alliance.

"NATO is a regional alliance, North America and Europe," Stoltenberg said. "And we will remain a regional alliance, North America and Europe. But this region faces global threats and challenges."

"The military buildup by China, and also combined with [its] closer and closer relationship with Russia, means that we have to take this seriously as an alliance of North America and Europe," he continued. "And also because China is coming close to us. We see them in the Arctic. We see them in Africa. We see them in cyberspace. We see China trying to control critical infrastructure, and we expect China to have fifteen hundred warheads on missiles that can reach the whole of Europe and North America by 2035."

To demonstrate NATO's growing look eastward, nations with capitals many thousands of miles away from Vilnius traveled in to discuss shared threats and interests as well as further cooperation.

"Our Pacific partners attended the NATO summit—the leaders, the heads of state and governments from Australia and New Zealand, Japan and South Korea," Stoltenberg said. "So, NATO will not become in alliance with members in Asia, covered by Article 5, but we need to work with partners in Asia, and we need to address the challenges that stem from Asia."

"NO LIMITS" PARTNERSHIP OF XI AND PUTIN

As the US and its allies were solidifying and expanding their alliance and creating new ones, China and Russia were strengthening their own, predicated on their shared view of western alliances as a threat to their interests and conviction that the existing world order and "rules-based international system" was built by the West and its allies solely in their interests.

China and Russia, like their leaders Xi Jinping and Vladimir Putin, are two very different nations. They are separated by different languages, cultures, histories, and continents. China's GDP is six to ten times larger than Russia's. Russia, with an estimated six thousand nuclear warheads, has about twenty times the nuclear weapons China does. The Chinese and Russian leaders are different in their backgrounds as well. Xi is Chinese Communist Party royalty, a son of one of the original leaders of the Long March at the CCP's founding. Putin was a mid-level KGB officer before he was quickly elevated to power under Boris Yeltsin.

Xi and Putin are, however, strikingly similar in their ambitions and worldview. Both see themselves as historic figures with a mission to right historical wrongs imposed on their nations and people by the West. For Putin, it is righting the collapse of the Soviet Union, which he has famously described as "the greatest geopolitical catastrophe of the century." The historical wrong Xi is destined to correct is older: what he and many Chinese view as the subjugation of China by the West dating back to the Opium Wars of the mid-1800s and a series of unfair treaties and conflicts that led China to cede territory under duress (see Hong Kong and Taiwan).

"Look at the nature of these men and what they believe and what they think they need to achieve in order to be successes," said Matthew Pottinger, Trump's deputy national security advisor. "These are hard-nosed people."

Their shared interpretation of the present world is influenced by a shared vision of the recent past. Putin and Xi both view the collapse of the USSR as a cautionary tale. In fact, senior Chinese officials study the events of 1991 to prevent the Chinese Communist Party from facing a similar fate.

How far would Xi and China be prepared to go? All the way to confronting and ending US dominance in Asia and perhaps beyond. "Beijing is accelerating the development of key capabilities that it believes the People's Liberation Army (PLA) needs to confront the United States in a large-scale, sustained conflict," the intelligence community concluded.

The 2023 *Annual Threat Assessment of the US Intelligence Community* put the Chinese leader's ambitions in stark terms: "China's Communist Party (CCP) will continue efforts to achieve President Xi Jinping's vision of making China the preeminent power in East Asia and a major power on the world stage."[6]

The assessment described Russian ambitions in similar terms: "Russia's unprovoked war of aggression against Ukraine is a tectonic event that is reshaping Russia's relationships with the West and China, and more broadly in ways that are unfolding and remain highly uncertain. Escalation of the conflict to a military confrontation between Russia and the West carries the greater risk, which the world has not faced in decades."[7]

PUTIN-XI SUMMIT

In late March 2023, Putin and Xi celebrated their partnership on the world stage with a lavish three-day state visit by the Chinese leader to Moscow. "Dear friend, welcome to Russia," Putin said to Xi as he arrived.

Two weeks after Xi had engineered a sham election in the National People's Congress to extend his presidency into an unprecedented—and until then, unconstitutional—third term, Xi noted upcoming elections in Russia, also a far cry from a democracy. Xi said to Putin, "You have elections next year, and I'm sure the Russian people will support you." Putin praised Xi's leadership as well, crediting him for propelling China to a "colossal leap forward."[8]

The timing of the visit was notable and meaningful. The Chinese president was standing beside the Russian leader—literally and figuratively—days after the International Criminal Court had accused him and Maria Lvova-Belova, Russia's commissioner for children's rights in the office of the president, of war crimes for deporting children from Ukraine to Russia, and more than a year into the most catastrophic decision of Putin's presidency: the invasion of Ukraine. China had not yet armed Russia for the war. But a summit in Russia's capital was perhaps equally meaningful. Ukraine had become a proxy war between the US and Russia—and now China was more firmly than ever on Russia's side. Not since the Korean War—when Stalin and Mao held power—had Russia and China been in such public lockstep on a war with the West.

In a highly visual diplomatic counterpoint, Japanese prime minister Kishida Fumio made a surprise visit to Kyiv just as Xi and Putin were meeting in Moscow. The Japanese leader announced his country would be making $30 million available to Ukraine via NATO trust funds to help Ukraine acquire nonlethal equipment. And in a joint press conference with Ukrainian president Zelensky, Fumio pledged that "Japan will continue providing seamless support" and that his "country will stay with Ukraine until peace returns to its beautiful land," as reported by Japanese broadcaster NHK. The leaders of all major NATO allies, including the US president, had already visited Kyiv to show support for Ukraine and Zelensky. But here was the leader of an Asian nation—its capital more than five thousand miles away from Ukraine's—demonstrating that just as China was wedding itself to Russian fortunes in Ukraine, Japan was now firmly with the US and West on the side of Ukraine.

Ostensibly, the Xi-Putin summit's agenda focused on economic cooperation and trade, which had skyrocketed by nearly a third, to $189 billion, over the previous year as Russian energy exports to China surged (and plummeted to Europe).[9] The two sides signed a joint declaration on economic cooperation, which Putin said would help propel trade above $200 billion in the coming year.[10] The visit, Putin's spokesman told journalists, would also include discussions of a resolution to the Ukraine war. In the weeks prior, China had proposed the outlines of its own peace plan, though Ukrainian and western officials doubted China's credibility as peacemaker.

Jointly declaring their shared outlook to the world, the two leaders published simultaneous articles on the eve of the visit: Putin in the Chinese-government-run *People's Daily*, and Xi in the

Russian-government-controlled *Rossiyskaya Gazeta*.[11] They described their relationship in glowing and historical terms. "Our two sides are implementing the concept of friendship passed down from generation to generation, and this traditional friendship is growing day by day," Xi wrote.[12]

"The Russia-China relations have reached the highest level in their history," Putin wrote, "and are gaining even more strength; they surpass Cold War–time military-political alliances in their quality, with no one to constantly order and no one to constantly obey, without limitations or taboos. We have reached an unprecedented level of trust in our political dialogue. Our strategic cooperation has become truly comprehensive in nature and is standing on the brink of a new era."[13]

That "new era," the leaders said, is marked by a new and growing threat—the US and the "collective West"—and a growing need for a new global order.

"Unlike some countries claiming hegemony and bringing discord to the global harmony, Russia and China are literally and figuratively building bridges," Putin wrote, citing a new railroad bridge between the two countries over the Amur River in eastern Russia.

For his part, Xi wrote, "There is no universal model of government and there is no world order where the decisive word belongs to a single country. Global solidarity and peace without splits and upheavals is in the common interests of all mankind."[14]

They made clear that their shared goal is a remaking of the global order, with Putin writing, "Our countries, together with like-minded actors, have consistently advocated the shaping of a more just multipolar world order based on international law rather than certain 'rules' serving the needs of the 'golden billion.'"[15] (The "golden billion" is a conspiracy theory that the world is ruled by a wealthy elite serving the interests of the richest one billion people.)

Even as the Russian invasion entered its thirteenth month, the Russian president claimed this new system "is not directed against third countries." It was a preposterous characterization, as it coincided with one of the bloodiest phases of Russia's war. At that moment, as Putin was feting Xi in the Kremlin, Russian forces were weeks into a devastating battle for the eastern Ukrainian city of Bakhmut. The UK Ministry of Defence estimated some thirty thousand Russian troops had by that time been killed or wounded on that single battlefield. As I read their declarations, I wondered if any of those Russian soldiers, many of them former convicts recruited by Putin's then ally Yevgeny Prigozhin for the Wagner Group, had heard Putin's words. Would they ever?

In short, Putin's article was a mission statement for a new world order built on his conviction that the US is the lone aggressor. "We can feel the geopolitical landscape in the outside world change dramatically," he wrote. "Sticking more stubbornly than ever to its obsolete dogmata and vanishing dominance, the 'Collective West' is gambling on the fates of entire states and peoples. The US's policy of simultaneously deterring Russia and China, as well as all those who do not bend to the American dictation, is getting ever more fierce and aggressive. The international security and cooperation architecture is being dismantled. Russia has been labelled an 'immediate threat' and China a 'strategic competitor.'"[16]

Here was the Russian president establishing common ground and shared victimhood with the Chinese people. In doing so, he argued that China faces a threat from the US and its allies in Asia as much as Russia is threatened by NATO.

"It is crystal clear that NATO is striving for a global reach of activities and seeking to penetrate the Asia-Pacific," Putin wrote. "It [sic] obvious that there are forces persistently working to split the common Eurasian space into a network of 'exclusive clubs' and military blocs that would serve to contain our countries' development and harm their interests. This won't work."[17]

Putin's worldview was infused once again with a geopolitical paranoia—which the US intelligence community believes the Russian leader shares with his Chinese counterpart. "Beijing sees increasingly competitive U.S.-China relations as part of an epochal geopolitical shift," the US intelligence community assessed, "and views Washington's diplomatic, economic, military, and technological measures against Beijing as part of a broader U.S. effort to prevent China's rise and undermine CCP rule."[18]

These were not new views or new geopolitical outlooks. Vladimir Putin had been telegraphing his hostile view of the West—and his view of the West as inherently hostile to Russia—in stark terms since his speech to the Munich Security Conference in 2007. To a shocked audience at the time, Putin took direct aim at the US-led world order: "It is a world in which there is one master, one sovereign. And at the end of the day this is pernicious not only for all those within this system, but also for the sovereign itself because it destroys itself from within."[19] Notably, the Russian invasions of Georgia in 2008 soon followed.

As I detailed in the Prologue, Vladimir Putin had for years been quietly building a historical pretext for his invasion of Ukraine as well. Through a series of steps, he strong-armed Russian academia and bureaucracy to endorse his artificial reading of maps and history to substantiate Russian claims on Ukraine. That is, Putin had been rewriting history to create a justification for war. And just as his military commanders and intelligence officials had told him what he wanted to hear regarding Russia's capability to quickly defeat Ukraine, his historians and archivists told him what he wanted to hear on Russia's supposed historical claims. As the invasion approached, in his conversations with the Finnish president, who was one of his closest foreign counterparts, Putin clung to his version of history and justification for war. It is a position he never wavered from as the war neared its third bloody year.

XI'S VIEW OF THE WEST

Putin and Xi often assume the worst of their adversaries. In 2014, one year after he became president, Xi delivered his assessment of the US and the West to Chinese security officials, describing them as committed to weakening China: "Western countries such as America increasingly feel fishbones in their throats and blade-tips in their backs, so are stepping up their strategy of Westernizing and splitting our country."[20] The US wasn't just China's global competitor, as observers and diplomats had come to describe the two nations in public conversation. In Xi's view, the US was a direct threat to China's rise and its very unity as a nation. Like Putin, a newly installed Xi quickly followed his words with action. Beginning in 2014, China detained some one million Uighurs in Xinjiang and accelerated the construction of man-made islands in the disputed waters of the South China Sea.

During my time as chief of staff to the US ambassador to China from 2011 to 2013, China was in the early stages of what would soon become a massive land grab in the South China Sea. Many in the State Department downplayed China's territorial ambitions, assuming that Chinese leaders were reluctant to suffer the diplomatic consequences of antagonizing not just the US but also the half dozen Southeast Asian nations that simultaneously claimed the area as at least partly their own. When Xi took over leadership, this assumption endured. And yet, even as China took concrete steps that contradicted that assumption—launching and then accelerating a massive infrastructure project to expand and then militarize the islands—US leaders still took Xi at his word.

As I recount in *The Shadow War*, Xi and Obama clashed over the islands on the Chinese leader's first official visit to the United States, in September 2015. As they stood together before the cameras in the Rose Garden, President Obama said, "I conveyed to President Xi our significant concerns over land reclamation, construction, and the militarization of disputed areas, which makes it harder for countries in the region to resolve disagreements peacefully."

Xi did not back down, restating China's version of the history of the islands as fact. "Islands in the South China Sea since ancient times are Chinese territory," he said. "We have the right to uphold our own territorial sovereignty and lawful legitimate maritime rights and interests."

However, Xi made what the US perceived as a promise as well, vowing that China would not transform the islands into military outposts. "Relevant construction activity that China is undertaking in the Nansha Islands [the name China uses for the Spratly Islands] does not target or impact any country, and there is no intention to militarize," Xi said.[21]

While the Chinese word for "intention" (*yitu*) may fall short of an overriding promise to refrain from militarization, US leaders took it as such. In the months and years that followed, Xi's "promise" proved empty.

The Chinese and Russian leaders have stated their positions in public with clarity for years—and those positions are increasingly reflected in the comments of senior Russian and Chinese officials down the line. As then foreign minister Qin Gang told journalists at the National People's Congress in 2023, "If the US does not hit the brake but continues to speed down the wrong path, no amount of guardrails can prevent derailing, and there will surely be conflict and confrontation."[22]

"There will surely be conflict." Listen to what they say.

In our conversations, then Joint Chiefs Chairman General Mark Milley dubbed this his "declaratory policy" of international affairs. "My read of history is, when foreign heads of state make declaratory policy and it's publicly stated and then repeated several different times, it is in people's interest to believe them—what I call declaratory policy in international politics," Milley told me. "When Saddam Hussein says publicly he's going to invade Kuwait, it's a good idea to listen to him, right? When Hitler says, and writes in *Mein Kampf*, I'm going to kill the Jews, you got to listen to him. When Kim Il Sung says, I'm going to invade South Korea, probably listen to him. When Mao Zedong says, If you get within twenty-five miles of the Yellow River, I'm coming across the border . . ."

Some current and former US officials see in Xi and Putin parallels to some of the most dangerous leaders of the last century—reminiscent in many ways of Mao and Stalin.

"Both of them have been in power a very long time," said former deputy national security advisor Pottinger. "We've had almost a quarter century of Putin. We've had a decade of Xi Jinping. If they believed that they could have achieved their aims earlier, they would've gone for it."

The most important point, Pottinger argues, is that the Xi-Putin challenge to the West is defining for them, requiring an equally defining change in perspective from the West.

"That's why we should also stop kidding ourselves," he continued. "This is a tried-and-true American pastime to assume that the rest of the world only acts in reaction to things that we say or do. There's a lot of that still going around. You see a lot of people saying, 'Well, geez, if we hadn't shot a fucking balloon, I'm sure that Xi Jinping would be angling for some kind of kind of peace-pipe moment right now.' It's preposterous."

Now, like the West, Russia and China increasingly see great power competition in global terms and are marshaling resources along the same dividing lines extended and increasingly defended by the West. Where their goals align, Xi and Putin will work together, including in targeting Europe.

"Let's not kid ourselves," said Pottinger. "China's strategy right now is to break apart Europe. That's why he signed that 'no limits' pact less than three weeks before Putin invaded."

RISING OR FALLING POWERS?

Russian and Chinese ambitions are one thing, and should indeed be heard and taken very seriously. But recent events have deflated cursory assessments of Russia and China as fully "ten-foot-tall" adversaries. Before the Ukraine war, Putin was—to some—a grand strategist too wise to order a full-scale invasion of Ukraine, and Europe too dependent on Russian energy to challenge him. And his military was destined to swallow Ukraine within days. None of this bore out. And the consequences for the security of the rest of Europe are lasting.

In early 2023, the US intelligence community's *Annual Threat Assessment* stated, "Moscow's military forces have suffered losses during the Ukraine conflict that will require years of rebuilding and leave them less capable of posing a conventional military threat to European security and operating as assertively in Eurasia and on the global stage."

Until recently, it was also conventional wisdom that China was on an unending rise. Again, the facts have pierced that bubble.

"China faces myriad—and in some cases growing—domestic and

international challenges that probably will hinder CCP leaders' ambitions," read the 2023 *Annual Threat Assessment.* "These include an aging population, high levels of corporate debt, economic inequality, and growing resistance to the People's Republic of China's (PRC) heavy-handed tactics in Taiwan and other countries."

China's economic growth has fallen back to earth. As a diplomat in China ten years ago, I saw close observers of the Chinese economy predict the negative trend lines. At the US embassy in Beijing, we knew that the Chinese government inflated its economic figures. What other country in the world forecast 7 percent economic growth every year and somehow managed to meet it down to the decimal point? Now, suffering under punishing debt loads and plummeting economic growth, the truth is out. Crucially, China's economy is coming back to earth before it has reached wealth levels consistent with those in developed nations and as the Chinese population is aging, further limiting its growth prospects.

US officials are acutely aware of the change. "On the one hand, of course, Xi has fully and further consolidated his power," Secretary of State Antony Blinken told me. "On the other hand, for reasons that are well-known, we're seeing China enter a very challenged period, where you have profound economic challenges. Some of those challenges are, in a sense, to be expected, given where China is in its development, moving from a development stage to a developed stage. And that typically brings growth rates down regardless. But they came down precipitously, and it's been exacerbated by Covid and by arguably some bad economic policy. But China making the adjustments from decades of eight, nine, ten percent growth to two or three percent growth is a huge challenge. You're seeing employment challenges. You obviously have a huge demographic challenge, with an aging population that's not being replaced. You have doubling down on state-owned, enterprise-focused economy and the restrictions that have been posed on the private sector.

"I'm not saying . . . that power is gone," Blinken cautioned. "But there are also certain constraints, based on where China is, that I think will come into play."

Internal weaknesses pose a threat to Xi greater, in some ways, than external ones. "We've now seen that he can be rattled when problems become political in nature domestically," said Pottinger, the former deputy national security advisor. "He was not rattled by the fact that his economy was cratering over the course of 2022. He doesn't appear to have been rattled by the fact that his Covid policy was not working in the end. But he was rattled evidently by the fact that Chinese citizens took to the streets in multiple cities around the country and were criticizing one of his signature policies and criticizing the Chinese Communist Party."

The question for leaders of rival great powers is, Do weaknesses make China and Russia more or less dangerous? At a minimum, many leaders I interviewed believe that both Xi and Putin feel the pressure of time. Putin feels required to act now, or find his country further relegated to irrelevance as a great power. Even when he is challenged, they warn, he will look for targets of opportunity against the West.

According to the intelligence community's threat assessment: "Moscow will continue to employ an array of tools to advance what it sees as its own interests and try to undermine the interests of the United States and its allies. These are likely to be military, security, malign influence, cyber, and intelligence tools, with Russia's economic and energy leverage probably a declining asset. We expect Moscow to insert itself into crises when it sees its interests at stake, the anticipated costs of action are low, it sees an opportunity to capitalize on a power vacuum, or, as in the case of its use of force in Ukraine, it perceives an existential threat in its neighborhood that could destabilize Putin's rule and endanger Russian national security."

The assessment also noted disturbingly that weaknesses were driving the Kremlin to rely more on unconventional weapons systems. "Moscow will become even more reliant on nuclear, cyber, and space capabilities as it deals with the extensive damage to Russia's ground forces," the assessment read.[23]

Putin is no brilliant adjudicator of when to strike, as the Ukraine invasion showed, but Russia's weaknesses have not coalesced enough to fully disable it. The Russian economy has suffered but not collapsed. The Russian military has been humbled but maintains the ability to arm and man a long war in Ukraine.

As for Xi, when it comes to the threat to Taiwan from China, and as he watches his economy suffer and Taiwan build its defenses, he may calculate that the sweet spot for action is now: as soon as the Chinese military is ready and before Taiwan can sufficiently shore up its defenses.

"We should take a little bit of comfort from the fact that they have been deterred so far, or at least up until February of last year, and that tells me that they are deterrable," said Pottinger. "But we sure as hell are running out of time. We're really running out of time to take steps that we need to take fast to reassert deterrents."

CHINA ARMS RUSSIA IN UKRAINE?

In early 2023, US officials began to warn publicly of what would be the most alarming demonstration of the "no limits" partnership between Putin and Xi: China was considering a more aggressive foray into the Ukraine war by providing "lethal support" to Russia for its ongoing invasion, to complement nonlethal aid it had already been sending.

This was a lot more than writing editorials in each other's papers. "We've been watching this very closely," Secretary of State Blinken told CBS's *Face the Nation* from the Munich Security Conference in 2023, noting the US had already observed Chinese companies providing nonlethal support to Russia, like trucks and semiconductors. "The concern that we have now is based on information we have that they're considering providing lethal support, and we've made very clear to them that that would cause a serious problem for us and in our relationship."[24]

To eliminate any doubt about what the US now believed Beijing was contemplating, Blinken described such lethal support as "primarily weapons," stating, "There's a whole gamut of things that fit in that category, everything from ammunition to the weapons themselves."[25] CNN reported soon after that US intelligence indicated such military aid would include, specifically, drones and ammunition for use in Ukraine.[26]

Sending military aid would be a momentous development. Though Xi and Putin had advertised their "no limits" relationship just before the invasion, China had stood by for a full year without taking such a step. This was despite the fact that Russia had first asked China for military support nearly a full year earlier, as my colleagues and I reported for CNN in March 2022, just weeks into the invasion.[27]

"We also are watching closely to see the extent to which China actually does provide any form of support, material support or economic support, to Russia," National Security Advisor Jake Sullivan told my colleague Dana Bash on *State of the Union* at the time. "It is a concern of ours. And we have communicated to Beijing that we will not stand by and allow any country to compensate Russia for its losses from the economic sanctions."

Crucially, as China had waited, it had observed Russia's war effort stumble into incompetence. A decision to jump in with weapons would have been a risky bet for Xi at that stage of the war, with the Russian military reeling. It would also almost certainly lengthen a war that has already claimed many tens of thousands of lives on both sides. Perhaps most important, it would expand Ukraine from what was already a risky proxy war between two great powers into one involving all three. It would become a great power conflict, albeit indirectly, unlike any the world has ever seen.

Chinese officials deflected the US warnings. Chinese foreign ministry spokesperson Wang Wenbin said in a briefing, "China has always taken a prudent and responsible approach to military exports and does not provide any arms sales to conflict areas or belligerents."[28] Instead, at the Munich Security Conference in 2023, China was talking up its peace plan for Ukraine.

US officials, making clear their Chinese counterparts had provided no details of their plan, expressed skepticism. "Just speaking generally and looking at what the Chinese have said in recent days, it would appear to us that the Chinese are trying to have it both ways," a US official said. "On the one hand, claiming that they would like to contribute to peace and stability in Ukraine, and yet on the other hand, taking these concerning steps to support Russia's war of aggression there."

In public comments, US officials began to characterize potential Chinese military support for Russia in Ukraine as a "red line" for the US.

"But we also have to be clear that if there are any thoughts and efforts by the Chinese and others to provide lethal support to the Russians in their brutal attack against Ukraine, that that is unacceptable," Ambassador Linda Thomas-Greenfield told my colleague Pamela Brown on *State of the Union.* "That would be a red line."[29]

Left unsaid, however, was how the US would enforce such a new "red line." The Biden White House was full of veterans from the administration of President Obama, who had infamously set a "red line" for Syria—that it never use chemical weapons—only to retreat when the Syrian regime crossed the line. How would President Biden, who was vice president when Syria crossed the line, make a new red line with China stick?

In the days and weeks that followed, US officials began to describe what those penalties might look like—specifically, economic sanctions targeting individuals and entities providing such support.

On a visit to Kazakhstan, Blinken said of his meeting with Chinese foreign minister Wang Yi in Munich, "We did very clearly warn China about the implications and consequences of going through with providing such support." He added, "We will not hesitate, for example, to target Chinese companies or individuals that violate our sanctions, or otherwise engage in supporting the Russian war effort."[30]

At the same time, using a tactic the US intelligence community had employed in Ukraine, CIA Director Bill Burns publicly disclosed US intelligence assessments that China was considering such military support.

"As Secretary Blinken has said, publicly, you know, we have begun to see—we have begun to collect intelligence suggesting—that China is considering the provision of lethal equipment. That's not to suggest that they've made a definitive conclusion about this," Burns said.[31]

This was a very public messaging effort by the US Defense Secretary Lloyd Austin spoke of the political and diplomatic damage China would suffer. "There's reputational risk, and of course, I'm sure China would love to enjoy a good relationship with all the countries in Europe," Austin told CNN. "And again, if you just look at the numbers of countries around the world, that really think that what Russia has done is horrible, I mean, adding to that, I think China—it would be a very ill-advised step for China to take."[32]

What was China's goal? Many in the West believed that Chinese leaders hoped to prolong the war in Ukraine in order to distract and weaken the US and its allies so as to make it less capable to respond to a potential Chinese invasion of Taiwan.

"If China can't help Russia win the war quickly, the second-best outcome for China would be to prolong the war in Europe as long as possible," former deputy national security advisor Pottinger told me. "The effects of prolonging that war would be to drain the US Treasury and our munition stockpiles, to create enormous strain on Europe and to see whether it can foment disunity about what has until now been an admirably unified response to Putin's aggression, and to create a major distraction at a time that [Xi's] getting his military and society geared up for war over Taiwan."

RUSSIA AND CHINA

How and where else could this military cooperation grow? In baseball terms, Russian military cooperation with Iran or North Korea is like a major-league franchise sharing talent with a double-A team. Russian military cooperation with China would be the equivalent of the Yankees merging organizations with the Dodgers—two behemoths in their hemispheres creating a partnership to take on the world. US officials and military analysts are watching one area of potential Russian-Chinese cooperation with particular concern: submarine technology.

As I detail in *The Shadow War,* following the fall of the USSR, Russia maintained its submarine forces even as it downsized and degraded its other conventional military forces. And though the Ukraine war has decimated broad swaths of the Russian military, its submarine forces have remained unscathed and advanced. China has also invested enormously in advancing its own submarine technology, though it remains behind Russia and the US, particularly in the ability to run silently and avoid detection by adversaries. That gap presents another opportunity for a confluence of interests in the new great power architecture.

In their essay "Putin's Ukraine Invasion: Turbocharging Sino-Russian Collaboration in Energy, Maritime Security, and Beyond?," Andrew Erickson, a professor of strategy at the Naval War College who has researched and written extensively on the Chinese military, and Gabriel B. Collins lay out a potential collaboration between Beijing and Moscow with global implications:

Regardless of the specific channel(s), additional Russian submarine technology and possibly operational expertise worth billions of dollars could be fed into China's military-industrial juggernaut. If that occurred, its capacity for assimilating foreign technology, adapting it to local needs, and producing at scale would be globally destabilizing and seriously inimical to U.S. national-security interests. China's massive investments in long-range antiair and antiship missiles already have eroded U.S. and allied surface and air forces' ability to operate near the PRC's periphery at a given level of risk, but American submarines and undersea warfare have hitherto been affected far less by these rapid improvements in counterintervention capabilities. As the sea surface, air, and space realms increasingly are contested, this remaining area of American undersea dominance offers increasingly irreplaceable options. Contributions from a Russia under duress, in theory, could offer a fast-tracked "great leap forward" for PRC undersea-warfare capabilities and acoustic intelligence to inform their employment, thereby shifting the Sino-American military balance of power significantly during this critical decade.[33]

"A Russia under duress." This captures the unavoidable imbalance in the Russia-China relationship: Russia needs China more than ever. China needs only what Russia can provide it in terms of helping to disrupt the western-led international order and advancing its military capabilities. Could China exploit that imbalance to squeeze Russia for perhaps its most precious military asset? Yes, many believe. One consistent appraisal I heard from intelligence chiefs is that China is the dominant partner in this relationship, with immense dangers for Russia.

As CIA Director Burns told me in Chapter 1, Russia faces the risk that "they are going to end up being an economic colony of China if they're not careful."

The danger for the world is that Russia's dependence would open new military ties between Russia and China—including on China's most sensitive nuclear submarine technology—which would only further entrench the "no limits" partnership, with consequences for the US and the world.

THE NONMONOGAMOUS MIDDLE POWERS

As Russia, China, and the US circle one another around Ukraine and, increasingly, Taiwan, and across the many new front lines, smaller powers are getting drawn into the fray. A long list of "middle power" countries are now expanding relationships with the great powers on either side of the divide, and sometimes, as CIA Director Burns described to me, on both sides.

"You've got a lot of middle powers out there right now who don't think that a kind of monogamous set of relations is the way you need to go," Burns told me. "So they're going to hedge. They're going to want to have decent relations, well, certainly with China, decent relations with us in another way. Some of them at least want to keep their doors open to Russia."

Some—such as Iran and North Korea—are gravitating toward Russia and China. Others—such as the members of NATO and US allies in the Pacific—are firmly on the side of the US and the West.

"There's a lot of other powers in the world that are very, very strong and very capable," said General Milley. "Think all the various countries of Europe perhaps, NATO. Think, obviously, things like Japan and South Korea are really significant regional powers, and economically, they're clearly global in nature."

British intelligence sees middle powers often playing the middle, so to speak, siding with one great power or another or neither, depending on how it suits their interests. This global picking of sides recalls the back-and-forth among the aligned and nonaligned nations of the last Cold War—only with three great powers to navigate and even longer dividing lines among them.

"The very short period of unipolarity has finished, hasn't it? That's very clear," Richard Moore, chief of the UK's foreign intelligence service, MI6, told me. "[It is very interesting to see] the way in which middle powers now are trying to avoid choosing between Russia, between the US and China, the way in which they are trying to exploit great power dynamics to try and expand their freedom of maneuver."

RUSSIA AND IRAN

As the US carefully watched for China's next move in Ukraine, a new military relationship was already developing between Russia and Iran. As soon as the second month of the invasion, US intelligence agencies began to see signs of military cooperation between Moscow and Tehran. And by July the US assessed that Iran was preparing to provide armed drones to Russian forces.[34]

Iranian drones had an immediate impact on the war, providing Russia with a lethal way to strike both military and civilian targets. With their ability to linger above a target before striking, they proved an effective and frightening weapon for terrorizing the Ukrainian population.

By February 2023, CIA Director Burns told Margaret Brennan on CBS's *Face the Nation*, "It's moving at a pretty fast clip in a very dangerous direction right now. In the sense that we know that the Iranians have already provided hundreds of armed drones to the Russians, which they're using to inflict pain on Ukrainian civilians and Ukrainian civilian infrastructure. We know that they've provided, you know, ammunition for artillery and for tanks as well."[35]

By July 2023, defense intelligence officials revealed to reporters at the Pentagon that Iran would soon help build a new drone manufacturing plant inside Russia, which those officials said would provide Russian forces with a supply of drones "orders of magnitude larger" than previously. The US released a satellite image of the planned location of the facility, several hundred miles east of Moscow, and noted it had already observed Iran sending equipment to Russia to help construction.[36]

Great power relations are often transparently transactional. The "no limits" partnership between Russia and China actually involved a number of such conditional exchanges—China's diplomatic cover for the Ukraine invasion in exchange for discounted Russian oil among them. Russia's "alliance" with Iran is no different. In March 2023, CNN reported that Russia was shipping captured US weapons to Tehran, with the apparent goal of allowing Iran to reverse engineer the weapons' technology to create its own versions. Among the systems Russia shared were advanced Javelin anti-tank missiles and Stinger anti-aircraft missiles.[37] As Burns highlighted this increasingly symbiotic relationship, he warned that Russia was considering more significant military help to Iran.

"What we also see are signs that, you know, Russia is proposing to help the Iranians on their missile program and also at least considering the possibility of providing fighter aircraft to Iran as well. . . . So it's, you know, quite [a] disturbing set of developments," Burns said on *Face the Nation*.[38] By late 2023 a Russian plan to provide ballistic missiles to Iran appeared to be on hold, but the US warned that could change at any time.[39]

Russia's growing military cooperation with Iran—opening the warehouse, in effect, of one of the world's largest militaries to a regional power threatening a disparate group of western allies, including Israel and Saudi Arabia—is the kind of new alliance in the new great power conflict that deeply alarms western officials: each nation equally authoritarian and equally interested in disrupting the existing world order.

What elevated even that threat was the nuclear dynamic: that one power owns the world's largest nuclear arsenal and the other has long been an aspiring entrant into the world's nuclear club. As of mid-2023, the CIA assessed that Iran's supreme leader had not yet decided to resume Iran's nuclear weaponization program. But the potential remained. And here we see two dangerous threads of the new great power competition merging: new alliances among powers eager to break the current world order and new cooperation among nuclear haves and have-nots.

In fall 2023, Iran and Russia identified a new opportunity to disrupt the current world order. The Israel-Hamas war, sparked by the devastating October 7 terror attacks on several communities in southern Israel, aligned Iranian and Russian interests once again. For Iran, Hamas remained a proxy force to exert pressure on Israel, in part to demonstrate that the Iranian regime was still working to deliver on its defining promise to end the State of Israel and, in part, to act as a deterrent against any Israeli military attack on Iran itself, including, most consequentially in the view of Iranian leaders, a potential strike on its nuclear facilities. As my CNN colleagues and I reported in the early days of the war, US intelligence assessments at the time doubted that Iran was directly involved in the planning, resourcing, or approving of the October 7 operation. In fact, the US collected specific intelligence indicating that senior Iranian officials were surprised by the attack.[40] However, Iran had long supported, armed, and trained Hamas fighters explicitly to threaten and weaken Israel. And Iran's supreme leader repeatedly celebrated the attacks and the chaos that followed. He called the depraved violence on October 7 "a courageous and self-sacrificing move by the Palestinians" and, as Israel's military offensive inside Gaza expanded, demanded an economic blockade of Israel, saying "Muslim governments must block the export of oil and other essentials to the Zionist regime." In the wake of terror attacks that stunned even many in the Muslim world, Iran was again staking its claim on the Hamas side of this dividing line, and with pride and clarity.

As I reported on the war from inside Israel that fall, Israeli officials told me they now saw the Kremlin as being openly on the side of Hamas as well. The war was, they said, in Russia's selfish interests.

"Russia is a friend of Hamas, not our friend," a former senior Israeli intelligence official told me. "They enjoy the rising price of oil and the diversion of attention from Ukraine."

As the war raged on, Russia made its position only more publicly definitive. In late October, a delegation of Hamas leaders traveled to Moscow to meet with senior Russian officials. Russia portrayed the visit as an attempt to mediate the crisis. Israeli officials believed otherwise. The Israeli Foreign Ministry called the Kremlin's invitation "a reprehensible step that gives support to terrorism and legitimacy to the horrific acts of Hamas terrorists."[41] And in fact it wasn't the first time Hamas had been welcomed in Moscow. Leaders of the terrorist group traveled to Russia in March 2023, according to Hamas leaders, at Russia's invitation. And the head of Hamas's political section, Ismail Haniyeh, met with Russian Foreign Minister Sergey Lavrov in Moscow the previous September.[42]

On November 1, before the UN General Assembly, Russia's ambassador Vasily Nebenzya said Russia recognizes Israel's "rights to ensure its security" but rejected Israel's right to defend itself against Hamas in Gaza. "The only thing they can muster is continued pronouncements about Israel's supposed right to self-defense, although as an occupying power, it does not have that power as confirmed by the advisory opinion of the International Court of Justice handed down in 2004," Nebenzya said.[43]

Behind the scenes, Russia's involvement was more consequential. In late October, the US gathered intelligence indicating that Syria would provide Hezbollah, Iran's proxy in Lebanon, with the Russian-made surface-to-air SA-22 missile system. According to US officials, the Russian mercenary group, Wagner, was the conduit for the exchange.[44] A senior US military official told me that such an exchange would not have taken place without the explicit approval of the Kremlin. This was a wartime gift to Hezbollah from Russia—and an

THE RETURN OF GREAT POWERS

impactful one, giving the militant group the capability to target Israeli warplanes over Lebanon.

Russia's military assistance to Hezbollah, just as Israel and the US
were attempting to prevent a second front in the war from opening
up on the Israel-Lebanon border, was a jarring blow to Israeli policy
from the preceding years. Israeli leaders had taken care to strike a
delicate balance in their relationship with Russia since its invasion of
Ukraine, loath to antagonize Moscow despite Israel's deep ties to
Ukrainian leaders—chief among them President Volodomyr Zelensky, who is himself Jewish. In this choice between two friends, Israel
appeared to pick Russia. Israel repeatedly refused to supply weapons
and ammunition to Ukraine out of fear of damaging its position with
Moscow. In particular, Israel prioritized maintaining its ability to
strike Iran-backed forces inside Syria where Russian forces held sway.
In the days after the Russian invasion, then Israeli Prime Minister
Naftali Bennett neglected to even mention Russia, instead calling for
a peaceful dialogue among all sides.[45] Now, as Israel was locked in the
largest war it had fought in decades—a war Israeli leaders saw as
existential—Russia was arming a dangerous adversary perched on its
northern border.

The US was not a bystander to the Israel-Hamas war. In fact, from
President Biden's first comments on the October 7 attack, it became
clear that a key focus of the US response, beyond supporting its close
ally Israel, was to deter other state and non-state actors from expanding the war. That message came in both words and action. When he
addressed the nation on October 18, Biden repeated what would become a frequent warning from US officials commenting on the war,
"My message to any state or any other hostile actor thinking about
attacking Israel remains the same as it was a week ago: Don't. Don't.
Don't."[46] The president backed up that warning with a ballooning
deployment of US forces in the region. The US sent two carrier strike

groups—the USS *Gerald R. Ford* and USS *Dwight D. Eisenhower*—to the Eastern Mediterranean, each carrier with the capacity to carry dozens of fighter aircraft and joined by other warships, including guided-missile cruisers and destroyers. And, in a highly unusual move, the US Navy publicly announced that it had sent an *Ohio*-class guided-missile submarine to the region. The movements of such submarines are among the most sensitive for the US military. To announce its arrival—in a tweet, no less—showed that not only was the US flooding the region with assets to respond to any expansion of the war, it wanted its adversaries to know it.

Israeli officials noticed. "For the first time since the withdrawal from Afghanistan—even the first time since 2003—the U.S. is advancing large military assets into a war zone—and engaging," Michael Oren, the former Israeli ambassador to the US, told me. And that message, Oren said, was being heard far beyond the Middle East. "Iran, Russia, China—they all drew conclusions about America's unwillingness to project power. Even in Ukraine, Biden wasn't willing to lose a single US soldier. That suddenly has changed."

To Oren's point, the US assets weren't silent. US warplanes struck Iran-backed militias in Iraq and Syria after they targeted US forces stationed there. And a US destroyer shot down missiles fired at Israel by Iran-backed Houthi rebels in Yemen. "America is going right at this axis—right at the vortex, the focal point that is Iran," Oren told me.

Whether that deterrence would work remained an open question. And—as CIA Director Burns warned in our own conversation—the danger remained that small encounters between the US and its adversaries in the region could escalate into something bigger.

RUSSIA AND NORTH KOREA

Great power geopolitics can make for strange strategic bedfellows. Later in 2023, as China hesitated to deliver the weapons Russia desired, Russia turned to the world's most isolated country, North Korea, for help. In September 2023, Vladimir Putin and North Korean leader Kim Jong Un performed a very public courtship, with Kim traveling to Russia, where he received a warm welcome from Putin. Kim's visit to Russia followed a visit to North Korea two months earlier by Russian defense minister Sergei Shoigu. The common focus of those meetings was enhanced military cooperation. The quid pro quo? North Korea would send much-needed artillery ammunition to Russia for use in Ukraine. The concern among US officials was that Russia would then need to return the favor with missile and space technology. It was therefore notable that Kim's visit to Russia included a stop at Russia's Vostochny Cosmodrome in the Russian Far East, a new Russian spaceport for launching some of the country's most sensitive military and intelligence satellites.

US officials described the arms negotiations between Moscow and Pyongyang as "actively advancing." "We have information that Kim Jong Un expects these discussions to continue, to include leader-level diplomatic engagement in Russia," National Security Council spokesperson Adrienne Watson told CNN.

Asked if he and Kim discussed military cooperation, Putin told state-controlled TV channel Russia 1: "Well, there are certain restrictions, and Russia complies with all these restrictions. But there are things that we can of course talk about, discuss, think about it. And here too there are prospects."[47]

At their state dinner, Kim in return delivered an endorsement of Russia's invasion of Ukraine, choosing language similar to what

Putin and Xi use to describe the US and its allies. Kim said he was "certain that the Russian people and its military will emerge victorious in the fight to punish the evil forces that ambitiously [sic] pursues hegemony and expansion."[48]

The gifts the North Korea leader received were telling. At the spaceport, Putin gave him a cosmonaut's glove—and later in his visit he received body armor and a set of drones. Could those personal gifts foreshadow the military equipment soon to change hands between the nations?

US AND AUSTRALIA

Of course, Russia and China are not the only great powers making new agreements with middle powers around the world. Between 2021 and 2023, the US and its allies in Asia signed a series of new agreements creating a new security architecture, further fortifying the dividing lines among the great powers. One of the most consequential developments in the new great power conflict took place five months before Russia invaded Ukraine and involved nuclear submarine technology as well. In September 2021, Australia, the UK, and the US signed the AUKUS agreement (an acronym based on the three partners' names), a security pact under which the US and the UK provide Australia with advanced nuclear submarines.

At the time, the deal made headlines in part because of an awkward snub of the ally effectively pushed out by the agreement: France, whose contract to sell diesel electric submarines to Australia was displaced by a new contract for Washington to instead sell nuclear submarines to Canberra. However, this was far more than a short-term military trade dispute. Rather, it signaled that Australia's decades-long policy of engagement and trade with China was over and, in great power terms, that the US and its allies had made a significant expansion of military power in Asia.

Australian leaders had previously calculated their future was equally as a citizen of Asia as of the West—and they had tweaked their country's trade and defense policies accordingly. Yes, China was authoritarian, but there was no questioning its growing economic and military power in the region. Better to get along. But Beijing had overplayed its hand, interfering in Australian politics and, when displeased with Australian trade and foreign policy, applying economic pressure by reducing purchases of Australian exports. By entering AUKUS, Australia threw its lot in fully with the US and the West—and the US and the West gained a powerful new means of projecting power in the region with a weapon, the fearsome nuclear submarine, that is seen as more and more likely to determine the outcome of any future military conflict among the great powers. By late September 2022, as *The Wall Street Journal* first reported,[49] the Biden administration was considering a plan to speed up the delivery of nuclear submarines to Australia in response to growing Chinese military aggression in the region.

EUROPE TO ASIA

As the West and its Asian allies have grown more alarmed at China's military expansion, European nations that had previously maintained little to no significant military presence in Asia began to change course. One by one, and somewhat out of the spotlight, European nations made new agreements and commitments in Asia.

In December 2022, the UK, Japan, and Italy announced plans to develop the next generation of fighter jets under the new Global

Combat Air Programme. In January 2023, the UK and Japan announced they were signing a "historic defense agreement" that allowed both countries to deploy forces on each other's territory.

"The Reciprocal Access Agreement is hugely significant for both our nations—it cements our commitment to the Indo-Pacific and underlines our joint efforts to bolster economic security, accelerate our defense cooperation and drive innovation that creates highly skilled jobs," said UK prime minister Rishi Sunak. "In this increasingly competitive world, it is more important than ever that democratic societies continue to stand together shoulder to shoulder as we navigate the unprecedented global challenges of our time."

At the same time, the West's Asian allies stepped up their own support to Ukraine against Russia's ongoing invasion. In that vein, NATO and Japan discussed opening a liaison office in Japan—the first of its kind for the alliance. While Japan still identified China and North Korea as its greatest threats, Japanese foreign minister Yoshimasa Hayashi told CNN in May 2023, "The reason why we are discussing this is that since the aggression by Russia to Ukraine, the world has become more kind of unstable, and I felt like something happening in East Europe is not only confined to the issue in East Europe and that it affects directly to the situation here in the Pacific."

"CAMP DAVID PRINCIPLES"

In August 2023, President Biden hosted the leaders of Japan and South Korea at Camp David to unveil a new trilateral partnership. It was a diplomatic achievement for Biden and the US. While Washington has maintained bilateral security relationships with Japan and South Korea for decades, relations between Seoul and Tokyo had remained troubled by lasting disputes over, among other issues, elusive

Japanese compensation for forced South Korean labor before and during World War II. As President Biden, Prime Minister Fumio Kishida of Japan, and President Yoon Suk Yeol of South Korea spoke to reporters after signing the "Camp David Principles," Biden said of their agreement, "This summit was not about China."

In fact, China was very much a unifying issue among the three nations, along with the growing nuclear and missile threat from China's ally North Korea. And each facet of the new agreement—annual multi-domain military exercises, enhanced cooperation on missile defense, and a new hotline to coordinate responses to military threats—were aimed equally at North Korea and China.

Their joint statement twice referenced their shared interest in defending the rules-based international order with specific references to ways China has done the opposite, including with its unilateral territorial claims in the South China Sea. "We share concerns about actions inconsistent with the rules-based international order, which undermine regional peace and prosperity," read their statement, which described China's expansion and annexation of islands in the South China Sea as "dangerous and aggressive behavior supporting unlawful maritime claims."

In addition, they expressed unity in opposing potential Chinese military action against Taiwan: "We reaffirm the importance of peace and stability across the Taiwan Strait as an indispensable element of security and prosperity in the international community."

What was equally striking was that the leaders were united in their response to a threat many thousands of miles away from East Asia, on the battlefields of Ukraine. Their position was clear: Russian aggression in Europe represented a direct threat to their own security in Asia.

"We believe the lasting lesson from this catastrophic war of aggression must be the international community's abiding will to uphold the principles of territorial integrity, sovereignty, and the peaceful resolution of disputes," the leaders said. "We reaffirm our view that when these foundational principles are rejected anywhere, they represent a threat to our region. We are unified in our intent to ensure that no such egregious acts are ever perpetrated again."

Not coincidentally, as the US, Japanese, and South Korean leaders met outside Washington, Russia and China were holding joint military exercises in the East China Sea, just to the southwest of Japan and South Korea. Japan's Joint Staff tweeted that Japanese fighter jets scrambled to respond to "a suspected intrusion into Japan's airspace over the Sea of Japan and the East China Sea." While this new trilateral partnership was forming, Russia and China were apparently sending a message.

New economic dividing lines were developing along with the military tensions. In the aftermath of the Ukraine invasion, Russia and the West effectively decoupled economically. The US, while not decoupling from China, is, in the new buzzword of US policymakers, "de-risking"—that is, ending economic ties in areas when the US deems doing so relevant to its national security interests. The days of turning your smartphone on in any country on the map and being immediately connected to a global network could soon be over. Technologically, the promises of a global internet, global technological standards, and global telecommunications networks are disintegrating as not only Russia but also China develop their own sequestered standards and systems.

It is a global order in which countries across the planet are siding with one or more of three powers as those powers and their allies then focus on lengthening and fortifying the dividing lines separating them from one another and their claimed spheres of influence. The challenge for the great powers and the world is that those spheres increasingly overlap and intersect—and at those intersections lie the potential flashpoints for a broader great power conflict in Europe and Asia.

PART TWO

PART TWO

CHAPTER THREE

FLASHPOINT BALTIC SEA

"INCOMING"

NATO's Very High Readiness Joint Task Force (VJTF in NATO shorthand) was in international waters just a few miles southwest of Kaliningrad when the German flagship FGS *Mecklenburg-Vorpommern* received a warning: "Incoming." A US P-8 Poseidon surveillance aircraft operating in the area had spotted two Russian jets and two Russian warships heading the task force's way. I had booked a weeklong embark on the VJTF patrol to explore the new reality on NATO's eastern front as the dividing line between NATO and Russia lengthened and hardened. But I had not banked on witnessing so quickly how "very high readiness" means more and more close encounters between Russia and NATO—and more and more chances for tensions to escalate.

Nestled between the Baltic states and Poland on the Baltic Sea, Kaliningrad is a detached remnant of the old Soviet Union, separated from the rest of Russia by the Baltic states, which declared independence after 1991. Despite its separation from the motherland,

Kaliningrad survives as an outpost for the former Soviet empire and for forces of the Russian Federation in the Baltic and North Seas.

NATO's growing presence here is not accidental. What Kaliningrad lacks in size and strategic depth, it makes up for in forward positioning as an observation post, base of operations, and location for some of Russia's most advanced weapons systems. In 2022, Russia positioned advanced anti-ship missiles in the oblast, including the Bal system (with a range of 70 to 160 miles) and the Bastion-P (with a range of 190 miles). Together, these weapons can strike shipping all the way to the Swedish coast, making the Baltic Sea a dangerous environment for NATO ships in the event of war.[1] More recently, the Russian military said it had deployed hypersonic missiles to the Kaliningrad region.[2] NATO believes it needs to operate here more often and in greater numbers—to lay claim to these key strategic waters.

"This makes our way of operating quite different between the Mediterranean and here in the Baltic Sea with the [Kaliningrad] oblast right in the middle of our operation area," Rear Admiral and Commanding Officer Thorsten Marx of the VJTF told me as we sailed just a few miles off the coast of Kaliningrad.

For Russia, Kaliningrad's strategic impact is significant. Imagine a detached piece of Russian territory between Massachusetts and New York with a naval base, a heavy deployment of ground forces, and missile batteries capable of hitting US military and commercial traffic on land and at sea. Kaliningrad is surrounded by the most powerful military alliance in the world, but it has a sizable capability to threaten and disrupt.

As relations between Russia and NATO have worsened, Moscow has looked for new opportunities to threaten and disrupt the alliance. In 2018, Russia deployed nuclear-capable Iskander missiles to Kaliningrad, according to Russian state media. The Lithuanian government has since publicly warned that Russia has put nuclear warheads into place as well. Secretary of State Antony Blinken and other senior US officials have told me the US believes Russia knows it cannot credibly take on the alliance. But do NATO commanders agree?

A NATO COMMANDER'S VIEW

"I hope that this is really the case," Rear Admiral and Commanding Officer Marx said. Like the seasoned commander he is, with more than three decades in the German Navy, Marx takes care to consider all possibilities. "If the regime is under so much pressure—so in danger—that it needs to take measures of last resort, then you never know what will happen in this regard. But at the moment, I think by clear strategic messaging, by making sure that the capabilities [are] available and operating in the vicinity, at least the communication and the messages are [delivered] in such a way that there is no room for misunderstandings."

After the collapse of the Soviet Union, there was a brief period in the 1990s of genuine cooperation across the old East-West divide. Marx took part in the first German-Russian exercises as an officer on a minesweeper in the mid-1990s. However, contacts intended to prevent miscalculations and escalation between the two sides have waned. While NATO makes its exercises publicly known and follows a regular annual schedule, Russia carries out its own training exercises without notice or warning.

Marx told me there is even less communication between the German and Russian navies today than there was during the latter years of the Soviet Union, when there was a brief opening during Mikhail Gorbachev's perestroika and glasnost initiatives.

"We do not have any more of this kind of established communication among us like we have seen in times of perestroika here,"

Marx said. "With the vocabulary they are using, it's not possible to work constructively with them anymore."

History—recent and more distant—weighs heavily on Marx. After beginning his naval career during the last Cold War, he watched with relief as tensions eased in the latter years of the old Soviet Union—and then were replaced by hope during new, friendlier interactions with his Russian counterparts. Now they were on opposite sides once again.

This is particularly meaningful territory for Germany. In the seven decades since its defeat in World War II, the German military has operated under strict limitations on both its size and capabilities. It is no accident, for instance, that the German Navy has no destroyers. Today, however, Germany is arming up again for a new era of great power conflict.

"World War I and World War II is pretty much on the mind of every German," Marx told me, our conversation taking a deeper, more thoughtful turn. "It's part of our history and also the lessons learned. We will learn from these dark times. And for me personally, it's unbelievable that we are seeing nowadays in Europe battlefields like we have seen in World War I. And this is not just my way of thinking—it's also now a common feeling across Europe. And nobody would like this kind of battlefield on their own soil."

Today, testing red lines has become a regular facet of the standoff between NATO and Russia in Europe—and testing capabilities and response times. Those approaching Russian aircraft were one such test. Each side claims to have a reasonable understanding of the other's limits. However, the Russian invasion of Ukraine proved such assumptions can be wrong. How many in the US and Europe remained convinced Putin was too calculating to order a full-scale invasion of Europe's largest country? With that misreading in mind, NATO leaders today emphasize the need for clearer communication of the alliance's commitments and capabilities. The VJTF is a sentry, in effect, on NATO's northeastern frontier.

ADEX

In the midst of the air defense warning, I had taken a rigid inflatable boat (RIB) from the *Mecklenburg* to another vessel in the group, the Portuguese Navy frigate NRP *Bartolomeu Dias*. It was a harrowing journey. With the *Mecklenburg*'s RIB hoist broken, German sailors had dropped a rope ladder three stories down the side of the frigate. As the waves of the Baltic bounced the RIB up and down like a cork, I gingerly climbed down the rope ladder with a white-knuckle grip, wearing a bulky dry suit in case I slipped. With seawater temperatures only just above freezing, I wouldn't have survived more than twenty minutes or so unprotected. At the bottom of the ladder, I jumped into the inflatable and grabbed the center console for balance with relief. Looking up, I realized that even a modest-size German frigate appears giant from the water.

On board the *Bartolomeu Dias*, where the RIB hoist was thankfully still working, I went immediately to the bridge. The watch officer had received another warning from the US Navy P-8. The Russian warships—two corvettes—were now seven nautical miles south of the *Mecklenburg*, ten nautical miles from the *Bartolomeu Dias*. And the jets were moving closer quickly. The P-8 identified them as Sukhoi Su-27 fighters.

The Russians' timing was impeccable. A short time earlier, the crew of the *Bartolomeu Dias* had been training for just such an encounter, running through a series of simulated air defense exercises (known as ADEX). Two Polish Air Force jets—Soviet-made Su-27 fighters just like the approaching Russian aircraft—had been playing the part of enemy aircraft. Scenarios that seemed far-fetched just a few years ago have taken on a greater urgency. The Polish jets had swooped low over the water and across the bow, imitating how Russian jets have often harassed NATO ships in these waters.

In the next phase of the air exercises, the same Polish jets lined up on simulated attack runs—taking two passes over the *Bartolomeu Dias*. The first mimicked a run with "dumb" bombs, in which pilots attack bow to stern to maximize their chances of a successful hit. The second run saw the pilots flying in from port and starboard as they would if firing anti-ship missiles. Such attacks could be potential deathblows to the frigate and its crew.

With each run, the *Bartolomeu Dias*, the *Mecklenburg-Vorpommern*, and their partner vessels activated multiple lines of defense. First, Sea Sparrow missiles, a short-range anti-aircraft and anti-missile defense system designed for threats more than eight miles out. As jets came closer, the ships simulated fire from their 76mm bow-mounted guns, also with a range of several miles. Even closer in, the ships activated equipment near the stern that throws up a cloud of metal chaff, or shrapnel, intended to fool incoming missiles into detonating at a safe distance. They call the last line of defense the "Goalkeeper"—a Dutch-designed air defense system that fires a fusillade of shells at a rate of four thousand rounds per minute to create a wall of gunfire for close-in threats. As the "enemy" jets flew at the ship from every direction, each line of defense sprang into action.

Now, with actual Russian aircraft on approach, the *Bartolomeu Dias*'s crew rapidly transitioned from training to active defense. At the rear of the bridge, an officer moved a tiny black "X" on a whiteboard from the white position, for normal, to the yellow position, signaling a potential attack.

Inside and outside the bridge, sailors searched the sky with binoculars. In the ship's operations center, two decks down from the bridge, far more powerful sensors were at work. At twenty different stations, officers were monitoring the threat picture with NATO's latest surveillance, data, and imagery technology. One station combined those data streams to create a comprehensive "air picture compilation." Another did the same for the surface. A third created a subsurface picture, since Russian submarines operated in these waters. They were not relying on just one vessel's view. Via a state-of-the-art NATO datalink, all the ships in the task force were sharing surveillance intelligence and combining it into the most comprehensive view possible of the world around them.

"With this, we have the big picture," a lieutenant commander told me, pointing to the dozens of screens in front of him. "All of the air, the surface, and the subsurface" in clear view, he said, and all the commanders and crew now operating on an attack footing.

As he watched, the *Bartolomeu Dias*'s commanding officer, a thirty-year navy veteran himself, lamented Europe's return to more tenuous times.

"We are getting back to the older times in the 1970s and 1980s," Captain José Rodrigues Pedra said. "Until a few years ago, Russia wasn't an adversary. Now our leaders start to see a risk from the east."

On the bridge, duty officers received another update: the task force had lost the Russian aircraft. The lieutenant commander told me there were two possibilities: the jets had dipped down low over the water to avoid radar, or they had "strangled" the radar via countermeasures. The Portuguese sailors kept searching the sky with binoculars and the naked eye. The threat warning level remained at yellow.

Since the Russian invasion of Ukraine, Russian aircraft and ships had become more aggressive across the European theater. Two weeks before I embarked on the VJTF, a Russian jet had harassed an unmanned US Reaper drone over the Black Sea. Caught on the UAV's video camera, the jet can be seen swooping in and dumping its fuel on the drone. On an even closer pass, it struck the drone's propeller, sending the Reaper crashing into the sea.

A lost UAV sends a signal, and is one thing. A piloted aircraft brought down would be another altogether. In April 2023, as my CNN colleague Oren Liebermann reported, US Central Command stated that Russian pilots were attempting to "dogfight" manned US jets over Syria. A US official told Liebermann that the US did not believe Russian pilots intended to shoot down US jets but might have been attempting to "provoke" and "draw us into an international incident." A video released by Central Command dated April 2 showed a Russian SU-35 executing what the US military described as an "unsafe and unprofessional" intercept of a US F-16. A second video, dated April 18, showed a Russian fighter flying within two thousand feet of a US aircraft.[3] Such close encounters looked less and less like outliers.

Virtually everyone aboard these ships had their own story of a brush with Russian ships or aircraft. The helicopter squadron commander, René (who gave only his first name for security reasons—yet one more indicator of the threat environment), was on another German frigate, FGS *Sachsen*, in March 2022 when a Russian fighter jet repeatedly harassed the ship. In a final flourish, the Russian pilot flipped his jet and flew upside down directly over the ship, like a scene out of *Top Gun*.

"The Russians came out to check on our activities and one of the MiG-29s [a Russian fighter jet] came inverted at two hundred feet over the ship," René told me. Two hundred feet is minuscule at flight speeds, reducing reaction times to near zero. "It was show of force," René said. A show of force and showing off, but an exceedingly dangerous way to do so.

Earlier in 2023, when the VJTF was taking part in the Joint

Warrior exercises (UK-led collective training for multiple threats) off Norway, Russian aircraft were again close by. Over lunch in the officers' mess, a German officer told me how it happened. In a standard red-on-blue exercise, the NATO VJTF was playing Russia—the "red" team—against another naval group playing NATO—the "blue" team. Just as the simulated engagement between the blue and red teams began, a Russian maritime patrol aircraft swooped in and began circling above. In one almost comical scene in this new Cold War, the real Russians were circling right above the fake Russians in a serious NATO readiness exercise. Intentional or not, the Russian aircraft's arrival meant NATO had to cancel the exercise immediately and divert the force back to the real-world mission of monitoring and defending against approaching Russian aircraft.

COMPETING RULES OF ENGAGEMENT

The two sides play by very different rules in these delicate encounters. NATO ships and aircraft operate under strict rules of engagement, maintaining at least five nautical miles' distance from Russian ships and aircraft. Russian pilots operate under different rules, or no rules at all. "They don't care," one pilot told me. While NATO aircraft fly with their transponders on—deliberately visible to the other side—many Russian aircraft do not. For René, the chopper squadron commander, the dangers of these behaviors and this new threat environment are very real.

"I have to be quicker in the air, more vigilant. We fly armed more often—always capable to defend ourselves and our force," René said.

The threat environment means a whole new mission for NATO forces in the Baltic. Before the Ukraine invasion, they told me they operated more like a coast guard. Now they are again a true navy.

"We changed back to our main missions: anti-submarine warfare, anti-surface warfare," René told me. "So we do multi-role missions for the frigate. We are the 'eagle-eye' view, and we extend the range of the maritime picture for the frigate. And we have to be capable to switch every hour from an anti-submarine mission to an anti-surface mission to passenger transport to deployment of special forces."

There is no question which mission set these pilots prefer. And such swagger is familiar. I heard it repeatedly from US military aviators in the Iraq and Afghanistan wars, where they relished the chance to fly missions over enemy territory. This is what they're trained to do, they say. It's a war fighter's mantra. The difference is that, in a military standoff among great powers, the enemy has comparable capabilities. There were no Taliban or ISIS jets, air defenses, or navy corvettes in the West's long wars in the Middle East. Russia, for all its failures in Ukraine, has hundreds of jets, flown by competent pilots, and dozens of naval vessels, commanded by competent commanders. Any potential conflict would be more evenly matched, making the danger for service members much greater.

NATO forces have not operated in such a threat environment in more than three decades, and now roles and relationships have been turned on their head. Like Rear Admiral and Commanding Officer Marx, René himself has a direct tie to the last Cold War, only on the opposing side. His father flew for the East German air force before the fall of the Berlin Wall in 1989, at a time when the frontier between East and West went right through his native Germany. Now, with the frontier shifted eastward, René is flying to defend a unified Germany and NATO against the same Russia his own father had trained to defend—and as more modern versions of the very same jets his father had flown (MiG and Sukhoi fighters) were at that very moment shadowing his own ship. I found reminders of Europe's history—distant and more recent—ubiquitous, circulating among

European military forces. The last Cold War may seem long past, but as in this German helicopter pilot's experience, it is just one generation behind us.

As Russian forces shadowed the ships under his command, Marx told me he does not believe these aggressive moves are the acts of rogue Russian pilots. Harassment by Russian warplanes and warships actually is another reminder of the new world order. As he noted, nothing happens in Russia without the explicit approval of higher-ups. It is not a system that encourages the lower ranks to take the initiative.

"From my point of view, it's difficult to believe that's just the individual that misbehaved because of their hierarchy within the armed forces," Marx said. "So I think it's coming from those officers in the ranks that try to test the waters towards the Western side and also show the West how prepared and ready the Russians are."

"VERY HIGH READINESS"

After an hour of rapid updates and rapid responses, the crews received a call from the operations center announcing the yellow alert over: the Russian jets had turned away, and the Russian warships were continuing on a course northwest and away from the NATO task force. This close encounter among the great powers would pass without incident.

This VJTF Maritime, comprising the NRP *Bartolomeu Dias*; the FGS *Mecklenburg-Vorpommern*; and their partner ships from Spain, Poland, and Denmark, was one of a growing number of forward-facing operations and deployments intended to project NATO unity and capability toward Moscow. The task force was twice as large as in preceding years, with twice as many NATO countries represented.

"Part of our task is just to be there," one German officer told me as we left port. "We're there. We're NATO."

Days earlier, the task force had taken a wide turn from port in Kiel, Germany, and headed north, with the *Mecklenburg* as flagship and Rear Admiral and Commanding Officer Marx as task force commanding officer. The *Brandenburg*-class frigate is a near antique of the Germany Navy, twenty-seven years old and built during a time when a hostile Russia was a thing of the past; her crew affectionately calls her an "old lady." In a mission of many firsts, this was the first time a German flagship led a NATO operation east toward Russia.

These are operations with more than just a symbolic purpose. The *Mecklenburg-Vorpommern*, named for a German state, like all vessels in its class, is a frigate designed for anti-submarine operations and striking air and sea targets. It is armed with an array of weapons including the Harpoon and the RAM, or rolling airframe missile. Despite its age, the frigate is now being fitted with a broad new range of systems and capabilities. Its sensors have four times the range they did originally and provide 3D imagery of targets and threats. Real-time data exchange among the flagship and its task force partners has also advanced considerably.

The *Mecklenburg-Vorpommern*'s schedule during a week in the North and Baltic Seas was crowded with live-fire drills, air defense exercises, and group maneuver training intended to prepare ships from multiple armed forces to operate in unison in a "very high readiness" environment. Like the task force, the leadership of the *Mecklenburg-Vorpommern* is multinational as well, with officers from Germany, the UK, Portugal, Spain, and Canada. The battle group would end their visit with a port call in one of NATO's most eastward-facing allies, Estonia. Aircraft from the Swedish Air Force would join exercises later in the week, playing the part of enemy aircraft. The ships, the aircraft, the task forces, and the missions are increasingly a family affair for the alliance.

Deterrence is the guiding philosophy among NATO allies for these perilous new times. A greater threat means greater resources. Marx tells me that a few years ago this same task force could muster only one or two ships from NATO allies. Today, he was commanding six vessels, meeting NATO's new requirements for such a task force. During major exercises, his command doubles in size again to a dozen or more ships. When sending a message to Russia, NATO believes there is strength in numbers.

And then there is before Ukraine and after Ukraine, in terms of operations and outlook. On board the *Mecklenburg-Vorpommern*, the Ukraine invasion remains a clear turning point.

"The attack on Ukraine really changed the mindset in all of Europe," Marx told me. "People realize the way the Russians are fighting the war in Ukraine—not caring about their own people."

"After the attack on Ukraine, our chief of the navy ordered that everyone who is available goes out and shows the readiness of the German Navy," Marx told me. "And this was similar to all the other navies during that time. And quickly they were more than two hundred ships available sailing around, indicating that the alliance is ready and can do any defense job that's required. And I think this was also a very strong signal towards the opponent: 'Do not even dare.'"

"Do not even dare"—his words struck me. The task force's designation Very High Readiness has meaning. Implemented by NATO immediately following the Russian invasion of Ukraine, it means this task force is ready to act in any mission at any moment.

"If the telephone would ring now, we would sail immediately," Marx told me in his quarters. "We are a complete package that can be used for any maritime operation within hours." "Any maritime operation" ranges from simply showing NATO presence, to blocking or deterring a hostile adversary, and up to defending territory if required.

To accomplish this mission, the *Mecklenburg-Vorpommern* and its fellow warships must sail equipped to be self-sufficient for a full month, with all the fuel, provisions, operational readiness, and armaments that may be required. Commanders and their crews take the mission set seriously—and train for it virtually every day. In a single twenty-four-hour period at sea, I watched the task force conduct a live-fire drill, an air defense drill, a red-on-blue tracking exercise, an onboard fire drill, and the genuine rescue of a stranded Zodiac whose engine had stalled on its way to a partner vessel.

They are prepared for other, more urgent steps as well. The flagship has its own emergency medical staff and a legal advisor on call in case the force goes to a war footing. They are preparing not only for casualties of war but also for any questions on rules of engagement that may arise. "They know who they are—and are ready to go to the airport to fly here if needed," Marx said.

As the task force commander repeated to me several times during the embark, these forces are tasked with the mission of defending NATO's eastward-facing frontier. As a new Iron Curtain has descended, a hardened line of defense has risen to mirror it.

"We are the first line of defense," Marx told me.

In the previous three months, the frigate had sailed some sixteen thousand miles with that mission in mind, a path taking it from its home port in northern Germany through the North Sea, the Baltic Sea, the north Atlantic, and all the way to the Arctic Circle. More broadly, the alliance itself conducted a series of readiness exercises. In late 2022 and early 2023 alone, such exercises have included Joint Warrior, Arctic Dolphin (dedicated to submarine warfare), Dynamic Mongoose (also submarine warfare), Formidable Shield (air and missile defense), and BALTOPs (US-led exercises for a broad set of missions), like the VJTF mission, also centered on the Baltic Sea.

For members of the task force, these exercises represent an enormous change in roles in the span of just a few years.

"Our focus was more on a constabulary role," Captain Rodrigues Pedra said. No longer. "Now the perception of the threat is increasing. It is disruptive because Europe hasn't seen a war [on this scale] since Czechoslovakia [when Warsaw Pact nations invaded in 1968] or even back to World War II. And for the navy, events of 2022 only accelerated preparations at sea."

RUSSIA'S "VERY CAPABLE" NAVY

The forces on the other side of the line of defense have implemented their own new level of readiness. The German officer's story of Russian aircraft shadowing 2022's NATO-wide Joint Warrior exercises was not isolated. Russian forces were watching closely throughout, sending aircraft down from north of Norway virtually every day to have a look. Of course, NATO forces are increasingly aware of Russian exercises as well.

"If you talk to the average sailor on board—it doesn't matter if I go to the Spanish, the Polish, German—they recognize that the geostrategic situation changed," Rear Admiral and Commanding Officer Marx said. "And they perform their duties even more seriously being aware that they are the front line and the first responders if NATO requires them."

In the Ukraine war, Russian ground forces have suffered devastating losses in personnel, equipment, and pride, but NATO commanders say that, outside Ukraine, the Russian Air Force and Navy have remained largely unscathed.

"If you look on the broader picture, of course we recognize the capabilities of the Russian Navy, what they have in the inventory and that they are more or less not really touched by the [war in] Ukraine," he said. "So they are still recognized as a very capable force. And this is also the reason why we show this level of resilience and reassurance within the Baltic Sea and the North Sea."

NATO commanders say Russian forces exhibit their greatest strengths in electronic warfare, underwater operations including submarines and unmanned underwater vehicles, and advanced missile systems. Many of those systems have been on display in Ukraine, including hypersonic missiles capable of evading even the most advanced missile defense systems. In late 2022, as I reported at the time for CNN, Russia had been preparing to test a new nuclear-powered torpedo before it scrapped the test because of possible technical problems.

Marx and others are deeply skeptical of any assessment that the West has deprived Russia of its ability to replace what it has lost and retool for a long war of attrition in Ukraine.

"Nobody, in my personal opinion, should underestimate the resources across Russia," Marx cautioned. "You can walk back in history when many, many people underestimated Russia in this regard. So I still think they have quite a lot of capacities and capabilities and they're doing everything in order to catch up now. It's a regime that can order from one day to the next a one-hundred-and-eighty-degree change using the whole society without fearing that they might lose the next election."

NEW TECHNOLOGIES, NEW MISSIONS

As I note in *The Shadow War*, US Navy commanders had for years been expressing growing awareness of—and respect for—advancing

Russian submarine capabilities. In March 2018, officers on board the USS *Hartford* during the ICEX submarine exercises in the Arctic shared how Russian submarines like the ones that were shadowing them at that very moment had been becoming quieter and therefore harder to detect. Just weeks after those onboard conversations, US submarine forces in the North Atlantic experienced an urgent wake-up call to those new Russian capabilities, as one of Russia's most advanced submarines evaded detection for weeks in the North Atlantic. In the years since, US and NATO naval forces have witnessed increased Russian submarine activity in and near their waters—and increased ability by those submarines to evade detection. As in the air and on the surface, the standoff between NATO's and Russia's submarine forces is growing more competitive and more dangerous.

Russia should not underestimate NATO either, Rear Admiral and Commanding Officer Marx emphasized. Putin had calculated that the invasion would divide the alliance. Many in Europe and the US made a similar assumption. Many also calculated the costs of a protracted war and a clean break with Moscow—in weapons, diplomatic capital, energy supplies, and economic growth—would be too high.

"What we have seen after February last year and the attack on Ukraine was really that the NATO allies gathered . . . with a common [view] of what needs to be done next," he said. "This is definitely something the regime underestimated."

To that end, the alliance is undergoing a constant expansion of missions and technologies. The *Bartolomeu Dias* carried two drones on board—a barebones arsenal for sure, but a sign of how alliance members are moving into systems they hadn't considered impactful just a few years before.

"UAVs are changing the way the navy operates," Captain Rodrigues Pedra said. This means both new capabilities and new threats, he explained, noting that he and his crew now have to be very careful on approach to shore—on alert for UAVs deployed by state and non-state, civilian actors.

Russia's navy learned this lesson to devastating effect in Ukraine. Ukrainian forces sank the flagship of its Black Sea fleet with the help of drones that had overwhelmed its defenses as two surface-to-surface missiles struck their mark. More than a year into the war, a senior US military official told me that the Black Sea had become a virtual no-go zone for Russian warships. Ukrainian unmanned underwater vehicles by then had paralyzed even the Russian fleet based at Sevastopol in Crimea, the main prize of Russia's 2014 invasion of Ukraine.

European allies face new threats as well as Russia increasingly targets civilian infrastructure. In response, NATO has created a division dedicated to protecting such infrastructure. As we sat in his stateroom, a British officer showed us a map of the web of undersea cables and pipelines radiating across the Baltic Sea, North Sea, and Atlantic. He then displayed a second slide showing the path of a particular Russian vessel that had conducted repeated passes above one particular cable over the course of several days. NATO believes Russian forces are scouting potential targets.

One new job for the task force is to track Russian air and sea forces to search for patterns of behavior that might indicate a threat to one or more of these critical technological and economic links—and take action if necessary. As I also discuss in detail in *The Shadow War*, Russia has for years deployed ships with underwater capabilities around critical undersea cables with the capability and apparent intent to destroy or disable them in the event of war.

Since then, this undersea front of the "shadow war" has only grown more severe and dangerous, with the threat emanating from both Russia and China (see Chapter 5). And, once again, while

Russian ground forces have proved themselves weak in Ukraine, Russian naval and, particularly, submarine forces remain in a different and more formidable category. Moreover, Ukraine has shown its own capability and willingness to strike undersea pipelines, with a September 2022 attack on Nord Stream pipelines carrying natural gas from Russia to Europe, which western intelligence over time attributed to pro-Ukrainian groups.[4]

TARGET: CITIES

NATO commanders have gleaned another alarming lesson from the Ukraine war and another alarming reality of the return of great power competition. As its scorched-earth campaign against Ukraine has made clear, Russia makes no distinction between military and civilian targets. In fact, leveling civilian areas and punishing the population have proved to be integral parts of its military strategy in the Ukraine war. Alarmingly, in the view of NATO commanders, this element of Russian military strategy is not isolated to Ukraine. Rather, they see civilian targets, including some of the largest and most populous cities of Europe, as potential Russian targets in a great power war. That frightening reality adds another front to defend for the VJTF and other NATO task forces standing up today.

For commanders I met on board, entire cities represent another piece of "critical infrastructure" NATO must prepare to defend. The VJTF has the capability to carry and operate theater ballistic missile defense, which would help naval forces defend populated areas from missile attack in the event of war. The VJTF as currently configured and armed does not carry such a capability but could be equipped with it in the event of impending attack. In the meantime, antimissile systems on board could help defend ports from missiles.

"For naval assets, I would say indirectly as we have also the ballistic missile defense with us, so we probably can protect certain areas in the port with our missile defense," Rear Admiral and Commanding Officer Marx said. "We can contribute definitely to the picture compilation and acting as a command-and-control hub of the coast."

These are the calculations and decisions NATO leaders face every day: how many forces to deploy and where and how much to arm them to carry out their duties. Today, on each decision, the alliance is trending toward more: more forces, in more places, more often, and with more readiness to respond to threats.

STANDING UP EUROPE

This VJTF mission is marked by more firsts than just being the first time this task force has sailed under a German flagship. It is also the first time Spanish and Portuguese vessels were sailing in the vicinity of Russia and Russian forces, with their commanders and crews therefore getting the real-world experience of operating in close proximity to the nation the alliance identifies as its greatest threat. The collection of new commands and new configurations is deliberate: NATO commanders are supremely focused on preparing their forces to operate seamlessly together in the face of threats from Russia.

The focus on integration is apparent at every level of the alliance. In this task force, the commander is German, and his chief of staff is Portuguese. On board are officers from the UK, Spain, Canada, and the Netherlands. In NATO's larger Maritime Command, the current commander is British, his deputy Italian, with chiefs of staff from Italy and Spain. Other senior commands are filled by officers from Italy, Spain, Germany, Portugal, Canada, Turkey, and Greece, while an American typically leads the submarine component given the US role in maintaining the alliance's nuclear umbrella.

"Sharing the burden of security is reflected in the staff, to show solidarity," Rear Admiral and Commanding Officer Marx explained.

True burden-sharing, while a spoken priority, is proceeding unevenly. German officers noted with obvious chagrin that the French Navy had sent one warship for these exercises but sent it on its way after just a few days.

Since the Ukraine invasion, Germany—representing Europe's largest economy—has taken both enormous strides and half steps. In short order, Berlin reversed decades of diplomatic engagement with Russia and dependence on Russian energy. The costs to German politicians and the German public were severe. Angela Merkel's legacy as chancellor was tarnished as the architect of an engagement policy with Moscow that ultimately failed. While Americans had to suffer through one summer of high gas prices, Germans have been remaking their entire energy supply.

Germany's president and former foreign minister and vice chancellor, Frank-Walter Steinmeier, had himself been a leading proponent of engagement. And as I sat speaking to Marx in his quarters, I noticed a portrait of Steinmeier smiling down on both of us.

I asked Marx whether he believed German leaders such as Steinmeier and Merkel had grossly miscalculated with their engagement policy. Had they missed the looming threat? Personally, he doesn't blame them for trying. He noted that NATO has a saying: "The best captain is on the jetty"—in football terms, the equivalent of Monday-morning quarterbacking. With a crystal ball, he said, "everyone could do the job."

"It's pretty hard, then, to judge those people who [said], Okay, let's try it," he said. "Because the desired outcome is far better than what we have right now." Marx, however, noted that there were people in the military who had warned of what was to come with Russia. "We had some voices who warned, 'This is not the true face [of Russia] we are seeing right now. What you are seeing, this is just on the surface.'"

German leaders had invested in engagement, believing not only that engagement was better than confrontation but also that Russia and Germany somehow understood each other. Rather than reciprocating, Russian leaders, in Marx's view, took the outreach as a sign of weakness from Germany and therefore an opportunity for Russia to exploit.

"The common belief in Germany . . . [was] that we had not a partnership but a special relationship with Russia and that we can cooperate on a certain level of trust with each other as they also belong to the old age of Europe," he said. "It turned out that all these beliefs are now history."

Of course, Russian leaders made their own miscalculations, including Putin's assumption the Ukraine invasion would divide the alliance. Marx spoke proudly of NATO's response, and Germany's as well, including its commitment to meet the NATO requirement to spend 2 percent of its GDP on defense and how Europe as a whole coped with cutting itself off from Russia's energy supply.

Germany's sudden diplomatic and economic change has yet to be matched by military transformation. The Ukraine invasion sparked a rapid reassessment of military needs and priorities. However, military procurement, recruiting, and defense industry capabilities have lagged behind the urgent public pronouncements.

In terms of force size, Europe lags far behind the US. Following the end of the last Cold War, European countries greatly reduced the size of their navies. The 2008 financial crisis and the resulting squeezing of national budgets exacerbated the decline. Between 1999 and 2018, the number of frigates and destroyers in European navies dropped by 32 percent, and the number of submarines by 28 percent.

As the German Council on Foreign Relations noted in an April 2020 policy brief, "Even though defense budgets slowly recovered toward pre-crisis levels after 2014, capabilities did not. Nationally as well as at EU and NATO level, significant gaps still exist."[5]

In July 2023, at the Aspen Security Forum, I asked Emmanuel Bonne, advisor to French president Emmanuel Macron, if Europe is now closing those gaps.

"We are now organizing our forces and building our capacities in a very consistent way," Bonne told me. "It's very much about how we combine all different capacities and how we not only build up the military, but how we exercise and how we are able to be engaged in high-intensity conflicts."[6]

Bonne said that money—specifically, meeting the much-discussed threshold of 2 percent of GDP dedicated to defense—matters, but that other changes are equally crucial. "The rest is so important: rebuilding our industries, funding innovation, being able to dispatch troops wherever they're needed," he said.

Bonne cited a recent example of what he described as NATO's growing capability to deploy forces quickly: "Romania wanted NATO to dispatch [an] expeditionary force in its territory after Russia triggered the war in Ukraine, and we were able to send our soldiers and have our contingent operational in Romania in one week. And this is not a question of money. It is very much a question of, you know, capacity."[7]

One of the biggest and most enduring challenges for the German military is that it is still struggling to keep up with demands for personnel. Among the commissioned and noncommissioned officers on board are the last men and women who entered the navy via Germany's national service program, which was abolished in 2011. Since then, the military in general and the navy in particular have had trouble maintaining even modest recruitment goals.

Several officers complained to me about the younger generation showing no interest in service and little understanding of what role the military serves today. An opinion poll conducted by YouGov and reported by *Die Zeit* in early 2023 asked young Germans if they would be willing to take up arms to defend their country. Only 11 percent replied yes, and only one in twenty said they would volunteer to do so. Nearly a quarter of respondents said they would flee the country to avoid service.[8]

"The new generations—Generation Z, or Y, or whatever—doesn't even know what we do," the frigate's weapons officer—an eighteen-year veteran—told me. When he was a teenage conscript, he said a life on the sea sounded like an irresistible adventure. Sailors on board the frigate were away from home 486 days the last two years—a price fewer and fewer young Germans seem to find attractive.

Some crew members describe the recruiting shortage as part of a larger problem in outlook, including the lack of a robust German military industry to manufacture the weapons needed in this new, more hostile security environment. "We were surrounded by friends," the weapons officer complained. "So we did not need new ships or new tanks or new weapons." He added, "We send a couple howitzers to Ukraine, and we don't have any left for training."

Recognition of these fundamental challenges has influenced Germany's strategic planning. Its latest plan—dubbed Fleet and Force Structure 2035+—envisions a navy less dependent on sailors and more so on unmanned vessels. In April 2023 the International Institute for Strategic Studies noted, "Berlin's Fleet and Force Structure 2035+ plan stresses that the Baltic Sea requires weapons systems with more uninhabited capabilities, and that 'mass matters', which refers to the need to increase the numbers of platforms and systems. The German Navy is therefore planning to acquire up to six large uninhabited underwater vehicles together with an unspecified number of uninhabited mine countermeasures systems. . . . The German Navy also appears to be planning to acquire up to 18 uninhabited surface vessels, currently dubbed the Future Combat Surface System, potentially to support other crewed platforms like the navy's corvettes, and boost its capacity in uninhabited aerial vehicles."[9] If you can't recruit the personnel, you plan to go to war without them.

"I think all the western nations tried to get the maximum out of this so-called peace dividend and save some money," Marx told me. "But the lessons learned now within one year across Europe, across all NATO allies, are also very, very impressive."

An Estonian defense official was less sanguine. "Russia put Europe to sleep in the 1990s," he said, "and it is struggling to wake up."

PORT CALL IN TALLINN, ESTONIA

Fewer than twenty-four hours to port, the VJTF picked up another Russian aircraft heading toward the ship. It was again a Sukhoi Su-27. The *Mecklenburg-Vorpommern* was in the midst of a difficult maneuvering exercise—practicing towing a stranded ship—when the announcement rang out over the bridge: Russian jet approaching, fifty nautical miles away. A few minutes later, it was just twenty nautical miles away and flying fast. Even with the best of practices, each close encounter creates a possibility for escalation.

On board the *Mecklenburg-Vorpommern* and *Bartolomeu Dias*, each "very high readiness" drill and each alert of incoming Russian aircraft or naval vessels gave me a feeling of foreboding. Were NATO and Russia unwittingly slipping, step by step, toward war, or at least creating the circumstances to do so? Commanders often recall the memory of the twentieth-century world wars as cautionary tales of unintended conflict. And Rear Admiral and Commanding Officer

Marx, whose career in the German Navy bridges the last Cold War and this emerging new one, fears the dangers of descending into old habits and reflexes. One can both accept the arrival of a new Cold War but also dread that acceptance.

"You can come to the conclusion that there are several similarities [to the last Cold War]. And if I would then agree that history repeats itself, I would also say, 'Okay, this will lead automatically to war.'" He cautioned, "And I hope that the societies and the politicians are smarter. We need to take the lessons we learned in the past and adapt them so that we are not overstepping and then coming to the final conclusion that we *need* to have war."

The VJTF ended this mission, fittingly, in the port of NATO's most vulnerable member, Estonia. Estonian leaders had been telling me since the start of the Ukraine invasion that they were Putin's next target. NATO leaders' repetition of the pledge to "defend every inch of NATO territory" was directed—perhaps equally—at Russia to deter and at the Baltic States to reassure. Yet, that pledge alone was proving insufficient comfort. VJTFs like this one are intended to back those reassuring words with action. But among NATO's eastern-facing members, the fear of Putin's next step is more raw. They had warned their western partners for years before 2022 to beware Putin's plans. And now the leaders of the Baltic States in particular were warning them again.

CHAPTER FOUR

RUSSIA'S NEXT TARGETS

TRIPWIRE FEARS

Estonia is an early-warning system for NATO, and Estonian leaders consistently deliver blunt warnings about the threat from Russia. In military terms, they are—quite literally—a tripwire for a Russian invasion. "Tripwire" is, in fact, how NATO describes its defense strategy for Estonia, Latvia, and Lithuania if Russian forces were to attack.

NATO's eastern-facing allies interpret and convey Russia's threat very differently than its western allies do. Estonian officials—presidents, prime ministers, foreign ministers, and military commanders—have been telling me for years, even prior to the 2022 Ukraine invasion, that "We are next" in Russia's crosshairs. They do so without melodrama and simply by pointing to history.

NATO's Very High Readiness Task Force dropped me off in the Estonian capital of Tallinn, where I was to meet with one of the most no-nonsense voices on Putin's Russia, Estonian prime minister Kaja Kallas. I was arriving the same day she was announcing a new coalition government, following elections her party had won the month before. We met in the downtown hotel where the new coalition's press conference would take place.

Estonia's role in NATO had been a central issue in the campaign. The country's far-right party EKRE had vowed to curtail Estonia's support for Ukraine. Kallas had promised to increase it. Sharing a coffee before she would join her coalition partners onstage, Kallas told me one of her first tasks in the new government would be to raise taxes to pay for increased spending on the nation's defense. Unlike her US counterparts in recent times of war, she was explicitly asking her citizens to make a financial sacrifice, to contribute above and beyond the military service most citizens are already required to perform.

Throughout the campaign, she had framed NATO's defense of Ukraine as essential to Estonia's own defense. In her view, Estonia's survival as an independent state is deeply intertwined with Ukraine's.

This is a case Kallas makes with equal fervor to her fellow citizens and to the leaders of Estonia's allies. She emphasizes that today's Russia sees Estonia and the other Baltic states as no more deserving of independence than Ukraine. In Putin's view, as former Soviet republics, they are all rightfully part of Russia or at least rightfully within Russia's sphere of influence and control. It's a reality that Kallas believes NATO's western-facing allies simply don't understand.

"They have much better neighbors," she said. "They don't deal with this. For them, the security issue is a nice intellectual conversation to be having. It's not an existential threat like it is for us."

I spoke with Kallas many times both before and after the Russian invasion of Ukraine—and her message has never wavered: Estonia is fighting for its survival as an independent state. Her fear is double-sided, fueled by both a cold assessment of Putin's ambitions and a lingering doubt about their allies' understanding of the threat's severity. Putin, too, has been consistent in his disregard for Estonia's sovereignty, while Europe has been inconsistent in its defense. With characteristic bluntness, she reminds her fellow European leaders often that they have abandoned Estonia before.

"The western world survived very well without us for fifty years," she told me.

Estonia, as an independent state, is remarkably young—just over thirty years old, dating to the collapse of the Soviet Union in 1991. Estonian Independence Day, celebrated on February 24, commemorates Estonia's first brief taste of freedom in 1918, before it was absorbed into the Soviet Union. Regardless, independence is not a theoretical issue for Estonians. Many of them, like Kallas, are young enough to remember living without it. To Kallas, the debate among western leaders about whether Ukraine should trade territory for peace with Russia is dangerous. If NATO is willing to watch Ukraine cede territory to Russia, might the alliance ask Estonia to do the same someday?

"If they are thinking that they are protecting themselves by sacrificing something that is not dear to them—a small country, 1.3 million people, who cares?" she said. "The US doesn't even know where we are."

Kallas is a leader deeply conscious of history. In two hours over coffee, she cited half a dozen books she'd been reading—on Russia, on Putin, on the history of World War II and the Cold War—a leader searching the past for lessons to save her country as an independent state.

Kallas has her own recent experience of history to draw on, growing up in Estonia when it still was a Soviet Socialist Republic. "We were suffering so hard," she told me. "And I am just afraid that they are not going to miss us this time. I mean, we missed the western world, really. Even I remember those times, and don't want those back."

Further back through the decades, Estonians have only cautionary tales about Russia. "Remember [Neville] Chamberlain," she said. "Everybody was convinced that he made the right decision, but the history shows that that was not the case."

Estonia's view of Russia is a product of its history and geography. From my first visits to eastern Europe, I learned an important geographical lesson. As an American growing up during the last Cold War, I had imagined great distances and a vast buffer zone between East and West. Take the three-hour flight from London to Moscow and that impression disappears. NATO and Russia are not only neighbors. They are also deeply intertwined.

Estonia is a tiny country, quite a bit smaller than the state of West Virginia, situated on Russia's western border. The distances between East and West are minute. Its capital, Tallinn, is more than 200 miles from St. Petersburg. Helsinki, capital of NATO's newest member state, is just 50 miles away; Stockholm, 264 miles. And the Russian enclave of Kaliningrad, which the task force had sailed by earlier in the week, sits right on the other side of the Baltic States of Latvia and Lithuania. Here, East and West are wrapped around each other.

Estonia's ties to Russia are about more than distance. Tallinn's population of fewer than five hundred thousand people is nearly 40 percent ethnic Russian. Estonia's *Guide for Friendly Forces*, distributed to NATO service members making port calls, advises that among ethnic Russians in eastern Estonia and some parts of Tallinn "support towards allied units' presence in Estonia is considerably lower compared to the rest of Estonia." Among the precautions the guide recommends for NATO service members is to select only Estonian mobile carriers for their cell phones and to avoid going anywhere near the Estonian border with Russia. Cross-border hostage-taking by Russia is not out of the question.

To that point, when NATO's Very High Readiness Task Force sailed into Tallinn on a sunny, spring day in April 2023, sailors going ashore were advised to wear civilian clothes to minimize any potentially difficult interactions with ethnic Russians and to make them less obvious targets for Russian intelligence. Many sailors communicated only via encrypted messaging apps. These all seemed like unusual protocols for a visit to a friendly NATO port, but this is a NATO outpost on Russia's doorstep.

Estonians describe the threat from Russia as existential, the way, say, Israelis see the threat from Iran. And so, Baltic leaders have been pushing NATO to develop defense plans for the Baltics that fit the threat. Until recently, they believe those plans fell far short.

Eastern European leaders felt somewhat vindicated at the NATO summit in Madrid in June 2022. The Ukraine invasion was proving them right in how far Russia was willing to go to remake the map of Europe. What they were now demanding was a qualitative change in the alliance's defense strategy for the eastern allies. Just before the summit began, Kallas declared her country would be "wiped from the map" under NATO's existing plans. Why? As she detailed to reporters in Madrid, the current NATO defense plan allowed for Estonia to be overrun by Russian forces in the initial phase of an invasion. Only then would NATO attempt to push Russian forces out, within 180 days.

"If you compare the sizes of Ukraine and the Baltic countries, it would mean the complete destruction of countries and our culture," Kallas told reporters. "Those of you who have been to Tallinn and know our old town and the centuries of history that's here and centuries of culture that's here—that would all be wiped off the map, including our people, our nation."[1]

With palpable disdain, Kallas dismissed tripwire as a plan "to lose it and liberate it afterwards," which she argued was no longer acceptable after the world had witnessed Russia's scorched-earth tactics in Ukraine and its war crimes in Bucha and beyond. "Now everyone sees that this tripwire concept doesn't really work," Kallas said.[2]

When she and I spoke in Madrid, Kallas told me NATO had to entirely reengineer its defense posture in eastern Europe.

"NATO's posture so far in the eastern flank and in the Baltic states has been a deterrence posture, and now we have to move to a defense posture," she said. "It's also important that the plans NATO has will be implemented fast, so not in words but in deeds."

Kallas was arguing membership in NATO alone was not a sufficient security guarantee. Europe post-Ukraine is a fundamentally different place.

"So far, nobody thought Russia would test NATO's unity, but we have seen that they have acted in conflict with all the laws that we might have," Kallas continued. "So, we have to be prepared. As Russia has boosted the level of aggression, we have to boost the level of defense also."

A more robust defense is, she says, in the interests of the alliance as a whole. The events of February 24, 2022, made that clear.

When Kallas complained about the tripwire posture to her fellow prime ministers, they had no idea it was the alliance's defense plan for the Baltics in the first place. At the European summit in May 2022 and later at the NATO summit in Madrid, she said several of her counterparts were just as stunned as she was.

"The same day we had the European summit . . . the majority of NATO prime ministers come to me and say, 'Oh my God! Is that the case? Is that the plan? I didn't know that. We have to change that,'" she told me. "And that was a week before the Madrid summit."

"They didn't know?" I asked with surprise.

"They didn't know," she said. "So, they came to me and said, 'Oh my God, we have to change that. It can't be like this.'"

The Estonian people didn't know either. So when Kallas went public with her criticism of the defense plan, she was met at home by surprise and fear.

"I was under so many attacks—Why did I say that? Is it really so?— because people were shocked," she said. "Six months. So, six months you have to survive, [then] NATO will come and liberate us? There would be nothing left here."

UPDATING THE TRIPWIRE POSTURE

A combination of Estonia's dire warnings and the harsh reality of Russian crimes in Bucha and beyond hit their mark. In the months that followed the Madrid summit, a new NATO plan for the Baltics' defense emerged.

NATO's new plan for Estonia and the other Baltic states involves a layered defense. NATO warships, in deployments such as the VJTF, form the first line of defense, coming to Estonia's aid immediately at the first sign of a Russian attack. NATO has also set up a dedicated ground component—a brigade-size quick-reaction force based elsewhere in the alliance—that would deploy to Estonia within hours of an attack. Military equipment, including US-made HIMARS and Norwegian-made National Advanced Surface-to-Air Missile Systems (NASAMS), are now pre-positioned in Estonia. And as part of NATO, Estonian and NATO forces are now unified under a single chain of command.

"They are designed to fight for us," Kallas told me, "which means that they exercise, they practice with our troops. They come here when we do the exercises. They are in the same chain of command, but they are not here permanently."

Is this new forward defense posture enough, though? I asked her. Could NATO forces get here fast enough to repel a Russian invasion before it overtakes the country?

"When we have had exercises, even from the US, they get here in seven hours—even five hours for the paratroopers," she said. "And you have the pre-positioned equipment. . . . If the NASAMS and the HIMARS are already here, it's easier."

These are the hour-by-hour calculations of a leader watching one war underway several hundred miles to the south while contemplating the possibility of another on her own nation's territory.

A senior Estonian defense official echoed the prime minister, explaining that Estonia's focus now is on what NATO does, rather than what it says. "We are quite happy to see how plans changed in the last several months after Madrid," this official told me. "But we have more to do. It is not enough to put plans on paper. We now need to fill the plan with forces.

"There is still huge work to do," the official continued, noting, like Kallas, the differing points of view among allies on the seriousness of the Russian threat. Some see the Russia threat for what it is, he explained, while others remain unconvinced. "All members need to acknowledge the threat," the official said.

OTHER TARGETS

Putin's territorial appetite for reclaiming old pieces of the Soviet Union extends beyond the Baltics and Ukraine. Moldova—nestled between Ukraine and NATO ally Romania—is not a member of the alliance, as its constitution establishes its "permanent neutrality." But as Russia has increasingly meddled inside its borders, Moldova and NATO have drawn closer, working together to upgrade and modernize Moldova's defenses. As NATO has stated, "In light of Russia's unprovoked invasion of Ukraine in 2022, NATO is increasing its support for partners, including Moldova, to help them build their capabilities and strengthen their resistance." At the 2022 NATO summit in Madrid, the alliance agreed to provide additional support "to help strengthen its national resilience and civil preparedness."[3]

Despite NATO's promises, Russia continues to test its limits. Putin sees Moldova, like Ukraine and the Baltics, as a part of the former USSR that belongs back in Russia's sphere of influence.

In February 2023, the threat to Moldova came into sharper focus following a disturbing public revelation by Ukrainian president Volodymyr Zelensky. In comments to European Union leaders, Zelensky said that Ukrainian intelligence services had intercepted Russian plans to destabilize Moldova, which he shared with Moldovan president Maia Sandu.

"I have informed her that we have intercepted the plan of the destruction of Moldova by the Russian intelligence," Zelensky said, describing plans showing "who, when and how" Russia planned to "break the democracy of Moldova and establish control over Moldova."[4]

Russia's plans for Moldova resembled its original plans to take Ukraine: Russian operatives would force out Moldovan leaders and replace them with others friendlier to the Kremlin. Moldova's Intelligence and Security Service confirmed it had been warned by Ukraine and announced it had found "subversive activities, aimed to undermine the Republic of Moldova, destabilize and violate public order."

Soon after, President Sandu went on national television to warn the public of a plot to destabilize the country using "saboteurs who have undergone military training and are disguised as civilians." In her address, Sandu said, "In the past few days, there have been discussions in our society about the security of our country. The statements of President Zelensky about the plans of the Russian Federation to destabilize the Republic of Moldova have been confirmed by our institutions."[5]

The plan was a textbook FSB influence operation, similar to a plot Russia had attempted in Montenegro in 2016. In that instance, Russian agents had hatched a plot to take over the country's parliament ahead of elections and even kidnap the country's then leader, Prime Minister Milo Đjukanović. The ultimate goal, a Montenegrin judge would later conclude, was to block Montenegro's effort to join NATO, which, despite the Russian plot, was eventually successful, as it gained admission in 2017.[6] In Moldova, Sandu said, Russian agents would have infiltrated "the so-called opposition" to attempt a coup.

"Russia's plan to carry out subversive actions on the territory of our state is not new," she added. "Attempts to destabilize the situation and undermine the state were also made last autumn, but they did not achieve their goal, thanks to the prompt intervention of our security and public order agencies."

Still, the warning sent shivers through the country. The next day, the government temporarily closed Moldovan airspace. The national carrier Air Moldova announced with grim understatement, "Dear passengers, at this moment, the airspace of the Republic of Moldova is closed. . . . Today's schedule will undergo changes"; it urged passengers to "keep calm and follow the information panels in the airport."

In exposing the plot to the public, the Moldovan leaders were following a strategy employed by US officials in the days leading up to the invasion of Ukraine. At the time, Russia's FSB intelligence service had hatched a series of "false flag" operations intended to manufacture a pretext for the Russian invasion, including a series of staged terrorist attacks, which Russia hoped to blame on Ukraine, thereby necessitating Russian intervention to "stabilize" the country. To deflate those plots in advance, the US declassified intelligence revealing Russia was behind them. The US tactic worked. When the bombs did go off, few believed they were genuine acts of terrorism. Now Moldovan officials were attempting the same.

With comical denial from a country by then nearly a year into its bloody invasion of Ukraine, Russian Foreign Ministry spokesperson Maria Zakharova said on Telegram, "We resolutely reject the insinuations about the alleged desire of Russia to 'undermine' the situation in the Republic of Moldova. Unlike Western countries and Ukraine, we do not interfere in the internal affairs of Moldova and other countries of the world."[7]

Russian foreign minister Sergey Lavrov, a seasoned spinner of lies in nearly two decades as Russia's top diplomat, accused the West of attempting to turn Moldova into "another Ukraine."

European leaders were alarmed—and used the moment to push for further steps to recognize and support Moldova's sovereignty. The president of the European Parliament, Roberta Metsola, sent an open letter stating the Parliament's "unwavering solidarity" with Moldova and declaring that "Moldova's place is in the European family," a reference to the nation's proposed membership in the EU.[8]

Again, however, the leaders of NATO's eastern-facing allies demanded more than words to defend Moldova. Speaking on CBS's *Face the Nation*, Polish prime minister Mateusz Morawiecki expressed the need for the EU to provide Moldova with the political and military support necessary to defend its sovereignty, stating, "Yes. I do see lots of fingerprints of Russian forces, Russian services in Moldova. This is a very weak, very weak country and we all need to help them."[9]

Morawiecki emphasized the unique threat faced by countries such as Moldova that remain outside the NATO alliance, making the case for admission for not only Moldova but also Ukraine.

Both Moldova and Ukraine had been granted candidate status for the EU in June 2022, but their membership in both the EU and NATO had become a diplomatic football. Aware of the gap between rhetoric and action, Zelensky appealed to lawmakers in Brussels to grant Ukraine entry into the European Union, saying that Europe is Ukraine's "home."

"It's not only about us," Prime Minister Morawiecki said. "It's also about creating stability around us in our direct neighborhoods. And if we fail to integrate Ukraine in NATO and [the] European Union, Ukraine will always be a buffer zone, which is not right," he added.[10]

At the Munich Security Conference, Zelensky chided allies for delaying support for Ukraine and Moldova. "Delay has always been and still is a mistake. While we negotiate how to strengthen our defense with modern tanks, the Kremlin is thinking, thinking about ways to strangle Moldova," Zelensky said.[11]

Days later, President Biden made a point to meet with Moldovan president Sandu in Warsaw. The White House said that Biden had "reaffirmed strong U.S. support for Moldova's sovereignty and territorial integrity" and "highlighted ongoing US assistance to help Moldova strengthen its political and economic resilience, including its democratic reform agenda and energy security, and to address the effects of Russia's war against Ukraine." The combination of NATO support and Russian fumbling appeared to mitigate the risk for Moldova for the moment, but few Moldovans believed it would be the Kremlin's final attempt to take their country.

And the entire region seemed unable to escape the idea of giving up parts of itself to achieve an uneasy peace. With NATO debating

Ukraine's future in the alliance, Prime Minister Kallas believes it was already forgetting the lessons of Russia's territorial aggression.

As we met in Tallinn in spring 2023, there were renewed rumbles about a land-for-peace formula to end the war. Emmanuel Macron had recently been in Beijing, deliberately putting daylight between himself and the US on Taiwan, not unlike his posture in the days leading up to the Russian invasion of Ukraine. Kallas was dismissive of Macron's peace efforts. And she confided in me that she had privately chastised the French president for imagining he could negotiate with Putin in a way other western leaders had failed.

Kallas herself is unmoved by the idea of land for peace. More than once as we spoke, she recalled Winston Churchill's warning about Hitler before World War II: "Appeasing the dictator is like feeding the crocodile, hoping that you are the last to be eaten."

GHOSTS OF HISTORY

Estonians had their own Chamberlains, leaders who believed they could negotiate with Stalin's Russia. In fact, if you read the history of Russia's peace "agreement" with Estonia in 1939 and its subsequent invasion and occupation the following year, you can see how Russia's twenty-first-century invasion of Ukraine echoes it. The earlier Russian assault on Estonia began with a pact disavowing military action. Within months, however, Moscow accused Estonia of "hostility" to Russia and sent in the tanks. Soon after, the Russian occupiers held "elections" in which only Soviet-friendly candidates were allowed to run.

"In 1940s, we had our president at that time [thinking] that we going to make an agreement with Russians so that they're going to spare us," Kallas recalled. But Russia did not "spare" Estonia. From the moment Soviet forces arrived, they began to erase its entire open society—its government leaders, politicians, diplomats, and journalists.

"We lost our country. We lost our freedom. We lost one fifth of our population," she said. Russia would remain in Estonia for more than fifty years.

Kallas told me there is a room in Tallinn's statehouse where she makes a point of taking visiting heads of state. "We call it the State Elders Room, where we have pictures of the people who were leaders of our country," she said. "And I always say, 'Please look at their dates of death.' They all were killed when the occupation started."

The biographies of each leader honored with a portrait in the Elders Room make for sobering reading:

Konstantin Päts, president from 1938 to 1940 and five-time prime minister, arrested by the Soviet secret police (NKVD) and deported to Soviet Russia, where he died in 1956.

Jaan Tõnisson, two-time prime minister from 1919 to 1920, captured and imprisoned by Soviet authorities in 1940, after which he was tried and disappeared in 1941.

Kaarel Eenpalu, two-time prime minister from 1938 to 1939, arrested by Soviet authorities in 1940 and deported to Russia, where he died in 1942 in a Soviet prison camp.

Otto August Strandman, one of Estonia's first prime ministers in 1919, committed suicide at his home in 1941 when NKVD agents came to arrest him.

Friedrich Akel, Estonian diplomat and state elder, arrested in 1940 and executed by the NKVD in 1941.

Jaan Teemant, politician and state elder, arrested by the NKVD in 1940 and sentenced to a prison camp, where he disappeared and was presumed executed in 1941.

Today, the names of Russia's enemies of the state have changed—updated to include Russian dissidents such as Alexei Navalny, Vladimir Kara-Murza, and the late Alexander Litvinenko. And the tactics have changed as well, with Polonium-210, Novichok, and errant "falls" from balconies and rooftops replacing the firing squad. The gulags remain, now as "penal colonies," where WNBA star Brittney Griner merited a stay. What has endured, too, is disregard for life and the law. The Kremlin's playbook—honed in the last century—is being put to brutal use once again today.

Russia is of course conscious of history as well, distant and more recent. In Kallas's view—and she is not alone—one of the most influential lessons for Putin was the West's muted response to Russia's previous invasion of Ukraine in 2014.

"If you see how they have evolved over time, first, they were ashamed that they were actually taking territory from their neighboring countries," she told me. She continued, "Then they saw that nothing happened. Nothing happened. So next time they were braver."

In the midst of the 2014 invasion, some western officials sounded warnings about the West's halting response—and the risk that it would encourage Putin to grab more territory. As I note in *The Shadow War*, then US ambassador to Ukraine Geoffrey Pyatt described a White House struggling to realize Putin's true intentions.

"There was nobody—nobody—in the US government who predicted that the Russian response would be so expansive and militarized," Pyatt told me at the time. "There was a failure of imagination because we were mirror-imaging."

Meaning US and European leaders persisted in believing Russian leaders wanted what they wanted: cooperation and integration with the West. Pyatt recalled continuing debates in the White House even as Russian troops were already claiming Crimea as part of Russia.

"There were lots of conversations with lawyers litigating over what is permissible under the Black Sea Fleet agreement and whether we call out the Russians for violating their treaty obligations," recalled Pyatt.

"There were lots of Russian experts who said he'll never annex Crimea. He would never do that," said Pyatt. "That would be far too provocative. He'll send some troops in to destabilize and send a message but he's not going to go so far as to actually change the borders of the Russian Federation."

But "That was Putinism. It was the most naked manifestation of his revisionist agenda," said Pyatt. "And he did it in a Dirty Harry way. 'What are you going to do about it?' He was using military force to establish a political fait accompli and then challenging all of us to do something about it."

Russia's testing and retesting of the West's limits reminded me of the pattern that played out in the run-up to Russian interference in the 2016 US election. Before Russia hacked Clinton campaign emails, it had hacked into the US State Department's email system in 2014 and 2015, remaining inside undetected for months. Richard Ledgett, who was deputy director of the National Security Agency at the time, recalled that while Russian hackers had in previous years tried to hide their fingerprints when the NSA discovered their activities, their behavior during the State Department and Clinton email hacks was different: they didn't even bother to hide.

"For a very long time, when we would find Russians and engage them in the network, do things in the network that would indicate to them that we knew they were there," Ledgett explained, "they would take defensive actions. They remove malware, things like that. They would disappear.

"They go deep, and they'd come back dressed completely differently, and you'd have to re-detect them again," he added. "They would change the way they looked so that we wouldn't recognize them next time. Their principal goal was not get caught."

That changed with the Russian attack on the State Department's email system in 2014. Now, when NSA technicians identified and engaged their Russian adversaries, the Russian hackers didn't leave. They would simply deploy new iterations of the same cyber tools and attack the network again. Russian hackers abandoned subtlety for blunt force.

"Beginning in 2014, their principal goal was get the data," Ledgett said, describing the Russian attitude as "We don't care if you know we're here."

Note the timing: in 2014, as the West accepted Russia's annexation of Crimea and Eastern Ukraine with only limited consequences, Russia's cyber warfare took on a more aggressive quality as well.

To Kallas, though, the historical context is that this has been Russian behavior for more than a century, never truly changing from 1919 to 1940 to 2014 and to 2022 and beyond: Russia takes what it can get and then pushes for more.

"That is the lesson we learned from history, and that is the lesson for Ukrainians as well: that they just can't stop, otherwise they're going to lose territory," she told me. "They have already lost people, but they're going to lose more if they give in to Russia. It's never going to stop."

NATO NEXT?

Russia's attacks on the former Soviet republics are one significant category of aggression. Putin has, after all, launched the bloodiest war in Europe since World War II.

However, would he go even further and take on the NATO alliance itself?

Secretary of State Antony Blinken is confident that even Russia is aware of its limits. "What has been the ultimate check or restraint is that they're having such a challenging time on the battlefield," Blinken told me. "They're spending so many resources, both human and material, that I think, from their perspective, it would be very challenging to handle anything broader."

"One of the ironies is, because Putin, whether out of mistake or intentionally, somehow believes that NATO poses a direct threat to Russia and would attack it—which it never will, it is not an offensive alliance—has to keep things in reserve, in his own mind, to deal with the potential for direct conflict with NATO, which means fewer things that he can use in Ukraine, which is also helpful," Blinken continued. "The bottom line is, Putin really wants to avoid doing anything that would broaden the conflict, because Russia would have trouble handling it."

"[Putin] could broaden it by trying to use some rump expeditionary force to attack NATO countries in the Baltics, but I don't think that will go well for him," said Matthew Pottinger, deputy national security advisor under Trump. "I have very little doubt that NATO will hold the line and be more galvanized than ever if he decides to trip that wire."

Estonian leaders aren't so certain. In 2007, Russia targeted Estonia with the biggest state-on-state cyberattack ever, three years after Estonia had joined NATO. The broad-based attack targeted government agencies, financial services, commerce, and more—a debilitating assault on a country dependent on digital technology. The cyberattack was coupled with violent protests by pro-Russian factions to further destabilize the country. Some Estonian leaders told me they feared the attack was the first wave of a full-scale invasion.

Estonia eventually fought off the cyberassault, though it had to cut itself off from the outside world for days to rebuild its critical systems.

It's not out of the question for some in the US military and intelligence community either.

"Putin does have a healthy respect for NATO's military power. I don't think he's looking to widen the war right now in Ukraine unless he feared that he was about to lose it decisively," a senior US official told me. "If he feared he was about to lose his grip on Crimea, then I'd say a lot of bets are off, because he's the kind of guy who could try to take the temple down with him."

"Try to take the temple down with him"—this is an alarming assessment of the Russian leader but one that the US government takes seriously. Putin—if he feels he is at the brink of what he sees as a catastrophic loss—could risk broader great power war.

Estonians' doubts—informed by more than a century of suffering under Russian broken promises, aggression, and subjugation—did not surprise me. But their doubts about their own allies did.

"They hope that this will go away, and they don't really realize that it's here to stay. That's a new normal. And we have to actually prepare," Prime Minister Kallas said.

Beyond talk of land for peace in Ukraine, Kallas sees worrisome precedents in NATO's sometimes halting military support for Ukraine. "What I'm worried about right now, when they say, 'Give Ukraine what you have,' and then they say that they don't have more, what if [Estonians] need help? Then they won't have the people or the equipment to come here."

In her press conference that day at the downtown Tallinn hotel, as she announced the new ruling coalition and made the case for tax hikes to pay for her nation's defense, Kallas described security as her government's greatest responsibility.

"Without security, we don't have to talk about anything else. That's why we're increasing our defense expenditure to three percent [of GDP] in the coming years," she said.

She went on to emphasize that all nations must "do everything possible to secure themselves," noting an article from the NATO treaty that doesn't get discussed as often as the Article 5 commitment to mutual defense.

"Before Article 5, there's Article 3. Article 3, in the NATO treaty, says that everybody has to make everything possible to defend themselves," she told me. That reminder seemed to me to be a not-so-subtle dig at NATO allies—many of them bigger and richer than Estonia—who have yet to meet the 2 percent commitment and whose armed forces lag behind the growing demands of the alliance.

To highlight her point, Kallas told me the story of an encounter with German defense industry leaders at the Munich Security Conference that February. Germany had just agreed to send fourteen Leopard tanks to Ukraine, following a long public debate about whether such weapons would be received as too provocative by the Kremlin. After the transfer was eventually approved, Kallas asked the German executives how many new tanks the German government had ordered to backfill the tanks they were sending to Ukraine.

"Germany, they are just talking, but they are not actually investing in defense," she said, noting that after Germany sent those fourteen tanks to Ukraine, it only ordered just over a dozen more to replace them. "Not hundreds," she said.

Germany sends a handful of tanks to Ukraine—for a conflict that has already seen hundreds of tanks destroyed—and replaces them with a handful more. More broadly, though it has pledged to meet the alliance's target of spending 2 percent of its GDP on defense, it modified its commitment in late 2023 to do so only as calculated on average over a five-year period.[12]

Kallas's study of history is intended to avert a war with Russia, not to start one. Throughout our many conversations, she expressed deep fears about how devastating such a new war with Russia would be for Estonia and for Europe. She wants to learn from her predecessors' decisions—good and bad—to help prevent another, and the hundreds of tanks aren't about offense, but defense and deterrence.

"We have fought together before," she said of Estonia and Russia. "I sound like we are going to have a war. I don't want to say that. I hope that we are going to avoid the war."

The history of this new great power competition in Europe continues evolving under our eyes and will into the next months and years. And so she and her fellow European leaders must make decisions today with outcomes that will become clear only years later—decisions such as how to defend Ukraine now, including how many tanks to send or whether to send fighter jets, and how to defend themselves and their NATO allies in the east.

"The dilemma that the prime ministers have," she said, "is that we have to make decisions. But we will [only] know if they are right or wrong in five years' or ten years' time. But you have to decide now, if we go and send the planes there, does it mean that the war will stop, or does it mean that the war will expand?"

More and more, she sees power in the alliance migrating toward allies with greater urgency about the Russian threat. "The center of gravity in NATO," she told me, "is moving towards the north."

Unfortunately, as the power center moves east and north, Russia remains uninterested in the kinds of contacts that might help deescalation. When I asked how often she speaks with her Russian counterparts, she answered virtually never.

"They want to talk to the big ones," she said, referencing the bigger NATO allies such as France, Germany, and the US. "They have always wanted to talk to the big ones. Even in the European Union, it's like, 'Talk to my hand.' This is the attitude. They say that 'we don't really care about the small ones, but the big ones.'"

So the Estonians do what they can and take pride in taking matters into their own hands. Fact is, their history requires self-reliance. And so, they embrace it. All Estonian men of military age are required to perform military service. For those not engaged in military service, many volunteer to contribute to national defense in other ways. The Estonian Defense League trains average citizens to join in the country's defense in the event of war. Experts in the high technology industries take part in the country's Cyber Defense Unit, which has successfully warded off countless Russian cyberattacks since 2007. Kallas says her husband, an investment banker, is a volunteer himself. The number of volunteers soared following the Ukraine invasion.

"After this war started, there were a lot of CEOs, masses of people really, both men and women, going to the Defense League," she recalled. "They have their firms. They have their villas in Spain, whatever. But one of them said, 'I can't imagine that I will be in my villa in Spain watching TV news, seeing what is happening here. I have to fight for this.' And this is something that I think majority will do, because we just don't want to lose this."

Lose what? Their very nation. That is the threat they see from Russia today, even with NATO membership. "I have to fight for this" originates, again, from two fears: Russia's ambition and their allies' ambivalence. It's a combination of fears that now extends all the way to Asia.

CHAPTER FIVE

TARGET TAIWAN

"IF YOU WANT TO TAKE TAIWAN, YOU HAVE TO TAKE PENGHU FIRST"

The mechanized infantry combat team stationed at Hen Hill Army Base on one of the ninety Penghu Islands is preparing every day for invasion. Taiwan's military is careful about allowing journalists access to its bases on this archipelago, strategically positioned in the disputed waters of the Taiwan Strait. While Taiwanese officials don't hesitate to make public warnings about the risk of a Chinese invasion, they're more reluctant to expose the details of their preparations for the island's defense. Accepting a rare invitation, I visited the army base as soldiers conducted an exercise simulating a Chinese airborne assault. This was not for show, but part of the Taiwanese armed forces' regular training.

Hen Hill hosts a company-size team of 119 soldiers ready for deployment at all times—a quick-reaction force for a Chinese assault. "We're confident we will be able to handle whatever the PLA [People's Liberation Army] throws at us," Colonel Chang Chi-Ming, the chief of operations on Penghu, told me, "All training has realistic scenarios in mind, so no matter when, no matter where, we can react to it in the shortest period of time."

This unit is built and trained for "combined forces" operations, drawing armored cavalry, mechanized infantry, artillery, and air defense units into a single, cohesive unit. These forces coordinate with their air force and navy counterparts to carry out operations across all branches of the military. Combined arms operations are the mantra of commanders across continents, including Ukraine. Ukrainian forces were proving themselves capable of such operations, while Russian forces were not.

The mood among the troops during the exercises fit their commanders' urgency. To maximize impact, commanders kept the location of the simulated assault a surprise to all units until the last moment. Once they received the intelligence, platoon commanders huddled around a 3D mock-up of the battlefield and recited their piece of the battle plan, shouting out each step of the maneuver. Armored personal carriers and battle tanks then fired up their engines and sped toward an airfield designated as the point of the Chinese attack.

In rapid succession, the combat team swarmed the battlefield in waves. Infantry spilled out of armored personal carriers, rifles leveled, moving toward the target, dropping to the ground, and then hopping up to move forward again. Behind the APCs, tanks emerged from the surrounding tree line. The dance continued for several minutes until platoon commanders declared the site, an airfield, secure.

This is the rhythm of defense planning here, across the Taiwan Strait from China. With such short distances—Penghu is just eighty-six miles from the Chinese coast, less than the distance from Florida to Cuba—Taiwanese forces must train to respond within minutes. To make them more difficult targets for any Chinese attack, Taiwanese military units are deliberately dispersed across the islands.

I found similar urgency at the nearby Magong Air Base, home to a rotating squadron of "indigenous defense fighters," the jets that form the backbone of the Taiwanese Air Force. There, squadron commander Lieutenant Colonel Pi Shih-Chuan—who, with *Maverick*-like bravado, shared his call sign, "Big"—explained that his squadron trains to scramble within five minutes, yet almost always gets airborne even faster.

"Sometimes it's reconnaissance. Sometimes it's training," Pi told me in Chinese. "Although we are performing readiness missions here, the training has never stopped."

When I then asked him if he's proud of his squadron's readiness, he answered that question in English: "Of course," he said.

The day I visited Magong, Pi's Coyote squadron got a real-world test of their readiness. More and more often, mainland Chinese jets had been infiltrating Taiwan's air defense identification zone, or ADIZ, an area extending twelve nautical miles around Taiwan and its territorial islands and from the median line between Penghu and the mainland. And that morning, four People's Liberation Army Air Force fighter jets had broken the line just to the southwest of the Penghus. Coyote squadron jets scrambled to intercept them, a delicate high-altitude encounter between warplanes from two countries not quite at war. The PLA jets eventually turned away back toward the mainland, their mission complete. These infiltrations were becoming almost daily events here, taking yet another jump in frequency since US House Speaker Nancy Pelosi had visited Taiwan the previous August. Beijing was not only testing Taiwan's air defenses but also sending a message to Washington.

The Penghu Islands are central to both Taiwan's and China's military planning. For Taiwan, the Penghus are a forward military outpost: home to early-warning radar, anti-ship and anti-aircraft missiles. There are bases for Taiwanese army, air force, and naval forces. And for China, they would be the first target in any invasion scenario.

"There's a saying, 'If you want to take Taiwan, you have to take Penghu first,'" Colonel Chang told me.

LESSONS FROM UKRAINE

As commanders here gaze warily across the strait, they are also closely watching the battlefields of Ukraine, thousands of miles away, for lessons they can apply at home. I found Taiwanese forces already implementing some lessons from Ukraine's successful defense against the Russian invasion. Forces in Penghu now deploy counter-measures against drones, following Russia's expansive use of drones to attack military and civilian targets in Ukraine. They are organizing their ground forces into smaller combat units to allow for greater mobility against a larger invading force. And they are expanding air defense systems to provide greater protection against missile attacks.

"We do incorporate [what we've seen in Ukraine] into our planning," Penghu operations chief Colonel Chang told me. And he added he's confident the Taiwanese military can defend itself, because it shares something essential with Ukrainian forces. "Our forces are high morale, with the will to fight," he said, crediting their morale to the advantage maintained by forces committed to defending their home. It's an advantage Russian forces have lacked in Ukraine, and one he believes mainland Chinese forces would lack in Taiwan as well.

"WE . . . FIND OUR WAY"

The talk on Penghu is of impending war. On Taiwan itself, however, I found a place far less alarmed about its potential fate than the armed forces or its supporters abroad. Capital city Taipei was reminiscent of Beirut for me: a city surrounded and defined by the prospect of war but getting on with life and often downplaying invasion fears as an outsider's obsession.

"For seventy years, they've been telling us China is going to invade," a taxi driver told me. "And here we are today, just fine."

Even some of the most senior Taiwanese officials echo that skepticism. "We people in Taiwan have lived under this circumstance for decades," Chern-Chyi "C. C." Chen, the deputy minister of economic affairs, told me. "My sense—[for] the majority of the Taiwanese people—we think the conflict definitely can be avoided."

Is that the wisdom of experience, or willful ignorance? In the weeks before my trip, a series of current and former US military leaders described Taiwan as if it were a close relative unaware of the gravity of his illness. "They'll need every bit of military training, I'm afraid," one former military intelligence officer warned with a sense of resignation.

But the alarmists are not outliers. Concern over a Chinese invasion is also the public position of the Taiwanese government.

"They seem to be trying to get ready to launch a war against Taiwan," Foreign Minister Joseph Wu had told me of China a few weeks before my visit, as the PLA carried out the largest military exercises around the island ever. "Beijing's way of handling the differences between Taiwan and China is true coercion, military threat. And the threat to use force against Taiwan.

"These are unacceptable," Wu continued. "And we condemn it."

The view among many Taiwanese I met is far more nuanced. Many—from journalists to business owners to political analysts to even senior officials in Wu's own administration—are far from a war footing.

"We sort of find our way," said Minister Chen. "So we know how to survive. And not only survive, we prosper. And because of our prosperity, the spillover effect also benefits China."

Taiwan's approach to mainland China involves a series of delicate balances: ask for more from the Taiwanese people in the form of longer military service but don't frighten them into believing they'll soon be asked to die for their country; celebrate a unique Taiwanese historical and political identity but don't force people to reject their cultural and familial ties to China; secure military, economic, and diplomatic support from allies but don't destroy an economic relationship with China that still accounts for 40 percent of Taiwan's total trade; and—perhaps most difficult—prepare for the possibility of war but don't provoke one.

"We are watching very closely how China will develop or evolve in terms of its society, its political system, its economic situation," said Chen. "That's something we have some concern about, but definitely not to the extent of a hot war. But we have to prepare ourselves. We avoid conflict by virtue of our prosperity, our self-defense, and our resilience. That's why we are preparing ourselves, not because we are foreseeing a conflict immediately."

The focus of Taiwanese officials is on one man: Xi Jinping. Ultimately, they believe the decision to invade or not to invade is his alone.

"Xi Jinping took office in 2012, and President Tsai took office in 2016," said Jan Jyh-Horng, deputy minister of Taiwan's Mainland Affairs Council, referring to Taiwan's president, Tsai Ing-Wen, who will step down in 2024 because of term limits. As leader of Taiwan's pro-democracy Democratic Progressive Party, perceived as more supportive of Taiwan's eventual independence from the mainland, Tsai has been a frequent target of Beijing's attacks. "Ever since President Tsai took office, mainland China has been engaging in all kinds of threats and warfare against us. However, like I said, we have remained safe, and we are still alive."

Taiwan lives on borrowed time and seems to be fine with it. And yet, as I listened to the doubters about the prospect of war, I couldn't help recalling the doubts I heard in Ukraine right until Russian tanks started to roll across the border. Many in Ukraine and the West saw Putin as a pragmatic leader—playing chess with his threats and military buildup—until the facts proved otherwise. Putin's ambition launched the largest war in Europe since World War II. Would Xi do the same in Asia?

"NO ONE DARES TO PICK UP THE PHONE"

In Taiwan's government, the Mainland Affairs Council is the primary agency for maintaining ties and communications between Taipei and Beijing. Started in the late 1980s, the council is now a cabinet-level department with a broad portfolio of cross-strait relations, ranging from trade to military-to-military communications.

President Tsai previously served as chair of the council. And Deputy Minister Jan has been in leadership roles on the council for more than three decades. He explained over tea in a reception room just outside his office that when he and other Taiwanese officials charged with cross-strait relations attempt to reach out to their mainland counterparts, there's often no answer.

"When it comes to official communication outside of these agreements, so far we haven't seen any, and even if we call them by phone, no one dares to pick up," Jan said. "Even if there were a hotline between the two sides, it wouldn't necessarily work in the times of need. And that's because even in emergency situations, mainland China would just arbitrarily decide that they won't pick up our call."

Today, there is no military hotline between the People's Liberation Army and the Republic of China Armed Forces. In fact, virtually all cross-strait communications at the official and unofficial levels have waned. This silent treatment across the Taiwan Strait is particularly dangerous in the military sphere, as it puts ships and aircraft of the Republic of China (ROC) Armed Forces into an increasingly delicate position. When PLA Air Force jets cross into Taiwan's air defense identification zone, ROC Air Force jets must now physically approach them, rather than communicating from afar.

"Even when we spot them, what we can do is very traditional," Jan explained to me. "We have to actually approach them. The military aircraft have to actually approach them and drive them away by radio. So that is very dangerous because, in these times, the airplanes run the risk of being shot down by them immediately."

"Shot down by them immediately"—it's a remarkable scenario for a senior Taiwanese official to lay out in detail. Such an encounter could very well be seen as an act of war by either side, which could then spark a larger military conflict. In today's new normal, the conditions for such a scenario are almost daily events. And more close contacts equals more chances for escalation equals more chances for war.

Of course, the Taiwanese and mainland Chinese armed forces are not the only ones operating in the area. US warplanes and warships regularly transit the strait, as do partner forces, in maneuvers carried out deliberately to demonstrate the West's commitment not just to keeping these sea-lanes open but also to maintaining the status quo for Taiwan. And yet communications between the PLA and western forces are equally irregular to nonexistent.

When the two sides aren't speaking, close encounters can become dangerous. In early June 2023, a Chinese destroyer deliberately cut in front of the USS *Chung-Hoon*, which was participating in a joint exercise with Canadian vessels in the Taiwan Strait. According to the US Indo-Pacific Command, the Chinese warship came within 150 yards of the *Chung-Hoon*, a near miss at sea. "Chung-Hoon maintained course and slowed to 10 k[no]ts to avoid a collision," read the statement from the US Indo-Pacific Command, which added that the Chinese ship's "actions violated the maritime 'Rules of the Road' of safe passage in international waters."[1]

According to Jan, Beijing often simply refuses to answer during these interactions, for Taiwan or the US and its regional allies.

"The US military sometimes wants to convey information or have emergency contact, but mainland China will simply just refuse to pick up the phone. Or between Japan and mainland China, sometimes Japan will want to say something, but mainland China will say, 'I'm sorry, this is beyond the scope of our hotline communication, so we will not pick up the phone.'"

"That's why I have no reason to be optimistic," Jan added. After the series of dangerous scenarios we had just discussed, I almost had to shake my head at the understatement. He was describing the makings of war.

FADING RED LINES

For years, each party has established and advertised its red lines. For Taiwan and the US, the red line has been a Chinese invasion, or any attempt by China to take Taiwan by force. For Xi, the red line has been Taiwan formally declaring independence or—less definitively—moving too close to independence for Chinese leaders' comfort. But in recent years, under an increasingly aggressive Xi, many fear China has lowered its threshold for military action. The Chinese leader, fresh off securing an unprecedented third term and dispensing with

China's decades-old term limits, simply *wants* to reunify the island with the mainland to solidify his historical legacy and is just waiting for the right time to do so at minimum cost.

Secretary of State Antony Blinken has watched the transformation with alarm.

"China has decided to move away from the status quo that prevailed for decades and that was instrumental in keeping peace and stability across the strait—by starting to exert real pressure on Taiwan, coercion, pushing it out of the international space, trying to sever its relationships with countries around the world, exerting more economic and military pressure on it," Blinken told me. "And we, of course, have made clear our opposition to that and the importance of maintaining the status quo.

"What China says to us is 'This is a sovereign issue. It's none of your business or anyone else's,'" Blinken continued. "Our answer is 'No, actually that's not true.'"

COSTS OF WAR

"Not only is it an understanding that preserving the status quo is vital to our own relationship, but we and countries around the world have a profound interest at stake in preserving stability across the Taiwan Strait," Secretary of State Blinken said. "Given the fact that fifty percent of commercial traffic goes through the strait every single day for the world, and seventy percent plus of semiconductors are made in Taiwan, well, that could be disrupted. We'd have potentially an economic crisis of global proportions."

Identifying the shared economic costs to the region and to the world is part of the case US officials make to allies and others in Asia and beyond. In short, if China disrupts the status quo on Taiwan, we all pay.

All sides are entering this precarious new reality with an awareness of the devastating costs of such a conflict. From an economic perspective, the costs to the US, China, the Asia-Pacific region, and the world would be monumental.

But while the potential economic costs of a war over Taiwan are severe, the military costs are heart-stopping. War games envisioning a potential Chinese invasion of Taiwan paint a horrific picture. In January 2023, the Center for Strategic and International Studies (CSIS) published the results of a war game it conducted, forebodingly entitled *The First Battle of the Next War: Wargaming a Chinese Invasion of Taiwan*. The study was comprehensive, drawing on historic battles from the Gallipoli landing to the Normandy and Falkland invasions as well as hard data on modern US, Chinese, and Taiwanese weapons systems. CSIS ran its model some two dozen times and published its results in "optimistic," "pessimistic," and "base" scenarios. None were pretty.

The CSIS report envisioned the onset of the war as follows: "The invasion always starts the same way: an opening bombardment destroys most of Taiwan's navy and air force in the first hours of hostilities. Augmented by a powerful rocket force, the Chinese navy encircles Taiwan and interdicts any attempts to get ships and aircraft to the besieged island. Tens of thousands of Chinese soldiers cross the strait in a mix of military amphibious craft and civilian roll-on, roll-off ships while air assault and airborne troops land behind the beachheads."[2]

In these war games, Taiwanese forces were not China's only targets. The PLA also unleashed a devastating barrage on US military bases in the region, followed by perhaps the largest, most lightning-fast naval engagement in history. In each iteration of the war games, the losses mounted quickly. In the base scenarios, "U.S. Navy losses included two U.S. aircraft carriers as well as between 7 and 20 other major surface warships (e.g., destroyers and cruisers)." In addition, the US lost anywhere between 168 and 372 aircraft, including navy aircraft deployed on carriers and ground-based aircraft at US bases in Asia. Taiwan lost roughly half its air force, all 26 ships in its navy, as well as 3,500 casualties in the Taiwanese army. The US and its regional allies would lose tens of thousands of service members at sea and on land. The scale of the projected battle had no comparison since World War II.[3]

The report projected China would suffer catastrophic losses of its own. Its navy, on average, would lose a staggering number of vessels: 138 major ships, including 86 amphibious ships and 52 other major surface warships. Chinese aircraft losses averaged 161. China's personnel losses, in killed, wounded, and captured, also numbered in the tens of thousands. The study found that at the end of such a conflict, China's "navy is in shambles, the core of its amphibious forces is broken, and tens of thousands of soldiers are prisoners of war."[4]

With notable similarities to Russian forces' experiences in Ukraine, Chinese forces would face immediate obstacles. According to CSIS: "The Chinese invasion quickly founders. Despite massive Chinese bombardment, Taiwanese ground forces stream to the beachhead, where the invaders struggle to build up supplies and move inland. Meanwhile U.S. submarines, bombers, and fighter/attack aircraft, often reinforced by Japan Self-Defense Forces, rapidly cripple the Chinese amphibious fleet. China's strikes on Japanese bases and U.S. surface ships cannot change the result."

Crucially, there was no clear winner in any scenario. In the final analysis, CSIS found, "no scenario resulted in a clear Chinese victory."

All three major participants would be left with their forces crippled and Taiwan still independent but deeply damaged.[5]

US military war games over Taiwan are classified, but according to US officials who have seen them, they paint a similarly grim picture to those conducted by CSIS. And US officials speak openly about the dire consequences of war.

In June 2023, at the International Institute for Strategic Studies' Shangri-La Dialogue in Singapore, Defense Secretary Lloyd Austin said, "Conflict is neither imminent nor inevitable. Deterrence is strong today—and it's our job to keep it that way." He went on to note: "The whole world has a stake in maintaining peace and stability in the Taiwan Strait. The security of commercial shipping lanes and global supply chains depends on it. And so does freedom of navigation worldwide. Make no mistake: conflict in the Taiwan Strait would be devastating."[6]

UKRAINE A LESSON FOR TAIWAN

With these war scenarios in mind, part of Taiwan's defense plan is to raise the costs for China, and, again, its leaders see lessons from the war in Ukraine. In fact, despite the focus on what Beijing has learned from the Ukraine war, Taiwan may be gaining the most important lessons from the conflict. Just as Russia's 2014 invasion sparked Ukraine to institute major military reforms, and the West to boost training of Ukrainian forces and the influx of weapons, the full-scale 2022 invasion of Ukraine sparked a similar rethinking of Taiwan's military preparations and defense.

Today, Taiwanese officials note that the Ukrainian military's remarkable defense against a far larger and better-armed Russian invading force was not accidental. Ukraine had been arming and training its forces for nearly a decade with the help of NATO allies. Over the course of that time period, Ukraine had created perhaps the most formidable military in Europe through a combination of advanced weapon systems and training in those systems as well as a focus on asymmetric warfare to compete against Russian forces, which would always maintain a size advantage. Many Taiwanese military leaders and their US counterparts concluded Taiwan would need to pursue the same combination to blunt mainland China's similar advantage in numbers.

A war over Taiwan would be markedly different from the war in Ukraine. An amphibious assault is widely recognized as the most difficult and deadly of any military maneuver. Instead of tank battles, artillery barrages, and trench warfare, planners envision lightning-fast air and sea combat, with rapid waves of missiles, including China's new hypersonic missiles, as well as anti-satellite weapons and cyberattacks disabling key military and civilian technologies in advance.

Unlike Ukraine, too, the US and its allies would have no ability to resupply and rearm Taiwanese forces after the onset of war as they have done for Ukrainian forces via supply lines overland. As an island in the sea, Taiwan has no overland supply routes, of course, and China would presumably block sea and air routes during military action. So Taiwan's allies must provide the help it needs now.

THE "PORCUPINE" DEFENSE

What does such help look like? Many in Taiwan and among its allies have settled on the "porcupine" strategy. Republican US senator Roger Wicker, ranking member on the Senate Armed Services

Committee, laid out the strategy in stark terms on the Senate floor in February 2023.

"We need to turn Taiwan into a porcupine so that Xi Jinping wakes up every day and concludes that an invasion is not worth the costs," Senator Wicker told his colleagues. "Now, why do you say a porcupine? Any wolf has the ability to kill a gentle porcupine. And yet such an attack rarely occurs in nature. The defense of the porcupine's quills, which can rip through the predator's mouth and throat, is the deterrent that protects it from attack by the wolves. That should be our approach for Taiwan's defense."

"Rip through the predator's mouth and throat"—stark words from a US senator, and ones Beijing certainly heard. But they capture the intention: to make an attack on Taiwan as devastating for China as it would be for Taiwan.

On the Senate floor, Wicker specified the kind of weapons the US increasingly believes Taiwan should focus on. "Their weapons purchases increasingly align with how our military experts envision a correct defense of the island, including with Harpoon anti-ship cruise missiles, Stingers, anti-aircraft missiles, and secure communication systems," Wicker said. "We should encourage this change in Taiwan's focus."

Today, most Taiwanese military leaders agree. Admiral Lee Hsi-Min served in the Taiwanese navy for more than four decades and rose to chief of the general staff, Taiwan's equivalent of the US chairman of the Joint Chiefs of Staff, making him the island's highest-ranking military leader, in which capacity he served from 2017 to 2019.

"According to the experience from Ukraine, we found out that asymmetrical is the key for the defender," Lee said. "So that means that Taiwan, to defend itself, needs a lot more of the mobile, distributed weapons—asymmetrical weapons systems. . . . Both the United States and Taiwan should concentrate on supplying and acquiring more asymmetrical weapons systems instead of big-ticket, highly advanced conventional platforms."

A successful defense requires not just a change in weapons systems but also an urgent acceleration in weapons supplies. "Because Taiwan is an island state, we just cannot continue to receive international support during wartime—we have no opportunity if the conflict has already started," Lee emphasized.

The war in Ukraine provides multiple examples of the importance of asymmetrical weapons and tactics against an invading army. Shoulder-fired Javelin anti-tank missiles helped force a Russian retreat from its early assault on Kyiv. Later, anti-ship missiles coupled with drones sank the flagship of Russia's Black Sea fleet, effectively rendering the Black Sea a no-go zone for the Russian Navy.

"They [the Ukrainians] used two Neptune missiles to sink the *Moskva*," Lee noted. "And they used Switchblade drones, Stinger missiles, Javelin missiles to hit lots of tanks and helicopters and aircraft. So they've already proved that asymmetry is the key for the defender."

LEE'S BATTLE

Though it's what is necessary, Taiwan's transition to a focus on asymmetrical warfare is relatively new and has not been easy. As chief of Taiwan's general staff, Admiral Lee ran into consistent roadblocks pushing the military to change. Taiwanese leaders—like their counterparts in the US—were often too enamored of big-ticket weapons systems.

There is a long list of cautionary tales. The Littoral Combat Ship, a warship designed for surface warfare, submarine hunting, and minesweeping in shallow coastal waters, was abandoned only a few years after the first few were commissioned. Decommissioning alone cost $4.5 billion—about five times the amount of US military aid Taiwan receives each year.[7] The US Army's Crusader self-propelled howitzer, a forty-three-ton armored, mobile artillery piece, seemed built for another conflict before it was killed off in 2002.[8] And the US Navy remains locked in an ongoing debate about the effectiveness of aircraft carriers, even as they grow increasingly vulnerable to more advanced submarines and anti-ship missiles.

But Lee sees the US adjusting the kinds of weapons systems it prioritizes for Taiwan—in effect, the right refocusing on providing more quills for the porcupine. "[The US] rejected helicopter arm sales and promoted coastal defense anti-ship missile system," Lee noted. "That is a good direction."

What's still missing, Lee worries, is a shared plan to fight together in the event of a Chinese attack. Without a mutual defense treaty, there are no joint military exercises like the US carries out with Asian allies South Korea and Japan.

"We cannot practice together," Lee said. "Then, asymmetrical defense is [the] only way that Taiwan can attack. But even if we want to develop asymmetrical capability, we still rely on the assistance from the United States. And for the past two years, I believe [the] United States is already aware of that importance for asymmetry to Taiwan."

"The United States and Taiwan should sit [down] together to discuss solely how to develop a common operation concept," Lee said, noting, "We have our own responsibility, and if United States wants to intervene, they can take care of certain parts of Taiwan's defense.

"*If* the United States wants to intervene"—that is one of the crucial, looming questions for Taiwan and for China and the US, and one very much dependent on understanding what is happening now and what might happen next.

SHADOW WAR ON TAIWAN

While the world awaits Beijing's next move, mainland Chinese forces already are making life increasingly difficult for Taiwan. In 2019's *The Shadow War*, I document the "gray zone" warfare China was waging against the US and its allies via a combination of cyberattacks, disinformation campaigns, a broad military buildup, and the exertion of military pressure just below the threshold of kinetic conflict. In Taiwan in 2023, I listened as Taiwanese officials described an expanding Chinese shadow war on the island.

"Gray-zone aggression is happening every day," Admiral Lee told me. "We have to deal with that, and we also have to prepare for the existential threat that is a full-scale invasion."

China's military exercises around Taiwan in April 2023—its biggest and most aggressive ever—fit the pattern. As an experienced military tactician, Lee saw the exercises less as training for a future war and more as an end in themselves.

"From [a] military point of view, it's not good tactics because, during wartime, if they really send warships close to the coast, they will be attacked by missiles or other weapons from the land," Lee noted. As a result, he viewed the operations as part of a pressure campaign on Taiwan. "It is still a coercive operation or gray-zone aggression," Lee said. "More or less symbolic rather than a really meaningful military action."

China is constantly intimidating and testing Taiwan. Almost every day, Chinese warplanes enter Taiwan's air defense identification zone, with Chinese commanders sending a variety of their most advanced aircraft—J-10, J-11, J-16, and Su-30 fighter jets; military drones; and Y-8 anti-submarine warplanes—sometimes dozens in a single day. Chinese forces take other actions as well. In early 2023, Taiwanese officials began to suspect China had severed two underwater internet cables that link the Taiwanese-controlled Matsu Islands, approximately ten miles off the mainland Chinese coast, to the outside world.[9]

The sabotage of undersea cables is increasingly recognized as a standard part of any military attack by China or Russia. When I embarked on NATO's Very High Readiness Joint Task Force in the Baltic Sea in April 2023, the flagship commander told me that monitoring undersea cables had become a new focus of NATO naval forces—and that those forces had observed increased Russian naval activity over key chokepoints for years. In 2019, I reported on Russian naval vessels and submarines designed and deployed explicitly to target such cables. Today, Taiwanese and US forces see similar activity by the Chinese navy in the waters around Taiwan. "The activity looks like targeted harassment by Beijing—or an exercise in preparation for cutting off the whole of Taiwan," wrote Elizabeth Braw in the magazine *Foreign Policy* in February 2023.[10]

"A PORCUPINE . . . CAN BE STARVED"

These shadow-war tactics point to another possibility: that China's pressure campaign is not signaling but is central to the plan. US and Taiwanese officials tell me that mainland China has an option short of a full-scale invasion that might still allow it to reclaim the island as its own. Via a combination of military pressure, political interference, and economic measures, the goal would be for Taiwan to give in on its own over time and accept that, in effect, resistance is futile and that reunification is recognition of the inevitable.

Congressman Jake Auchincloss (D-MA), a member of the US House Select Committee on China, has visited Taiwan and is regularly briefed on the latest US intelligence on China and Taiwan. In his view, Xi would be less likely to order a full-scale Chinese invasion of the island given the enormous military challenges and the prospect of sparking a war with the US.

"Much of the war-gaming assumes PLA missile strikes on US Marines followed by an amphibious invasion that transitions to urban warfare," Auchincloss told me. "In some ways, this is the simple scenario, because it leads directly to war [with the US]." Many US officials believe that, like Putin with Europe, Xi does not want a war with the US if he can avoid it.

How does Xi then achieve his aim of reunification without going to war? Call it the "asphyxiation scenario," or, as some in the intelligence community refer to it, the "boa constrictor scenario."

"It's more likely to be a combination of energy asphyxiation plus disinformation in order to engineer reunification from within," Auchincloss told me. "As one KMT [Kuomintang, Taiwan's right-wing party, perceived as less supportive of Taiwanese independence] official said: 'A porcupine can't be eaten, but it can be starved.'"

A potential Chinese plan to "starve" rather than invade Taiwan was causing growing concern among US officials and lawmakers focused on the island's security. Republican congressman Mike Gallagher (R-WI) told me in August 2023 that he had heard a similar warning on his visit to Taiwan months earlier and that it continued to "haunt" him. "I left thinking we needed to pay more attention to the blockade scenario, the economic coercion scenario," Gallagher said. "In fact, you can make a case that sort of economic and cyber invasion of Taiwan has already begun."

"Consider a scenario where CCP ramps up gray-zone harassment such that Taiwan can't import LNG," Auchincloss explained. (Taiwan imports some 99 percent of its natural gas, according to Taiwan's Ministry of Economic Affairs.) "Simultaneously they are spreading disinformation about who's to blame via TikTok, YouTube, and traditional media. If done when the KMT is in power, it could force an agreement that puts Taiwan on Hong Kong's glide path."

This is a theme the congressman returns to frequently: that—in Chinese's gradual suppression of Hong Kong and Russia's brutal invasion of Ukraine—the world has already witnessed the two potential endgames for Taiwan.

"They can be Hong Kong and gradually be absorbed," Auchincloss said. "Or Ukraine and choose to fight."

China's massive military exercises around Taiwan following Nancy Pelosi's August 2022 visit offered an alarming model. For days, Chinese jets and warships swarmed the island. Missiles flew. Chinese forces were war-gaming an encircling maneuver around Taiwan. And even during a simulated maneuver, the Taiwanese economy was feeling the effects. Local manufacturers had trouble meeting orders as air and sea transit in and out of Taiwan suffered delays. Business leaders called partners overseas to help meet demands. If an exercise over days could begin to disrupt the supply chain for the world's twenty-first largest economy, how would one playing out over weeks or months impact Taiwan? Would it push the island to relent without a single directly fired shot?

In keeping with its practice of testing and extending the limits, since those early 2023 exercises, the PLA had set a new standard for military harassment. "Prior to the Pelosi visit," Deputy Minister Jan of the Mainland Affairs Council told me, "PLA fighter jets and PLA ships would stay west of the Taiwan Strait median line. However, after the Pelosi visit, even until today, the PLA fighter jets and warships have stayed close to Taiwan on a daily basis." PLA jets had done exactly that while I was visiting Penghu, forcing Taiwanese pilots into an almost daily ritual of scrambling to intercept them.

And in April 2023, China launched a new round of drills, which the PLA's Eastern Theater Command described as training "to seize control of sea, air and information under the support of our joint combat system," as CNN reported. Note the language: "to seize control." As those exercises came to a close, the PLA Joint Operations Command Center declared them a success, as having "simulated joint precision strikes on key targets on Taiwan Island." Again, note the language: "precision strikes on key targets on Taiwan." Taiwan's defense ministry reported detecting dozens of mainland Chinese warplanes crossing the median line and entering Taiwan's air defense identification zone.

Before I left Hen Hill Army Base on Penghu, Colonel Chang, its chief of operations, said that there is one unwavering fact of this standoff: whether China decides to asphyxiate or invade, Taiwan belongs to the Taiwanese people, and they will fight to defend it. He pointed out a mural on the wall of his conference room. The eight bold Chinese characters, painted in red, read: "We share this island. We will fight until the end."

The question remains: How will Xi Jinping react to that vow?

CHAPTER SIX

TAIWAN'S EXISTENTIAL QUESTIONS

WILL XI OR WON'T XI?

A potential Chinese invasion is an existential threat to Taiwan. Visiting there, I found the invasion question is actually multiple questions. The first, as it was for Ukraine before Putin ordered a full-scale invasion, will Xi or won't Xi? Will his desire to make history by reunifying Taiwan with the mainland outweigh his pragmatic interest in avoiding the military, diplomatic, and economic costs of invasion? And, simplest of all, does he believe China can actually take Taiwan successfully?

Recent history shows that Xi Jinping is a Chinese leader with greater ambition and less restraint than his recent predecessors. He has repeatedly proved himself willing to accept high risks for what he perceives to be his and the Chinese Communist Party's interests. In addition to incarcerating more than a million Uighurs in Xinjiang, he crushed popular protests in Hong Kong, antagonized a crucial trading partner in Australia, and imposed an aggressive zero-Covid policy on his own population despite significant political and economic damage. Each move was ruthless—and each was dismissed as unlikely until it became a reality. Would Xi again damn the consequences to take Taiwan?

VIEW FROM PENGHU

During my visit to his army headquarters on Penghu, Colonel Chang Chi-Ming told me his own analysis of the threat of a Chinese invasion is largely political. Chang, like most US military officers I meet today, is a student as well as a soldier, and in addition to years in active military service, he wrote his graduate thesis on the Chinese Communist Party structure.

He sees deep similarities between Xi Jinping and Vladimir Putin in their decision-making and leadership style. Noting that the Chinese and Russian Communist Parties were deeply intertwined in their structures and often educated each other's leaders, he sees Xi and Putin as creatures of the same system.

"They were trained in the same system, so they are leaders in the same model," he told me. That model favors the leader's survival over all else and disincentivizes dissent. The West had watched how the Russian system prevented any doubts about the Russian military's ability to seize Ukraine from penetrating Putin's bubble, feeding his overconfidence and enabling miscalculation. Chang sees a similar bubble engulfing Xi regarding Taiwan.

Chang can't predict whether Xi will follow Putin's example. But he believes Taiwan has to be ready. "I have faith we are ready for anything," he said.

VIEW FROM TAIPEI

In the capital Taipei, it's also believed the answer to the invasion question lies largely with Xi alone. In a mainland system built more and more around the ambitions of one man—China's president for life—judgments about Beijing's next move have spawned a modern Chinese version of Kremlinology. On that topic, Deputy Minister Jan Jyh-Horng of the Mainland Affairs Council is a devoted student. And he sees the trend lines bending toward conflict.

"All we can do is to ensure that we do everything we can to prevent a conflict," he said. "However, judging from the current situation over the past ten years, while Xi Jinping is in office, the situation is really not optimistic."

Through his more than thirty years on the Mainland Affairs Council, Jan has watched as relations deteriorated, primarily, he believes, because of a change in leadership in Beijing. "When Xi Jinping's two predecessors, Jiang Zemin and Hu Jintao, were in office," Jan said, "we were more sure of the situation and we were more optimistic."

A system that had been built on consensus among senior members of the Chinese Communist Party leadership is now markedly top-heavy, with Xi's views trumping those of all others.

"We feel that the decision-making for these three leaders is very, very different from each other," Jan told me. "When Jiang Zemin and Hu Jintao were in office, they took into account information from staff or from the bureaucratic system."

This is more than a change in leadership style. It is a fundamental change in how China operates in the world. China has long been a one-party authoritarian state, with power concentrated among a small group of senior CCP leaders. Now the People's Republic of China is in effect a one-man state. In June 2023, Joe Biden faced criticism for calling Xi a dictator, but Taiwanese leaders do not hesitate to do the same.

"Xi Jinping is very keen about maintaining his dictatorship," Jan told me. "So he believes that he is the only one who can make the call and no other people can make decisions for him."

XI AND PUTIN

The parallels between Xi and Putin fuel parallel concerns about Ukraine and Taiwan. When I asked Deputy Minister Jan if he—like many other China and Russia observers—saw similarities between Xi and Putin, he answered quickly, "I couldn't agree more."

Jan also places some hope that Russia's stumbles in Ukraine will make Xi think twice about invading Taiwan. "I'd say that there is one thing that is lucky for Taiwan," Jan said. "And that is now the whole world has already seen how Russia has suffered from its invasion of Ukraine."

It is a tense waiting game in Taipei. Yet, while Taiwanese officials cannot guess what Xi will decide and when, they already see damage from Xi's leadership style.

Not long ago, ties across the strait spanned multiple sectors.

"Over the past thirty years, the two sides across the strait have had a lot of chances for exchanges—mainly between citizens, between businesspeople, between scholars, across the two sides," Jan said. "We've seen some intense interaction between the two sides and these interactions present very good opportunities for communication."

These interactions—often described as "track two" communications, since they take place outside official government channels—helped keep the peace. And while Xi's predecessors Jiang Zemin and

Hu Jintao also vowed to eventually "reunify" Taiwan with mainland China, they deliberately kept these track-two channels open. No longer.

Xi's predecessors also sought counsel from lower-level officials and the party bureaucracy, which Xi resists. "So, at that time, we tried to convey our information through these intellectuals and staff," Jan told me. "And that's why, even at that time, the two governments didn't have direct channels of interaction, [but] we still had various ways to communicate. I believe that communication is key in our efforts to avoid conflicts."

Under Xi, these contacts have tapered off, and when they do take place, Taiwanese officials worry the substance of those communications does not make its way up to Xi himself. Meaning that in a country where only Xi matters, those contacts are far less useful.

"The situation at the moment is that we have tried to engage with them [mainland Chinese contacts] or communicate with them through the past connections that we've built. However, it seems that our opinions haven't been able to go all the way up to Xi Jinping through the staff or the bureaucratic system," Jan told me. "And that's why communication between the two sides seem to be quite indirect, and sometimes it seems that [those communications] need to take several turns before they get across. However, still, we don't have one hundred percent certainty that our opinions will certainly come across to Xi."

"POLITICS TRUMPS ALL"

If these conditions were the product of a bad period in China-Taiwan relations, or simply the style of one in a series of Chinese leaders,

Taiwan could wait out the storm and hope for a change and a chance to defuse the tensions. Today, however, Taiwanese leaders see them as systemic.

This new dynamic played out during China's handling of the Covid pandemic. When Chinese officials attempted to take a "milder approach" to lockdowns than the state had laid out, they were removed or demoted. The message was clear: challenge Xi, and you will pay a price. This dynamic infects every major decision of the CCP, Deputy Minister Jan believes, including its approach to Taiwan.

"A lot of people in the bureaucratic system are concerned that their decisions, if these decisions turn out to be bad decisions, then they may be penalized," he said.

"What I'm really concerned about is that Xi Jinping is still, at the end of the day, the head of an authoritarian state," Jan explained. "So he believes that only his own thinking and his own decisions can lead the direction of the entire country."

There is a conventional wisdom among many China observers that Xi and Putin are different in one fundamental aspect: that while Putin has brushed off his country's economic isolation resulting from the Ukraine invasion, such costs would be less acceptable for China and Xi. It is true that the economy is a powerful driving force for the Chinese leader. The CCP's power and legitimacy depend, in part, on its ability to deliver economic prosperity to its people. However, cracks are emerging in that convention. Jan's case in point: China and Australia.

"In Xi Jinping's time, I won't say that the economy is such an emphasis for him," Jan told me. "One of my most favorite examples is relations between mainland China and Australia."

China and Australia had a robust economic relationship for years. But Australian leaders bristled at Chinese economic pressure and interference in its politics, fraying relations. And in a fit of diplomatic pique, Beijing imposed deep economic sanctions on Canberra.

The spark was an Australian investigation into the origins of the Covid pandemic in early 2020, launched by the prime minister at the time, Scott Morrison. Soon after, the Chinese embassy in Canberra deliberately leaked a list of perceived wrongs by Australia against China, titled "14 Grievances." Included on the list was not just the Covid origins investigation but also Australia's decision to ban Chinese telecommunications manufacturer Huawei from supplying its 5G network, blocking some Chinese foreign investments in Australia, and, in the words of the document, "the incessant wanton interference" in Chinese activities in Taiwan, Hong Kong, and Xinjiang. China also pointed to Australia's statement before the UN criticizing Chinese activities in the South China Sea.[1] It was a diplomatic jeremiad against the whole of Australia's relationship with China on economic issues, human rights, and China's territorial claims abroad.

China followed the publicization of the list by ordering Chinese companies to stop importing a series of Australian products, worth billions of dollars, including wine, beef, barley, timber, lobster, and coal.[2] Taiwanese officials took note.

"Mainland China imposed bans on Australian lobster, Australian wine, and Australian coal, et cetera," Jan recalled. "These products are all things that the mainland Chinese people and the mainland Chinese economy needed, but still, Xi Jinping made that decision, and that decision was to cut off these imports."

Jan has observed similar behavior from Xi regarding trade between Taiwan and mainland China, which still accounts for nearly a quarter of Taiwan's total trade. That trade has helped keep the peace in the past, in Jan's view, but is no guarantee of peace in the future, especially under Xi's leadership. And, as with Australia, Beijing has used trade as a cudgel to punish Taipei.

"For cross-strait relations, of course, a certain level of economic ties is really helpful in reducing the possibility of having a conflict,"

Jan said. "And this has definitely been my observation over the past thirty years. Xi Jinping, however, has also been making very good use of these economic ties to retaliate against us or to enforce his own form of economic coercion. And that's something that he has also done to the US and to some US companies."

Together, Xi rules by hard power *and* he is willing to use that absolute power at home and abroad even when it costs his nation and people. Another way that Xi's track record mirrors Putin's.

"[Xi] will make these decisions sometimes at all costs. We have seen that in how he has dealt with Xinjiang, with Hong Kong, and also how he dealt with the protesters against the zero-Covid policies," Jan said. "He made the orders and didn't really care about the cost."

"Essentially, Xi Jinping's message is 'If you don't behave, if you don't listen to me, then you better not conduct any business with mainland China anymore,'" he said. "So I will say that, all in all, the logic is that, for Xi Jinping, politics trumps all."

TAIWAN'S (RECENT) AUTHORITARIAN PAST

Taiwan observes China with the experience of its own dictatorship. This is not distant history for Taiwan. Taipei began to dismantle its military dictatorship only in the late 1980s. Yet, unlike mainland China, Taiwan doesn't airbrush its past. In downtown Taipei, one can visit the former prison where dissidents and other perceived enemies of the state were tried, imprisoned, and sometimes executed.

As I toured the site, which is now the National Human Rights Museum, I was reminded of a similar walk through the Hanoi Hilton in Vietnam. Here in Taipei, the simple cinder block barracks housed tiny, bare cells, which had been filled with up to a dozen inmates each. There were torture rooms, shackles bolted to the floor, and walls marked by the graffiti of those condemned to torture and death. Inmates were forced to work in sweatshops, laundering and ironing clothes for a nearby hospital.

Taiwan's "White Terror," as it came to be known, was a decades-long campaign of repression against dissidents. Many victims of the repression are now serving in government. Today, Deputy Economics Minister C. C. Chen sees clues as to mainland China's future in Taiwan's own past.

"We were under martial law. We were under an authoritarian regime," Chen told me. "In our experience of how an authoritarian regime will function, it would open up to a certain extent, then it will contract because the ruler always, always has to control everything lest [he or she] endangers his or her position. So I don't know how Xi Jinping will rule China in the near future, but now it seems we are witnessing a big, long historical trend of opening up and then contracting."

THE TAIWAN MILITARY'S VIEW OF XI

Judging Xi's calculus is a focus of senior Taiwanese military leaders as well. Admiral Lee Hsi-Min, former chief of the general staff, believes that the primary deciding factor for a potential Chinese invasion is less China's military preparedness than the ambitions of the Chinese president and the promises he has made to the Chinese people.

"The first [factor] is Xi Jinping itself, his personality," Lee told me. "And secondary is the China dream. . . . Because Xi Jinping promised the Chinese people the China dream—that he would bring the people to the top of the world."

Xi introduced his concept of the "Chinese Dream" soon after ascending to the leadership of the Chinese Communist Party in 2012, declaring it "the great rejuvenation of the Chinese nation." The Chinese Dream, as he envisioned it and as it was widely publicized in Chinese official statements and state media, encompassed a "Strong China," in its economy, politics, science, and military affairs; a "Civilized China," defined as denoting equity and fairness, rich culture, and high morals; a "Harmonious China," with good relations among different social classes; and a "Beautiful China," with a focus on a clean environment, especially reducing air pollution.[3]

Xi's Chinese Dream also set two key goals: China would become a "moderately well-off society" by about 2020, when the CCP would mark its one hundredth anniversary, and China would achieve fully developed status by 2049, when the PRC would celebrate the one hundredth anniversary of its founding.[4] Yet, more recently, as the Chinese economy has come down to earth, the dream seems more like a mirage.

And the fading Chinese Dream, Lee argues, has put added pressure on Xi to act boldly. It's a promise that helped justify his unprecedented third term, breaking term limits the CCP had imposed to prevent the rise of another Mao. If Xi doesn't live up to that dream—at home and abroad—the Chinese public may sense weakness.

"So I believe that if his position is not so firm, he would take action," Lee said.

VIEW FROM THE US

The view in the Pentagon, like that in Taiwan, is that Xi Jinping is deeply invested in seizing Taiwan.

"It is absolutely clear that China believes that it's a core vital national security interest to unify Taiwan and the People's Republic of China," said General Mark Milley. "And it is also clear that that is a lifelong ambition, political ambition, of President Xi. He wants to do this on his watch. And he's said that multiple times."

Xi would prefer to take over Taiwan without war. China's "win without fighting" approach, dating back to Sun Tzu's *The Art of War*, and which I detail in *The Shadow War*, holds true with Taiwan—and particularly so given the extreme difficulty of seizing Taiwan by force. The military difficulties are clear.

"To conduct an amphibious invasion to seize the island of Taiwan, which is the most complex of all military operations, is a combination of amphibious, airborne assault—think Normandy—that's a really super complex thing," said Milley. "And the Chinese military has not trained to that level yet, and they don't have the military capabilities to do it yet."

The US believes Xi has instructed his military to achieve those capabilities by 2027 to give the Chinese leader the option at least to put those capabilities into action.

"He wants to get it done. So he is preparing his military to have options, military options, available to achieve his desired outcome," Milley said. "He wants to have military options available. So he has challenged the PLA to develop the military capability to invade and seize the island of Taiwan by 2027. . . . It used to be in the 2030s, middle 2030s, and he accelerated, 2027."

Milley told me the invasion is "extraordinarily high-risk" for Xi, and he views the Chinese leader as a Machiavellian assessor of risks, loath to lose a gamble with his power at stake. However, if Xi calculates the risk is worth it for him and for China, he may very well act. For the world, that means the risk of a great power war.

"If they were to attack to seize, or if they were to shell, bomb, or conduct violent activity toward Taiwan, as a minimum, there's a risk of a great power war," Milley said. "I'm not predicting that there would be one, but as a minimum, the risk is there."

UKRAINE LESSONS

Were Russia's stumbles in Ukraine forcing a rethink over Taiwan? In the spring of 2023, as the war in Ukraine entered its second year, CIA Director Bill Burns said that Russia's struggles on the battlefield had likely led Chinese leaders to reconsider plans to take Taiwan by force.

"I think what it means is that today, President Xi and the PLA—the People's Liberation Army—leadership have doubts about whether they could pull off a successful full-scale invasion of Taiwan at acceptable cost to them," Burns told the Aspen Security Forum in July 2023. "You know, no foreign leader, I think, has paid more careful attention to Putin's experience in Ukraine than President Xi has as he thinks about Taiwan. I think that's probably reinforced some of those doubts too, not only in the way in which an objectively smaller military has had incredible success in fighting back with a great deal of motivation against a bigger military but also some of the flaws in Russian weapons systems."

Burns said he believes the West's response to the Russian invasion likely also chastened the Chinese leader.

"The fact that, I think, certainly Putin, but, I think, also President Xi underestimated the speed with which President Biden would be able to put together a strong coalition in support of Ukraine and the solidarity of the West in being willing to accept some economic costs to inflict damage on Russia—all of that, I think, gives pause to the Chinese leadership," Burns said. "But having said all that, I don't think any of us at CIA or in the US intelligence community underestimate President Xi's commitment eventually to try to control Taiwan."

The danger is that Russia's stumbles in Ukraine accelerate rather than deter Xi's invasion plans for Taiwan. Xi may calculate, Burns said, that his chances of success will diminish over time, so the time for action is now.

Xi, "sort of like Putin with Ukraine, starts to worry that his window is closing to achieve what he believes is his destiny, which is to control Taiwan," Burns told me. "That can lead to autocrats—especially in the absence of a lot of contrary views in their inner circle and anything else—to make the kind of stupid decision that Putin made in Ukraine."

"You think of how intelligence needs to change in this new era," Burns continued. "One of the things is not to underestimate the sense that an autocrat's destiny can drive decisions that might not seem logical at all to us."

The focus of the US and its allies now is lengthening the timeline for any potential military action by China against Taiwan—hopefully, indefinitely.

"I don't think that's a given," Secretary of State Blinken told me. "Particularly if we're effective in either finding a way to diffuse their ambitions in one way or another, or certainly to build up, in a variety of ways, deterrence, so that he ultimately calculates the costs of taking that step are simply too great, at least in that time frame."

Over time, the Biden administration has been enlisting allies around the world to help discourage the Chinese leader from making a decision to invade, emphasizing the benefits of peace and the costs of war. The administration's goal, as Blinken described it to me, is expansive. It hopes to convince Xi Jinping that the costs of a war over Taiwan could not be contained to the island or even to the region. In Blinken's words, such a war would "implicate the interests of virtually every country on earth."

"I think all of that has been, in a sense, reinforced by what's going on in Ukraine," Blinken told me. "And one of the reasons that so many countries in Asia have been speaking out forcefully and acting in concert with countries in Europe against the Russian aggression is precisely because they see the potential implications, depending on what happens in Ukraine, for Asia and, for that matter, other parts of the world."

Hope and fear intertwine in this framing. Hope that the world has succeeded to a large degree in Ukraine by stifling the invasion and punishing Russia for it. Fear that if the world fails to do either, the floodgates will open for Taiwan and beyond.

"I think there's a strongly held view among a number of countries that if Putin is allowed to get away with this aggression with impunity, it potentially opens a Pandora's box where other would-be aggressors say, 'Well, if Russia can do it and get away with it, so can we,'" Blinken said, before adding, "And of course, one of the countries of concern would be China when it comes to Taiwan."

SHORT-TERM DELAY FOR TAIWAN

When I ran this deterrence theory past several current and former Taiwanese and US officials with long experience on China, I heard deep skepticism.

While Admiral Lee believes Russia's military failures in Ukraine— and the international community's relatively unified condemnation of the invasion—might delay Chinese military action against Taiwan, he does not think it has extinguished Chinese aspirations and planning.

"From the strategic point of view, I think Russia's experience in Ukraine will make China less likely to take the military action on Taiwan sooner rather than later," Lee told me. "However, I don't think Russia's [experience] in Ukraine will totally affect the Chinese leaders' decision."

Matthew Pottinger, deputy national security advisor under Trump, shared Lee's skepticism.

"I think that the fact that Putin has stumbled has probably surprised Beijing and will inform the approach they take in prosecuting their global strategy, but I don't see any indication yet that it has tempered Xi Jinping's intentions and broader ambitions," Pottinger said.

"I think that his timeline was informed," Pottinger continued. "In fact, I think he's behind schedule, so I don't think that our actions are what's really driving the clock. I think that it is more about Xi's timetable as a leader who's now got another five-year term. I think he wants to get a lot done geopolitically, including trying to annex Taiwan in this five-year term."

WILL THE US FIGHT?

Taiwan's second crucial question is actually one for the United States: Will the US go to war to defend Taiwan?

Over the course of his administration, President Biden has effectively created a new US-Taiwan policy. For decades, the US had maintained a "One China" policy, which recognized the People's Republic of China as the "sole legal government of China," after Washington ceased to recognize the Republic of China, Taiwan, as such in 1979. Striking a delicate balance, however, the US refused to endorse Beijing's claim of sovereignty over Taiwan. And to highlight this balance, Congress passed the Taiwan Relations Act (TRA), also in 1979, to establish unofficial diplomatic relations with Taiwan and to allow the US to provide Taiwan with weapons to defend itself. Whether a US president would or could order US forces to go further—to take military action to defend Taiwan—remained, by design, an open question. In theory, "strategic ambiguity," as this policy came to be known, left just enough doubt to avoid provoking China while also deterring an invasion.

Though the TRA does not commit the US to intervene to defend Taiwan militarily in the event of an attack, as China has increasingly threatened military action against Taiwan and as relations between Beijing and Washington have deteriorated, the president has said, yes, in fact, the US would defend the island militarily.

In August 2021, in an interview with ABC News, Biden grouped Taiwan in with US allies with which the US has explicit mutual-defense agreements. "We made a sacred commitment to Article Five that if in fact anyone were to invade or take action against our NATO allies, we would respond. Same with Japan, same with South Korea, same with Taiwan," Biden said.[5]

In October 2021, as CNN prepared for a town hall with the president, I suggested that my colleague Anderson Cooper follow up on Biden's comments in Tokyo and ask him if the US would indeed come to Taiwan's defense in the event of an attack by China. Not once, but twice, the president answered yes.

"China just tested a hypersonic missile. What will you do to keep up with them militarily? And can you vow to protect Taiwan?" Cooper asked.

"Yes and yes," Biden answered, adding, "Militarily, China, Russia, and the rest of the world knows we have the most powerful military in the history of the world. . . . I don't want a Cold War with China. I just want to make China understand that we are not going to step back. We are not going to change any of our views."[6]

"So, are you saying that the United States would come to Taiwan's defense if China attacked?" Cooper pressed.

"Yes," Biden answered, repeating, "Yes, we have a commitment to do that."[7]

Almost the moment the president uttered those words, White House aides claimed he was not altering US policy on Taiwan at all. The One China policy and strategic ambiguity remained intact. But over the succeeding months, as US-China relations suffered further, the president repeated the pledge to defend Taiwan, over and over.

In May 2022, during a press conference in Tokyo, Biden was asked if the US would come to Taiwan's defense. His answer? "We may." The president continued: "Here's the situation. We agree with the One China policy. We signed on to it and all the attendant agreements made from there. But the idea that it can be taken by force—just taken by force—is just not appropriate."[8]

In September 2022, Biden appeared on CBS News's *60 Minutes*, where he committed the US to defending Taiwan, not once but twice.

The *60 Minutes* correspondent Scott Pelley asked, "But would US forces defend the island?"

"Yes, if in fact there was an unprecedented attack," Biden answered.

"So unlike Ukraine, to be clear, sir," Pelley followed up, "US forces, US men and women, would defend Taiwan in the event of a Chinese invasion?"

"Yes," the president answered.[9]

General Mark Milley served as the top uniformed military officer throughout Biden's pledges to defend the island. So I asked him how the world should view Biden's statements: Has the US committed itself to defend Taiwan? And is the Pentagon making and enacting military plans for the island's defense?

Milley told me it's not his place to know for certain—it was his job only to "execute lawful orders." But when I pressed him—more than once—he repeated what he calls his "declaratory policy of national leaders," or what I refer to as the "Listen to what they say" rule.

"I would just tell you that, going back to a declaratory policy of national leaders, when a national leader says, 'I will do A, B, or C,' it's worthwhile believing them—that's my read of history," said Milley. "When foreign heads of state make declaratory policy, and it's publicly stated and then repeated several different times, it is in people's interest to believe them. The old saying is 'Great powers don't bluff.' Typically speaking, these guys do not bluff, and they say what they mean."

TAIWAN "STRUGGLING" WITH US POLICY

Does Taiwan believe him? In April 2023, I put that question to Taiwan's foreign minister, Joseph Wu: "Does Taiwan believe that the US would come to Taiwan's defense militarily if China were to invade?" His answer reflected Taiwan's difficult position resulting from the contrast between the president's words and official US policy.

"Well, there are different things the United States can do in an event of a Chinese military attack against Taiwan," Wu responded, notably not saying yes.

Wu went on to repeat what had become a standard Taiwanese government talking point when the issue of US military intervention came up: that Taiwan's defense was, first and foremost, Taiwan's job.

"We have also made it very clear defending Taiwan is our own responsibility. It's our freedom and it's our democratic way of life and it's our sovereignty. And we want to defend ourselves," Wu told me.

Deputy Minister Jan of the Mainland Affairs Council echoed Wu: "We always have this belief that in order to defend ourselves, we can only rely on ourselves, instead of relying on any other countries, even if they are friendly. . . . Exactly how other countries can come to our aid, I think that is the decision for the US government."

And this was Deputy Economics Minister C. C. Chen: "It's right to give Taiwan the ability to defend itself. That's the main thing."

As Admiral Lee put it: "There is no one that would like to help those people who do not want to help themselves. That is very important."

The furthest Wu would go on the question was to note that the US had grown more steadfast in its commitment to help ward off a Chinese invasion. "The United States seems to be more determined than ever in the creating a situation that China would know that its military attack against Taiwan is going to be associated with a heavy cost. And we appreciate the United States for having this posture," Wu told me before once more emphasizing Taiwan's preeminent role in its own defense. "But I need to stress again, defending Taiwan is our own responsibility. And if we don't want to defend ourselves, we have no right to ask any other countries to defend Taiwan."

What does this all mean? Does Taiwan believe the US has actually changed its policy?

"Taiwan is struggling about the US policy on the Taiwan issue," Admiral Lee told me. "It's still a debate in the United States. . . . From Taiwan's point of view, I don't think we should always expect the United States troops will come if there is the conflict. Because this is dangerous thinking."

That's not exactly a vote of confidence in the pledge of a sitting US president. In some respects, Taiwan has learned from Ukraine's success against Russia in another way—and that is that a robust self-defense is the price of admission for greater US military support. "Taiwan has to rely on itself to develop and establish a very strong self-defense capability," Lee said. "Because only Taiwan can show [the] United States that we are doing everything we can to establish that self-defense.

The connection is clear. Remember: On the dawn of the invasion, US intelligence agencies predicted the Ukrainian capital would fall within three days. They gave Ukraine little chance of fending off the Russian invasion. As Ukrainian forces far outperformed US and NATO assessments of their capabilities, only then did they receive greater and greater US and western military support. There's no better sales pitch for military support than winning.

One more precarious quality of this looming conflict is that, in effect, Taiwan must operate under the assumption that the US will *not* come to its defense.

THE "ONE CHINA" FICTION

In moments of candor, Taiwanese officials will say out loud what casual observers of US-China relations might recognize: the US's One China policy is, at best, precarious.

On this point, Taipei and Beijing may be in agreement. In the view of Deputy Minister Jan, Beijing long ago stopped believing the US's One China policy still held: "We know that the US has always been saying that its One China policy remains unchanged, but mainland China has responded by saying that 'we think that what you say is not in line with what you do. And we don't believe you.'"

Former deputy national security advisor Pottinger, long a cautionary voice on China's growing aggression and its designs on Taiwan, believes there is no question about what the US should do, and that is defend Taiwan or find itself losing more and more ground in the Asia-Pacific region and beyond.

"I think that if we don't defend Taiwan," he told me, "we are going to find that we're going to be desperately trying to defend a perimeter that is much, much bigger and much closer to home. So in short, yes"—the US *must* come to Taiwan's defense.

Regardless, the decision to go to war over Taiwan may not be up to the US. "I think that Beijing will attack us first, and it's in their doctrine," Pottinger told me. "If it rolls the iron dice and moves to take Taiwan, [Beijing] will do everything within its power to ensure success, the success of a fast invasion."

What would help ensure an invasion's success? Preemptively

eliminating the US's means to defend Taiwan by targeting US military bases in the region in advance of invading Taiwan.

"I think there are many indicators pointing to the likelihood that China will attack US forces in the western Pacific in order to buy itself time to complete the invasion," Pottinger said.

Is Pottinger an outlier? I asked Admiral Lee, who looked to history for a potential precedent.

"I believe anything would be possible," Lee said. "Like 1941, the Pearl Harbor raid. The United States didn't expect that Japan would do that, so we should not rule out any possibility."

That said, Lee believes China is far more likely to engage the US only *after* a US decision to intervene on its own. At that point, a Chinese attack on US military bases would be a natural and predictable decision from a military perspective.

"If the United States decided to intervene militarily, . . . then it will be very possible that the United States military bases in Japan [would] be attacked," Lee said. "Because the best strategy or operational plan is to destroy the military bases and make [US] aircraft and naval ships difficult to operate on the battlefield."

Regardless, either of these scenarios would mean a larger war between the great powers themselves.

The threat of a great power war over Taiwan is one the US takes very seriously—and despite public pronouncements by US military leaders that the US military is second to none, honest conversations deliver honest appraisals. China has designed its military around neutralizing US advantages. China has developed entirely new anti-ship missiles and strategies to deploy in order to put US carrier groups and other naval forces at risk and force them farther away—"over the horizon"—and farther out of striking range. This doctrine, under the banner of "anti-access, area-denial" (A2-AD), is the bedrock of Chinese military doctrine, with the US Navy as its target.

"China possesses a lot of long-range, medium-range, and short-range missiles," Lee noted, adding, "China now has the largest navy in the world—three hundred and fifty ships, compared to United States with two hundred and ninety. So there are a lot of disadvantages for the United States."

These disadvantages for the US must factor into Taiwan's own defense plans. Taiwan cannot rely on the US, one, to intervene militarily to defend the island *and*, two, to be successful if it ultimately would decide to do so. "So even [if the] United States is willing to intervene," Admiral Lee said, "we cannot just say that, well, the United States is coming, and Taiwan just stands on the sideline to see the US and China fighting each other."

A related question is not *will* the US fight to defend Taiwan, but *should* it? And, more pointedly, is the US public ready to send American men and women to fight and die there?

"As I have told people," John Kelly, the former Marine Corps general and Trump's chief of staff, told me, "we go to bed and wake up the next day and we've got two aircraft carriers gone with all hands, seven or eight other destroyer-type ships gone with most people killed, a couple of hundred airplanes maybe shot down. And that's the first day. You're talking about twelve, fifteen thousand casualties overnight. And the war games all indicate that we're not ready to do that."

The US hasn't experienced losses on that scale since World War II. Would the American people stomach those losses of sons and daughters, fathers and mothers, in defense of a distant, non-treaty ally? To date, the public discussion of going to war over Taiwan has been limited to grandiose but vague references to a US military "commitment" to Taiwan without an acknowledgment of the human costs.

"This war, potential war, over Taiwan would just be so big," Kelly said. "And as I say, if you don't convince the American people it's worthwhile and have that national debate. And it may be that the national debate turns out that no, we don't want to go to war over Taiwan."

Kelly speaks with the emotional weight exclusive to Gold Star parents like himself. His son, twenty-nine-year-old First Lieutenant Robert Kelly, died in Afghanistan in November 2010 when he was struck by an IED while leading Marines on patrol. I've met many Gold Star parents. And when I do, their voices can change, and their eyes seem to picture the faces of their lost children.

In one of those moments, Kelly told me of the prospect of war in Taiwan: "It's just like the Iraq and Afghan wars. Washington lost interest in the wars and decided that we're going to pull them out. And I tell you, there's huge consternation inside those of us that fought there and the families of people lost. It's a great deal of confusion, if nothing else, about why the hell would we do that?"

"We are a democracy, and we're not supposed to be lied to [to] get us into wars," Kelly said pointedly. "And in all of the wars, with the exception of the first Gulf War, people like me were told, 'This is important. Defend your country. Every red-blooded American boy is going to go and do his part.'"

That confusion—and pain—intensified after the US withdrawal from Afghanistan—a decision driven in part by President Biden's calculation that the US public would not and should not tolerate sending more Americans to die there.

"We are certainly a different people today than we were even after 9/11. There's much more questioning about our international involvement. Mr. Biden, whether you agree with him or not, made the case that we were wrapped up in a war in Afghanistan that was doing us no good and the American public couldn't take the casualties. When you think of it, there was over twenty years, my son included, two thousand four hundred deaths in Afghanistan."

Two thousand two hundred and nineteen deaths over two decades in Afghanistan versus many thousands of deaths in the first twenty-four hours in Taiwan.

"Right now, I would argue that we have not had a national discussion about going to war over Taiwan," Kelly said. "There's back-and-forth comments by the White House and people on the Hill that that's a decision that's already been made. We will go and help. But the American people should get a vote in this."

AND WILL TAIWAN FIGHT?

Whether Americans are willing to fight and die for Taiwan is one question. Whether Taiwanese are willing to do the same is another—perhaps a defining one for Taiwan. And the answer is not clear. In Taiwan, I did not encounter a population girding itself for war. And cross-strait ties in trade, family relationships, history, and culture run deep—not unlike the ties traversing the border between Russia and Ukraine.

"We have a problem with ideology and national identity," Admiral Lee told me. "We are divided. Some people say we should not invest too much in defense. And some speak evocative language to China."

Admiral Lee believes—or, more accurately, hopes—Ukraine has taught Taiwan a useful and inspiring lesson.

"I believe the Ukraine war provides a lesson learned to Taiwan," Lee said, citing the stark difference between Ukraine's submissive response to Russia's 2014 invasion of Crimea and its fierce defense following the full-scale invasion in 2022. "The most important difference is their will to defend themselves. The lesson we can learn is we have to be unified, and we have to have strong will to defend ourselves," he said.

Still, it is a mistake to see Taiwan as entirely united on the issue of China or China's relationship with the US. In fact, as tensions between the US and China have worsened, and their respective rhetoric over Taiwan has grown more bellicose, some senior Taiwanese leaders have made public their fears that Taiwan is caught up in a superpower conflict not of its own making.

In a February 2023 interview with Taiwan's *CommonWealth Magazine*, Defense Minister Chiu Kuo-Cheng said the US had made China its "imaginary enemy," adding that "Taiwan is caught in the middle and is also involved."

"The advantage of being caught in the middle is that Taiwan is interconnected with Japan and Southeast Asia, and the stakes are clear," Chiu told *CommonWealth*. "The downside is that China feels betrayed that 'we are of the same language and race, but Taiwan is helping outsiders,' and there are no good channels of communication between the two sides of the Taiwan Strait."[10]

His mention of a common language and race was notable. A refrain I heard often during my visit to the island is that Taiwan and China remain deeply intertwined.

TAIWAN'S "TRICK"

If war over Taiwan is indeed up to one man, Xi, some Taiwanese officials see one cause for hope. If Xi equals China, and China fails in Taiwan, then Xi himself is a failure.

"One characteristic of Xi Jinping is that he is face-loving," said Deputy Minister Jan. "He doesn't want to be humiliated."

Xi is exuberantly confident in his own power and abilities. But like many authoritarians before him, he fears his own people. And the hope among some Taiwanese is that he fears how his own people would react to the economic costs and risk of military failure with a full-scale invasion.

"He will not condone the situation where his decisions are likely to be assessed by the public as a mistake," Jan said. "Because we know that Xi Jinping has this personality, all we can do is to make him believe that he is not going to succeed in trying to resolve the issue in his tenure, because we know that if Xi Jinping actually turns his thoughts into action, then he will go all the way until he succeeds. And I think if he actually does that, then it will be catastrophic for both sides across the strait."

"There's this trick that we've learned," Jan said. "And that is we need Xi Jinping to know that our cross-strait policy has remained incredibly consistent, and that is we won't go provocative, and we won't do anything that's really surprising for him. But we also let Xi Jinping know that Taiwanese people are incredibly determined to defend ourselves."

That "trick" has worked for Taiwan for more than seventy years. But will it still make the difference between war and peace today? It's a question only Xi Jinping can answer. And like so many questions of this new era, the great powers appear less restrained by the limitations of the past, even when it relates to their most powerful weapons.

PART THREE

CHAPTER SEVEN

"NO LONGER UNTHINKABLE"

NUCLEAR ALARM BELLS

Late in the summer of 2022, US officials began picking up signs and intelligence that Russia was preparing for a shocking escalation of what was already the bloodiest war in Europe since World War II.

"I don't think many of us coming into our jobs expected to be spending significant amounts of time preparing for a scenario which a few years ago was believed to be from a bygone era," one senior administration official told me.

That scenario was the potential Russian use of a nuclear weapon in Ukraine, specifically a tactical or battlefield nuclear weapon—the first such use of a nuclear weapon in war and the first nuclear attack of any kind since the US dropped atomic bombs on Hiroshima and Nagasaki nearly eighty years before. Senior Biden administration officials I spoke with recalled a frightening stretch of weeks from late summer into the early fall in which the unthinkable had become thinkable.

"We had to plan so that we were in the best possible position in case this no-longer-unthinkable event actually took place," the same senior administration official told me.

What led the Biden administration to such a startling assessment was not one indicator, but a collection of developments, analysis, and—crucially—highly sensitive new intelligence. The degree of US concern—and the seriousness of contingency planning—has not been reported in such detail before.

The administration's fear, a second senior administration official told me, "was not just hypothetical—it was also based on some information that we picked up." That is, new information that US intelligence agencies gathered as they watched Russian fortunes deteriorate on the battlefield. Inside the White House, administration officials told me, the National Security Council began "preparing rigorously" for worst-case scenarios.

The US was not alone in its alarm. Senior officials in several European countries told me they shared the US assessment—and joined in preparations for worst-case outcomes. "When leaders of a terrorist country are threatening to use a nuclear weapon, we have to take it seriously," a senior Estonian defense official told me. "After all, they already invaded Ukraine."

Alarm was growing on Capitol Hill as well. In September 2022, a member of the House Intelligence Committee told me that Putin is "capable" of such a strike. A former CIA officer explained that Putin simply viewed nuclear weapons differently than western or even Chinese leaders did—that nukes had "always been on the table" for him.

RUSSIANS SURROUNDED

Late summer 2022 was proving a devastating period for Russian forces in Ukraine. Ukrainian forces were advancing on Russian-occupied Kherson in the south. The city had been Russia's biggest prize since the invasion. Now it was in danger of being lost to the Ukrainian counteroffensive. Crucially, as Ukrainian forces advanced, they were putting entire Russian units in danger of being surrounded. For Russian commanders—and for the Kremlin—this was unacceptable.

At the National Security Council, US officials were keenly aware that Russian military doctrine allows for the use of battlefield nuclear weapons in a number of circumstances, including direct threats to Russian territory or the Russian state. Russia claimed Kherson and the surrounding area as Russian territory, despite having seized it by force, in violation of international law. Such a significant loss of territory could—potentially—be perceived by Russian leaders as a direct threat to the entire military operation and therefore to Russia itself. The view inside the administration was that such a catastrophic loss could be a "potential trigger" for the use of nuclear weapons.

"If significant numbers of Russian forces were overrun—if their lives were shattered as such—that was a sort of precursor to a potential threat directly to Russian territory or the Russian state," the first senior administration official said. "In Kherson at that time there were increasing signs that Russian lines could collapse. Tens of thousands of Russian troops were potentially vulnerable."

As the US intelligence community saw it, Russian forces were getting routed in Kharkiv and Kherson. If they were broken, and—crucially—if Russia perceived that Crimea was threatened as well, Putin might order a nuclear strike to stem his losses and attempt to turn the tide.

■

Gauging Russia's calculus on nuclear weapons is an inexact science. Russian military doctrine has changed repeatedly in recent decades and is unclear on which specific circumstances would trigger a nuclear attack. In 1993, following the collapse of the Soviet Union, the Russian Federation abandoned the USSR's no-first-use policy. Since then, it has revised and adjusted the doctrine, appearing to rely more, not less, on the potential use of nuclear weapons. This has sparked a debate among Russian experts as to where the policy stands and, therefore, uncertainty at even the highest levels of the US government. As the Congressional Research Service (CRS) has noted, "This evolving doctrine seems to indicate that Russia has potentially placed a greater reliance on nuclear weapons and may threaten to use them during regional conflicts."[1]

The April 2022 CRS report *Russia's Nuclear Weapons: Doctrine, Forces, and Modernization* found that the latest Russian state document on nuclear weapons use left crucial questions unanswered: "As with previous official statements, this document does not call for the preemptive use of nuclear weapons during conventional conflicts. But it does not completely resolve the question of whether Russia would escalate to nuclear use if it were losing a conventional war. It notes that, 'in the event of a military conflict, this Policy provides for the prevention of an escalation of military actions and their termination on conditions that are acceptable for the Russian Federation and/or its allies.' Analysts have assessed that this means Russia might *threaten* to escalate to nuclear use as a way to deter a conflict that would threaten the existence of the state."[2]

Of course, Russia was then losing ground inside Ukrainian sovereign territory, not inside Russia. But US officials were concerned that Putin saw it differently. He had told the Russian people that Kherson was now part of Russia itself, and, so, might perceive a devastating loss there as a direct threat to him and the Russian state.

"Our assessment had been for some time that one of the scenarios in which they would contemplate using nuclear weapons [included] things like existential threats to the Russian state, direct threats to Russian territory," the first senior administration official said.

In this assessment, Russia could view a tactical nuclear strike as a deterrent against further losses of Russian-held territory in Ukraine as well as any potential attack on Russia itself. This was one sobering consequence of the decimation of Russia's conventional military forces in Ukraine: a greater dependence on nonconventional weapons, including both chemical and nuclear weapons. Russia had already been accused of using banned phosphorous weapons, which create fire devastating to civilians, in Ukraine. Would Putin escalate further by ordering a nuclear strike?

NUCLEAR FALSE FLAG

Fueling concerns about a potential nuclear strike, the US was picking up other disturbing signs as well. Going back to the very beginning of the invasion, Russia had orchestrated false flag operations in an attempt to justify its own military operations, like the series of bombings in Eastern Ukraine before the war, for which Russian authorities attempted to place the blame on Ukrainian "terrorists." As noted in Chapter 4, the objective, US officials told me at the time, was to use the false flag attacks as a pretext to invade Ukraine under the guise of a counterterror operation.

Now Russia's propaganda machine was circulating a new false flag story—this one about a Ukrainian dirty bomb—which US officials feared could be intended as cover for a Russian nuclear attack. Russian officials at the highest levels peddled the story to their counterparts. In October 2022, Russia's defense minister, Sergei Shoigu, made a series of phone calls to defense officials in the US, the UK, France, and Turkey, telling them that the Kremlin was "concerned about possible provocations by Kyiv involving the use of a dirty bomb."[3] US and other western officials rejected the Russian warnings. Still, Russia's UN ambassador delivered a letter directly to the United Nations detailing the same alleged threat.[4] Russia's story went like this: Ukraine would build and detonate a dirty bomb against Russian forces and then blame the attack on Russia. Russia also raised the possibility of a Ukrainian bioweapon, which Ukrainian and western officials similarly dismissed.

US officials dismissed the Russian warnings but feared the motivation behind them. "Russian public messaging came way out of left field on the potential for Ukraine to use a dirty bomb, which we saw not grounded in reality," the first senior administration official told me. "More concerning" to this official was that the Russians would say these things "either as a pretext for them to do something crazy or as a cover for something they themselves were looking at doing. So that was quite alarming."

Each of these indicators—the details of Russian military doctrine, the potential Russian losses in Kherson, and the disinformation about a Ukrainian dirty bomb attack—formed the building blocks of an intelligence assessment that the nuclear threat was real. But there was one more piece that raised such concerns to a new level. Western intelligence agencies had received information that there were now communications among Russian officials explicitly discussing a nuclear strike.

As the first senior administration official described it to me, there were "indications that we were picking up through *other means* [which is often shorthand for communications intercepts] that this was at least something that lower levels of the Russian system were discussing."

US access to Russian internal communications had proved capable before. In the run-up to the Ukraine invasion, the US had intercepted Russian military commanders discussing preparations for the invasion, communications that formed part of the US intelligence assessment—proved accurate—that an invasion was imminent.

RISK BEYOND "ANY OTHER POINT IN TIME"

I've covered the US military and intelligence agencies for more than twenty years. And for two years, as chief of staff to the US ambassador to China, I had the highest-level security clearance, Top Secret/ Secret Compartmented Information (TS/SCI), which allows access to some of the most sensitive national security intelligence. During my assignment, I read numerous classified intelligence assessments. And one lesson I learned reading them is that they are rarely, if ever, 100 percent certain. Most often, they are based on a combination of concrete intelligence, including imagery and communication intercepts, and analysis, to generate what are essentially informed estimates. Some assessments lean more on analysis than hard information. For instance, US assessments of Russian plans to invade Ukraine, which turned out to be correct, relied in large part on imagery of a massive buildup of Russian forces around Ukraine and intercepted communications among Russian commanders discussing an invasion. The US assessment of Iraq's nuclear weapons program prior to the 2003 Iraq invasion leaned far more on the latter, with a heavy dose of political influence to imply certainty where there was none. But this new assessment of a possible Russian nuclear attack included substantial doses of both hard intelligence and analysis.

"It's never a cut-and-dry, black-and-white assessment," the first senior administration official told me. "But the risk level seemed to be going up, beyond where it had been at any other point in time."

What the US had not yet detected was intelligence indicating

Russia was taking steps to mobilize its nuclear forces to carry out such an attack.

"We obviously placed a high priority on tracking and had some ability at least to track such movements of its nuclear forces," this senior administration official told me. "And at no point did we ever see any indications of types of steps that we would've expected them to take if they were going down a path toward using nuclear weapons."

However—and this alarmed me—US officials were not certain they *would* know if Russia was moving tactical nuclear weapons into place. Unlike strategic nuclear weapons, capable of destroying entire cities, tactical or battlefield nuclear weapons are small enough to be moved quietly and could be fired from conventional systems, including artillery and missile systems, which were already deployed to the Ukrainian battlefield.

"If what they were going to do is use a tactical nuclear weapon, particularly a very low-yield tactical nuclear weapon and particularly if they were only going to use one or a very small number, it was not one hundred percent clear to us that we necessarily would have known," this senior administration official continued.

In short, administration officials worried that Russia could be ready to launch a nuclear attack and the US wouldn't be aware.

And then there was the public threat. As Russian commanders privately discussed a potential nuclear attack, Russian leaders publicly had been raising the prospect of nuclear war for months. The former Russian president, and now deputy head of Russia's Security Council, Dmitry Medvedev, often led the rhetorical charge.

In April 2022, Medvedev warned that Russia would "more than double" its nuclear forces on its western flank if Sweden and Finland were to join NATO. "It will no longer be possible to talk about any non-nuclear status of the Baltic. The balance must be restored," Medvedev said, if the two Scandinavian nations were admitted to the alliance.[5] And yet, only two months later, at the NATO summit in Madrid, alliance members voted unanimously to do just that and welcome Sweden and Finland in.

In September 2022, President Putin himself appeared to raise the threat of a nuclear strike. In the same address in which he announced a partial mobilization of the Russian population to boost the Ukraine war effort, Putin said, "The territorial integrity of our homeland, our independence and freedom will be ensured, I will emphasize this again, with all the means at our disposal. And those who try to blackmail us with nuclear weapons should know that the prevailing winds can turn in their direction."[6]

The inclusion of the imagery of "prevailing winds" turning against the West disturbed me, seeming to evoke the prospect of nuclear fallout wafting toward Europe in the event of a Russian nuclear strike.

Weeks later, Putin again raised the prospect of nuclear war. Speaking in December in Moscow at a human rights council meeting, of all places, Putin said, "Such a threat is growing, it would be wrong to hide it." Then he cautioned: "We have not gone mad. We are aware of what nuclear weapons are. We aren't about to run around the world brandishing this weapon like a razor."[7]

Still, soon after, he mentioned the possibility of changing Russia's no-first-strike nuclear posture, blaming any such potential change— as he so often does to justify his threats—on the US.

"They [the US] have it in their strategy, in the documents it is spelled out—a preventive blow. We don't. We, on the other hand, have formulated a retaliatory strike in our strategy," Putin said at a news conference in Kyrgyzstan. (In fact, while the US has not adopted a no-first-use policy regarding nuclear weapons, it gives the president a "launch under attack" option, which allows missiles to be fired if "multiple, independent sensors" detect an incoming attack. Beyond that,[8] it has not specified all the circumstances under which it would use nuclear weapons, except "to defend the vital interests of the United States or its allies and partners.")[9]

"So, if we're talking about this disarming strike, then maybe think about adopting the best practices of our American partners and their ideas for ensuring their security. We're just thinking about it. No one was shy when they talked about it out loud in previous times and years," Putin continued.

"If a potential adversary believes it is possible to use the theory of a preventive strike, and we do not, then this still makes us think about those threats that are posed to us," he said.[10]

The nuclear saber-rattling continued into the next year. In January 2023, Medvedev delivered another not-so-veiled threat as the US and its allies were preparing another weapons package for Ukraine. Medvedev's words seemed to corroborate a substantial part of the basis of US concerns the previous fall: he declared that if Russian forces were pushed to the brink of defeat, Russian leaders retained the nuclear option.

"The loss of a nuclear power in a conventional war can provoke the outbreak of a nuclear war," said Medvedev. "Nuclear powers do not lose major conflicts on which their fate depends," he said, adding with apparent disdain, "This should be obvious to anyone. Even to a western politician who has retained at least some trace of intelligence."[11]

"PREPARE RIGOROUSLY"

Inside the White House, Biden administration officials were now preparing a comprehensive response to head off what they saw as a credible worst-case scenario.

"That's what the conflict presented us, and so we believed—and I think it's our right—to prepare rigorously and do everything possible to avoid that happening," the first senior administration official told me.

With concerns escalating, the US and its allies sprang into action, developing a plan to try to deter Russia from unleashing a nuclear attack, and initiating contingency planning for how the US would respond if deterrence were to fail. They were taking the latter possibility extremely seriously.

What would that response look like? Given the extreme sensitivity of such an outcome, US officials were reluctant to detail every step, except to say that the response would involve steps in the diplomatic, economic, and military spheres.

"We convened a number of meetings to put [together] a contingency plan internally for what types of things we would do in the event of either a very clear indication that they were about to do something, attack with a nuclear weapon, or if they just did, how we would respond, how we would try to preempt it, or deter it," the first senior administration official told me.

Part of the US message to Russia was that the use of nuclear weapons in Ukraine, including a low-yield tactical nuclear device, would spark a devastating military response by the US and NATO. The communications were classified. But over the course of those nervous months in late 2022 and early 2023, multiple US military officials described them to me in broad terms as follows: if Russia were to attack Ukraine with a nuclear weapon, the US and its allies would for the first time engage Russian forces in Ukraine directly, targeting those forces with a devastating campaign of air strikes and missiles. The US warning also appeared to include threats to attack elements of Russia's Black Sea fleet. A Ukrainian strike in the third month of the war, in April 2022, had sunk the flagship of the fleet, the cruiser *Moskva*. That attack, with two Ukrainian-made Neptune anti-ship missiles, had already chased much of the Russian Navy a safer distance from Ukrainian shores and scuttled the seaborne front of Russia's planned assault on Odessa. The message was Russia would pay dearly.

The US's European allies were aware of the warnings to Russia. In the words of a senior Estonian military official, "There was a backdoor channel that it would not end very well for the Russians."

As to whether the US would respond to a Russian nuclear strike with a nuclear attack of its own, that first senior administration official told me, "Without proscribing or limiting the president's decision space, I think that that is highly unlikely."

A FLURRY OF PHONE CALLS

With contingency planning in motion for the worst outcome, US officials went to work on an aggressive effort to deter Vladimir Putin from launching the world's first nuclear attack in generations. The most direct line in this pressure campaign was to the Kremlin itself. And US officials at the highest levels communicated directly with their Russian counterparts, one, that the US was aware Russia was considering a nuclear attack and, two, that Russia would pay a heavy price if such an attack were to go ahead.

Multiple senior administration officials took part in this urgent outreach. Secretary of State Antony Blinken communicated US concerns "very directly" with Russian foreign minister Sergey Lavrov, according to senior administration officials.

Joint Chiefs Chairman General Mark Milley called his Russian counterpart, General Valery Gerasimov, chief of the general staff of the Russian Armed Forces and author of Russia's "Gerasimov Doctrine," envisions a constant conflict with Russia's great power adversaries on multiple fronts.

Going into the call, Milley believed the risk of a Russian nuclear strike on Ukraine remained low. However, in keeping with his "declaratory policy" of reading geopolitics, the many public comments of Russian leaders rattling the nuclear saber concerned him.

"When people say they're going to use or might use or could use [nuclear weapons], I think you have to take them seriously, right?" Milley told me. "So, 'worried'—I wouldn't use that word. But take them seriously and have some concern about the potential use, absolutely."

Milley was aware that Russian nuclear doctrine allowed for the use of nuclear weapons in multiple circumstances, including a significant battlefield setback. So, during their call, his ears perked up when General Gerasimov brought up his country's nuclear doctrine.

"He talked about that, and he said, 'Look, we'll use nuclear weapons under certain conditions that are available in our nuclear doctrine,'" Milley recalled.

Was Gerasimov's intention to reassure the US by communicating that current conditions in Ukraine did *not* meet Russia's requirements for a nuclear strike? Or was he hinting current conditions might meet those requirements? Or did Gerasimov deliberately want Milley to leave the call not knowing for sure?

"I don't know if it was to reassure or just a statement of facts," Milley said. "I mean, he stated what he stated, and of course they are adversaries, so you have to always be skeptical as to what they say. Are they telling you the truth? Are they attempting to influence? Are they not?"

US officials continued receiving mixed signals during their senior-level outreach to Russia. According to a senior US official,

Biden sent CIA Director Bill Burns to speak to Sergey Naryshkin, the head of Russia's foreign intelligence service, in Turkey to communicate US concerns about a nuclear strike and gauge Russian intentions. At their meeting, Naryshkin told Burns that it was not Putin's intention to launch a nuclear weapon. However, when Burns asked Naryshkin to outline the Kremlin's vision of a potential agreement to end the war, Naryshkin said that Putin intended to keep all territory Russia had gained so far as part of any peace agreement.

So as US officials were attempting to defuse one crisis in Ukraine—the alarming prospect of a nuclear attack—another more lasting crisis loomed: little apparent path to peace.

"QUIET CONVERSATIONS WITH CORE ALLIES"

Given the deep and expanding fissures in US-Russia relations, the Biden administration did not leave its warnings purely to direct US-to-Russia contacts. Its goal was to marshal the international community—in both public and private—to warn the Kremlin away from a nuclear escalation by making clear the consequences for Russia in military, economic, and diplomatic terms.

In what administration officials describe as a central feature of Biden's foreign policy, the US worked closely with its allies both to develop contingency plans for a Russian nuclear attack and to communicate warnings to the Russian side about the consequences of such a strike.

"We conducted a number of quiet conversations with core allies to go through our thinking," a senior administration official told me. "That's a hallmark of our entire approach—that we are better and stronger doing this stuff when we're totally aligned with our allies."

To that end, on October 11, 2022, the G7 nations released a joint statement condemning Russia's "irresponsible nuclear rhetoric" and warning of "severe consequences" if it were to use chemical, biological, or nuclear weapons in Ukraine. "We deplore deliberate Russian escalatory steps, including the partial mobilisation of reservists and irresponsible nuclear rhetoric, which is putting global peace and security at risk. We reaffirm that any use of chemical, biological, or nuclear weapons by Russia would be met with severe consequences," the statement said.[12]

NATO Secretary General Jens Stoltenberg was watching the threat unfold with concern as well. "We saw Russian nuclear saber-rattling. We saw nuclear rhetoric from the Russian side, which was quite threatening, and we saw it again and again," Stoltenberg said. "So, of course, this was something we had to take seriously because these are . . . such serious matters."

NATO leaders, like US officials, conveyed to Russia a common warning that a nuclear strike was unwinnable. "We sent the message to Moscow . . . that nuclear war cannot be won and must never be fought," Stoltenberg said.

Meanwhile, the US enlisted not only close allies in its push but also nontraditional partners and even competing great powers to use their influence with the Kremlin to avert the "unthinkable." "One of the things we did was not only message them directly, but strongly urge, press, encourage other countries, to whom they might be more attentive, to do the same thing," a senior administration official told me.

Who would the Kremlin be "more attentive to"? US officials believed the key to deterring Russia went, in part, through China and India. This would, they hoped, become a great power full-court press against a Russian nuclear strike. "We thought about countries we believed could be potentially influential," another senior administration official told me.

Once again, this effort involved both public statements and private conversations. In early November 2022, German chancellor Olaf Scholz traveled to Beijing to meet with Chinese president Xi Jinping. Russia's nuclear threat in Ukraine was a central topic of their meetings. And following their talks, Scholz told reporters, "President Xi and I agree: nuclear threats are irresponsible and incendiary. By using nuclear weapons, Russia would be crossing a line that the community of states has drawn together."[13]

China's official readout of their meeting contained a similar warning using similar language. China's state-run Xinhua News Agency reported the two leaders had agreed to "oppose the use of or the threat to use nuclear weapons, advocate that nuclear weapons cannot be used, and that nuclear wars must not be fought, and prevent a nuclear crisis in Eurasia."[14]

Prime Minister Narendra Modi of India was even more forthright in his public criticism of Russia and its nuclear threats. At the Shanghai Cooperation Organization Summit in Uzbekistan that September, during a bilateral meeting with Putin, Modi seemed to chide the Russian leader, saying, "Today's era is not of war" and encouraging him to "move onto a path of peace."

According to the magazine *Foreign Policy*, many at the summit were surprised at his directness. India later voted in favor of a resolution to allow President Zelensky to address the UN General Assembly.[15] Then, in December, Bloomberg reported that Modi canceled a planned summit with Putin because of Russia's nuclear threats. "Trumpeting the friendship at this point may not be beneficial for Modi, said a senior official with knowledge of the matter," Bloomberg reported.[16]

"One of the things we know to be true is that we are not always the best direct messenger to countries like Russia, or China for that matter," the first senior administration official told me. "So, on this one, we thought about countries that could potentially be the most influential, starting with India."

Among the public messages from India, the Biden administration pointed to a speech before the UN Security Council in September 2022, when Indian minister of external affairs Subrahmanyam Jaishankar warned about the danger of nuclear escalation in Ukraine.

"The trajectory of the Ukraine conflict is a matter of profound concern for the entire international community. The future outlook appears even more disturbing. The nuclear issue is a particular anxiety," Jaishankar said.[17]

"He called out the danger in letting the Ukraine conflict escalate into the nuclear realm," said the first senior administration official, referencing the speech. "Only one side of that conflict has nuclear weapons, so it was obviously a pretty direct message to Russia. And we know that the Indians messaged with Russia directly and privately."

China was central to this effort as well. US officials calculated that Beijing was equally invested in preventing a nuclear escalation by Russia in Ukraine—and not so much as a favor from one great power to another, but as a shared interest in preventing nuclear war.

"We believe their private messaging to the Russians had been quite responsible," the first senior administration official told me. "I don't think they want to see Russia use nuclear weapons. That would certainly be a complicating factor in their support for Russia and in their 'no limits' partnership."

Looking back, US officials say they believe the pressure campaign worked. "I think we believe showing the international community the concern about this, particularly the concern from key countries for Russia and the Global South, was also a helpful, persuasive factor and showed them what the cost of all this could be," the first senior administration official said.

"I think the fact that we know China weighed in, India weighed in, others weighed in, may have had some effect on their thinking," the second senior administration official told me. "I can't demonstrate this positively, but I think that's our assessment."

Why the rare instance of cooperation between the great powers, US and China, to deter another great power in Russia? To paraphrase Lord Palmerston, the US and China were certainly not perpetual allies, but they did appear to have perpetual shared interests.

"I'm not sure how using nukes will advance Putin and Xi Jinping's joint aspirations," said former deputy national security advisor Matthew Pottinger. "They're deeply aligned in many respects, but if Putin decides to uncork the nukes, it may not improve his battlefield position in Ukraine, even if he used them, for one. And second, it will demonstrate once and for all that China and Russia are pariah states together, and they got into this thing together, and they will sink together on their little boat."

A WORLD WITHOUT TREATIES

The US has been navigating this nuclear scare as the world enters a new period with fewer and fewer treaties or even the outline of treaties to govern the expanding conflict. There are no cyber arms control treaties. There is no comprehensive agreement governing the weaponization of space. And two of the most crucial nuclear arms control treaties between the US and Russia—the Intermediate-Range Nuclear Forces (INF) Treaty and the Anti-Ballistic Missile (ABM) Treaty—no longer hold. The US withdrew from ABM under President George W. Bush in 2002 and from INF under President Trump in 2019, accusing Russia of repeated violations.

"We need at some stage to reestablish arms control," NATO Secretary General Stoltenberg told me, "because all the big arms control agreements that we were able to reach, actually during the Cold War and in the years after the Cold War, have just been dismantled."

Such agreements take years to negotiate under the best of circumstances. Yet there are no current, substantive efforts to restart these negotiations. As war has raged in Ukraine, the prospects for doing so have seldom looked poorer. Moreover, new weapons from cyberspace to outer space have created new fronts in great power competition with no treaties at all to help prevent conflict.

"We've had some technological leaps forward over the last decade, and as a result, new technologies that have military or security applications or implications, and no frameworks in place to regulate them or, on one level, to regulate them even internally or among friendly countries, never mind with competitors or adversaries," Secretary of State Blinken told me. "That is one of the big challenges at the moment."

BACKWARD PROGRESS

In February 2023, just as the nuclear scare was dissipating, Putin took another step in the unmaking of nuclear arms control. In his state-of-the-nation address, Putin announced that Russia was suspending its compliance with the New START Treaty on nuclear arms reduction. One again, the Russian leader assigned blame to the US and the West, explaining that Moscow was justifiably responding to western threats.

"They want to inflict a strategic defeat on us and claim our nuclear facilities. So, I'd like to make the announcement today that Russia is suspending its participation in the START Treaty," Putin declared to the sound of applause. "Let me repeat. We're not withdrawing from the treaty. No, but we're suspending participation."

The New START Treaty, signed in April 2010, has two essential elements: one, it places limits on the number of nuclear warheads each nation can deploy to 1,550 as well as limits on the number of launchers and nuclear-capable bombers; and, two, it allows both nations to conduct inspections to confirm compliance with the limits. Inspection visits had been paused because of the Covid pandemic in 2020. And prior to Putin's announcement, the US State Department had already determined that Russia was no longer in compliance with the treaty.

Soon after the speech, the Russian Foreign Ministry issued a statement describing the decision as "reversible," adding, "Washington must show political will, make conscientious efforts for a general de-escalation and create conditions for the resumption of the full functioning of the Treaty and, accordingly, comprehensively ensuring its viability."

However, the next day, the Russian parliament, a reliable source of rubber stamps for the Russian leader, made Putin's decision official. The State Duma, the lower house, passed a bill codifying the suspension after it was introduced by Putin. Then Russia's Federation Council, the upper house, unanimously passed the bill as well, reported the Russian state news agency TASS.

"Russia is not complying with its obligation under the New START Treaty to facilitate inspection activities on its territory. Russia's refusal to facilitate inspection activities prevents the United States from exercising important rights under the treaty and threatens the viability of U.S.-Russian nuclear arms control," a US State Department spokesperson had said in January 2023.

President Biden, in Europe following a surprise visit to Kyiv, was asked by reporters about Russia's decision as he entered a meeting at the Presidential Palace in Warsaw. He called it a "big mistake."

The question for his administration, and for the world, was

whether the move was symbolic, given Russia's existing lack of compliance, or a signal that Russia would make a hard break with New START's limits on deployed warheads. That is, had Russia initiated a new nuclear arms race?

"Without New START, there would be less transparency about US and Russian strategic nuclear systems," said Marion Messmer of the UK-based think tank Chatham House in a statement reacting to Putin's move. "This could lead to further arms races as each side is left to speculate about the other's abilities. This is also happening in the context of China expanding its nuclear arsenal."[18]

"While Putin has not made explicit his intention to extend the limits imposed by New START, it could send a signal about future intention: to increase the number of deployed strategic launchers and warheads, thereby reducing the time needed in order to launch them," Messmer warned. "Russia has also been investing in its hypersonic missiles, some of which were counted under New START limits. The suspension could signal ambitions for further investment into these capabilities."[19]

The world soon received a hint. The same day Biden was visiting Kyiv, Russia tested a new intercontinental ballistic missile—the SARMAT, nicknamed "SATAN II" in the West. That test failed, preventing Putin from mentioning it in his address.[20] However, the test showed Russia was making a shift in words and action.

Days later, Putin signed the new law formally suspending Russia's participation in the START Treaty. "The Russian Federation suspends the Treaty between the Russian Federation and the United States of America on measures for the further reduction and limitation of strategic offensive arms, signed in Prague on April 8, 2010," the text of the law read.

Like Putin, a Russian senator assigned blame to the US side. "In these conditions, the President of the Russian Federation noted that the consistent failure of the US to fulfil its commitments under the treaty is a fundamental change of circumstances," said Senator Konstantin Kosachev. "This is a reason to stop or suspend international treaties, and this is what is happening in this case."[21] Soon after, Deputy Foreign Minister Sergei Ryabkov told Russian state media RIA Novosti that Moscow had delivered an official note to US officials communicating the suspension of Moscow's participation in the treaty, as reported by RIA.

Russian officials did again say that the suspension was "reversible" and that Russia would remain under the treaty's limits on deployed nuclear warheads. Ryabkov also said that channels remained open on the possibility of restarting treaty negotiations. "We have had quite a lot of discussions lately, including through closed channels, and there is no reticence on our part, there are no open questions," he said, according to a CNN translation.

However, when I asked Andrea Kendall-Taylor, former Russia intelligence officer for the National Intelligence Council and the Office of the Director of National Intelligence, if Russia's move could signal the end of the era of nuclear arms control, she told me, "Yes, I'm afraid that's what it's looking like. I think it bodes poorly for the future of arms control." She added, "The fact that Putin has now suspended Russia's participation suggests that we are coming to the end of this era, and that is not in the interest of the United States nor in Russia's."

Speaking to me the next month on CNN, Jon Wolfsthal, who served as senior director for arms control and nonproliferation at the National Security Council during the Obama administration, agreed that the US and Russia had entered a truly dangerous period.

"In my view, we are at the most dangerous point in terms of our nuclear relationship with Russia than we were since before Gorbachev in the mid-1980s," he said. "We no longer have confidence that Russia is going to act in a reasonable way."

Even without an immediate violation of treaty limits on warheads, Russia and the US had lost a crucial asset: transparency. And, oddly enough, Russia stood to lose more than the US.

"Russia is increasingly flying blind because their intelligence is not as good as ours. Their satellites aren't as good as ours, so they need this information," Wolfsthal explained. "In fact, I would argue . . . I don't think we should just say to Russia, 'Okay, you're going to pull back, [so] we're going to pull back,' because they're the ones who benefit if the world gets closer to the nuclear brink, not us."

PROLIFERATING THREAT

The dissolution of nuclear limits has implications far beyond Ukraine. As Russia rattled the nuclear saber in Europe, China continued to expand its nuclear arsenal, North Korea further confirmed its status as the world's newest entrant to the nuclear club, and Iran, unleashed from the 2015 nuclear agreement, continued to expand uranium enrichment—bringing it closer to "breakout" when it would be able to build its own nuclear bomb. As one senior US diplomat remarked to me in March 2023, "Imagine how it would be if Iran had a tactical nuke."

At the same time, other nations, from Saudi Arabia to Japan to South Korea, were reconsidering their own nuclear postures. The driving question for their leaders: In a world without rules, what answer do non-nuclear powers have to territorial aggression by a nuclear-armed neighbor? To that point, would Russia have invaded Ukraine if it were still a nuclear power?

Together, these developments pose the biggest threat to nonproliferation in decades—and with fewer treaties in place to limit the danger and more nations interested in launching their own nuclear programs. The US intelligence community views the risk of such proliferation as genuine. A senior US official told me that that the IC sees a potential domino effect among the middle powers if a country such as Iran breaks out, thereby sparking an arms race with other middle powers in the region and beyond. It is, this official said, "a real threat."

Russia's full-scale invasion of Ukraine, though utilizing only conventional weapons, was in the view of some western diplomats, in essence, a nuclear escalation of its own. Among many dangerous precedents it set, Russia's invasion marked the first time that a nuclear-armed power had invaded a neighbor. And although Russia had not yet utilized a nuclear weapon in Ukraine, Russian leaders repeatedly dangled the threat of nuclear escalation. It was nuclear brinksmanship on a grand scale. In the view of Canadian foreign minister Mélanie Joly, by the very nature of its having nuclear weapons, Russia had threatened not just Ukraine but all of Europe.

"It's an existential threat not only to a given country," Joly told me. "It is an existential threat to all countries. From the moment that nuclear powers are not abiding by international rules, nothing can stand and there can be no trust in this world. And so that is why the question of Russia invading Ukraine is so important, because it's the first time since the Second World War that a nuclear power is invading its sovereign neighbor."

"NOT BEYOND THE REALM OF POSSIBILITY"

In the months since the nuclear scare of late 2022, I asked US and European officials if they had identified any similar threat. The threat had diminished as the war entered a period of relative stalemate in the east. However, the US and its allies remained vigilant.

"We have been less concerned about the imminent prospect since that period, but it's not something that is ever far from our minds," a senior US official told me. "We continue to refine plans, and . . . it's not beyond the realm of possibility that we could be confronting at least the rising risk of this again in the months ahead."

As Ukraine prepared a massive counteroffensive in the summer of 2023, western officials made clear that another Russian setback on the battlefield could be just the spark for escalating the conflict. A senior French military official told me that a "catastrophic loss" on the part of Russia would reignite the nuclear threat. The unthinkable remained thinkable in Ukraine.

And in June 2023, as Wagner chief Yevgeny Prigozhin was carrying out a brief mutiny against Putin, US officials communicated directly with their Russian counterparts, not just to make clear the US was not involved in the attempted coup but also to discourage Russia from using nuclear weapons in response. Russian foreign minister Lavrov publicly described those messages on Russian state media at the time.

"When US Ambassador [Lynne] Tracy spoke with Russian representatives yesterday, she gave signals. These signals were primarily that the United States had nothing to do with it, that the United States very much hopes that nuclear weapons will be in order, that American diplomats will not suffer," Lavrov said.

At each tense moment, both sides were openly discussing the nuclear risk.

MEMORIES OF PEACE

There is a nostalgic quality to conversations with NATO leaders whose lives and careers bridge the last Cold War and this new one. Like me, they remember the relief that followed the fall of the Berlin

Wall and the hope—since proved fleeting—that the threat of nuclear conflict had receded into history.

"I'm part of a generation that grew up during the Cold War, where [there was a] very present fear of a potential nuclear conflict," NATO Secretary General Stoltenberg told me, noting that that fear began to diminish even before the collapse of the Soviet Union and Warsaw Pact. "I had the privilege of seeing a number of walls coming down with those big new agreements between Reagan and Gorbachev in [the] 1980s," including the INF treaty banning intermediate-range missiles and, later, the first Strategic Arms Reduction Treaty (START I), which led to the dismantling of some 80 percent of the world's nuclear weapons.[22]

"We all felt relieved. We felt safer," Stoltenberg said. "We felt this is really the world moving in the right direction, not only reducing but banning a whole category of dangerous nuclear weapons. And now we are going the opposite direction."

The "opposite direction" has taken the world into a new era of increasingly open nuclear threats, with the great powers rethinking limits on their nuclear arsenals and middle powers considering nuclear programs of their own. The sobering result is that the unthinkable is now thinkable once again.

RUSSIA'S NUCLEAR BLUFF?

Some NATO leaders see a different danger in the West's reaction to the Russian nuclear scare: that overreaction might end up incentivizing further nuclear threats.

Prime Minister Kaja Kallas of Estonia recounted a dinner she attended with other senior officials from NATO allies during the Munich Security Conference in February 2023.

"We had a very interesting dinner regarding Russia," she told me. "What was interesting was that I heard very high officials from Germany and Luxembourg [and other] countries, say, 'Oh, we can't do this because it would provoke them to use the nuclear weapon.'"

In the meeting, Kallas responded with a mild scolding. "I said there that if Russia is going to use [a] nuclear weapon, it's going to be either on Ukraine or on us, but not on Germany, not on Luxembourg. If we are not afraid, so shouldn't you be. If Ukrainians are not afraid, you shouldn't be either."

Russia, she argued, stokes and capitalizes on those fears to its advantage. "So they know. They use this threat because they know that the westerners really are afraid of this. And if you look at the damage that they have [already] caused in Ukraine, it's bigger than any nuclear bomb."

Kallas believes that the risk of falling victim to Russian nuclear brinksmanship extends beyond Ukraine—that by retreating in the face of Russian nuclear saber-rattling, the West will empower authoritarians around the world.

"Some are saying we shouldn't talk about accountability, because then Putin is going to be the rat in the corner, and he has nothing to lose. So he will use [a] nuclear weapon, because he has no way out," said Kallas. "But I don't really buy that argument, because then you say that if you [make] nuclear threats, you are beyond the law, and you can do anything. And that is a message that you don't want to send to all the dictators around the world, that 'Well, we're not going to touch you if you have a nuclear weapon.'"

So how does the West walk that fine line? Secretary General Stoltenberg described the difficult balancing act NATO leaders are forced to perform in reaction to Russia's repeated nuclear threats.

"We take it seriously, but at the same time we need to react in a calm and measured way, to not exacerbate the situation or actually to give President Putin what he aims to achieve, because this nuclear rhetoric is about trying to divide NATO allies, is about trying to scare us to prevent us from providing support to Ukraine," he said.

"And that's the reason," he continued, "why it is important to be aware of the risks, follow closely what they do, take it seriously when they have such threatening language, but at the same time not over-react, because [it's] then actually that President Putin will achieve what he wants—that is to make us afraid."

The nuclear front is the most frightening area of potential escalation among the great powers, but it is by no means the only one.

CHAPTER EIGHT

A MULTIFRONT WAR

NEW FRONT: NEAR SPACE

An early 2023 standoff between China and the US exposed a new technological front. Events in January and February that year, in an ethereal no-man's-land sixty thousand feet over the continental US, would enter a new phrase into the vocabulary of great power conflict: "near space."

As CIA Director Burns warned in our interview, one of the greatest risks of great power conflict is the danger of relatively small collisions escalating into something bigger. And any incident that ends with one superpower firing at another is rife with danger. And over several tense weeks in early 2023, the great powers China and the US traded rhetorical shots that, for a time, portended a further breaking of perhaps the world's most impactful great power relationship.

The US first detected an enormous object drifting over Alaska in late January. US and Canadian early-warning assets—comprising a network of satellites, ground-based radar, airborne radar, and fighter jets—span the northwestern parts of the continent. It is the job of the North America Air Defense Command (NORAD), a joint division of the US and Canadian militaries organized in the 1960s to look out for Soviet nuclear missiles, to detect, validate, and warn of attack "whether by aircraft, missile or space vehicles" on the US and Canada, as NORAD says, and, in the event of danger, to "engage any air-breathing threat." Fighter jets stationed at Joint Base Elmendorf-Richardson in Anchorage regularly scramble to intercept Russian warplanes testing US air defenses.

This particular approaching "space vehicle" was something different. At two hundred feet tall and with a suspended payload of electronic equipment and solar panels some sixty feet wide, it wasn't small. And following prevailing winds, it wasn't particularly fast. However, balloons, despite their size, can present a relatively small radar picture, making detection more difficult.[1]

On February 3, the Pentagon revealed that it had been tracking the balloon for several days. Pentagon spokesman Brigadier General Patrick Ryder took pains to downplay any threat from the balloon, noting it was "traveling at an altitude well above commercial air traffic and does not present a military or physical threat to people on the ground."[2]

However, as it drifted slowly over the continental US, visible to passing aircraft and even to those people on the ground, the Chinese balloon transformed from a relatively new instrument of intelligence-gathering to a political football more than half the height of the Statue of Liberty and three school buses wide. Republicans chided President Biden for standing idly by through what they described as a grave national security threat. As it drifted over Montana, many took note that the US stations many of its ICBMs there, a juicy intelligence target for any foreign power.

The Republican former South Carolina governor Nikki Haley tweeted, "Shoot down the balloon. . . . Biden is letting China walk all over us. It's time to make America strong again." Republican senator

Marco Rubio of Florida, a member of both the Senate Foreign Relations and Intelligence Committees, demanded Biden order it shot down "over a sparsely populated area," adding, "This is not some hot air balloon, it has a large payload of sensors roughly the size of two city buses & the ability to maneuver independently."[3]

The Pentagon pushed back against the outrage, with a US military official telling CNN that the administration was simply following a "risk-reward" process in its decision-making. "Why not shoot it down? We have to do the risk-reward here," the official told CNN. "So the first question is, does it pose a threat, a physical kinetic threat, to individuals in the United States in the US homeland? Our assessment is it does not. Does it pose a threat to civilian aviation? Our assessment is it does not. Does it pose a significantly enhanced threat on the intelligence side? Our best assessment right now is that it does not. So given that profile, we assess the risk of downing it, even if the probability is low in a sparsely populated area of the debris falling and hurting someone or damaging property, that it wasn't worth it."[4]

Following the Pentagon's advice, Biden ordered the military to bide its time. And for several days, US military leaders choose instead to monitor the balloon, attempt to mitigate or block its collection and transmission capabilities, and wait for the balloon to drift over coastal waters, where it would be safer to take it down.

CLEAR AND PRESENT DANGER?

From a national security perspective, the degree and immediacy of the danger from the balloon was not clear. China has multiple satellites surveilling the US twenty-four hours a day. Satellites in low earth orbits pass over the entire continental US every ninety minutes, with an ability to gather intelligence from sensitive US sites and installations to a degree comparable to that of the balloon. Pentagon officials described the balloon's surveillance capability to me as "limited." However, an airborne vehicle at that altitude has advantages in gathering images and collecting signals intelligence. Distance matters.

During and after the days of the flight, Pentagon officials told me that the US had successfully mitigated the balloon's surveillance capabilities during its overflight of US soil and had even managed to extract some intelligence from the balloon's equipment. The US has highly capable jamming technology, which it operates from aircraft and ground stations, and it utilizes such technology regularly against surveillance assets from China, Russia, and other nations. Given such technology can be deployed against supersonic spy aircraft, a slow-moving balloon would presumably be a relatively easy target.

The Pentagon's sanguine appraisal changed in April, when the US assessed that the balloon had in fact transmitted information back home. Two months later, in June, the US reversed its assessment again, concluding the balloon had not been able to collect or transmit data while over US soil.

"We believe that (the balloon) did not collect while it was transiting the United States or flying over the United States, and certainly the efforts that we made contributed," Ryder told reporters at a briefing.[5] That is, according to the Pentagon, its initial assessment that the US had mitigated the balloon's collection had been accurate.

Once the balloon eventually drifted off the coast of South Carolina, the US military, under orders from the president, was ready to take action. On a Saturday afternoon in February, at a time when many TVs in the US were tuned to college basketball, television networks interrupted their broadcasts to air video of a US F-22 Raptor firing an AIM-9X Sidewinder air-to-air missile at the balloon, popping it like an enormous white bubble and sending it and its massive array of solar panels and other equipment plummeting into the sea. People on the ground who had been watching the jets circle the balloon prior to the missile strike were now treated to a bizarre aerial display—like slow-motion Fourth of July fireworks.

The military had waited for the precise window when the balloon had passed beyond the US mainland but was still inside US territorial waters—minimizing the risk to people and structures on the ground while preserving the ability to gather the wreckage at sea. As the F-22 fired its missile, US Navy ships were already in the area to swoop in.

ESCALATION

Standoff over. Or was it? Within hours of the shoot-down, the Chinese Ministry of National Defense issued a protest. A statement from Defense Ministry spokesman Colonel Tan Kefei read, "The US used force to attack our civilian unmanned airship, which is an obvious overreaction. We express solemn protest against this move by the US side." Tan then noted that China "reserves the right to use necessary means to deal with similar situations." Beijing appeared to be warning that US surveillance aircraft would face similar danger if they strayed into Chinese airspace.

Soon after, China's newspaper *Global Times*, a propaganda arm of the Chinese government, published an editorial quoting Tan and carrying the conversation further. The editorial's authors wrote:

It is widely known that US aircraft, appearing in civilian or military purposes, operate around China much more frequent than Chinese aircraft do around the US, Lü Xiang, an expert on US studies at the Chinese Academy of Social Sciences, told the Global Times on Sunday.

If the US does not differentiate between civilian and military aircraft, then it has made a very bad precedent in treating the China-US relations, Lü said.

The US frequently conducts close-in reconnaissance on China's doorsteps in the South China Sea, the Taiwan Straits and the East China Sea, sometimes in civilian disguises, according to think tanks and media reports.

"If the US does not make the difference, should China make a difference? Should China also take reciprocal measures? The US must carefully consider the consequences" Lü said."[6]

If the Defense Ministry's ominous words hadn't been enough, the *Global Times* put them in boldface. China was reserving the right to retaliate.

When I asked the Pentagon for its response, General Ryder first emphasized that US surveillance aircraft do not enter Chinese airspace: "Let's be clear: the PRC surveillance balloon was in U.S. territorial airspace, a violation of our sovereignty. We do not conduct such operations in Chinese airspace. So, there is no 'similar' situation."

Ryder then issued a pledge of his own, that US surveillance aircraft and naval vessels would continue their operations around China or anywhere else unabated: "The United States will continue to sail, fly, and operate anywhere international law allows."

CHINA'S "HUGE" CHALLENGE

The US and China had opened a new front in a growing great power standoff, somewhere between airspace and orbital space. More broadly, the balloon standoff was yet more evidence of the particular challenge China presents the US and its allies in intelligence gathering, a great power competition all its own.

"We're all pretty frank about the challenge," a western security official told me. "This is the big challenge. You have a rising power . . .

which is a repressive regime prepared to really focus on trying to keep it secret."

"They are highly active and frequently more than we would like them to be," this official continued. "The scale of challenge for us collectively as Five Eyes [the US, the UK, Canada, Australia, and New Zealand], as western intelligence powers, is huge."

In the view of Richard Moore, chief of the UK foreign intelligence service MI6, China takes an entirely different approach to intelligence gathering against its great power adversaries, on a scale unique to the PRC.

"They have such a completely different approach to it," Moore told me. "We're very conscious of only focusing on stuff which is genuinely secret. We are very conscious of what our state department or foreign colleagues can generate themselves and try not to duplicate that because that would be a waste of really expensive intelligence resources. So it's all very selective and it's very focused."

China, however, more than any other nation in the world, approaches the intelligence front of great power competition on an incomparable scale in both resources and targets. Moore says Chinese intelligence agencies simply vacuum up enormous amounts of data.

"For the Chinese, it's just a massive vacuuming operation," Moore explained. "While we draw neat distinctions between material which is classified as top secret, or material which is just held discreetly on governmental systems, they'll just hoover the lot up."

"GREAT GAME" IN THE ARCTIC

As the Chinese balloon traveled through near space into the continental United States, it first soared over another field of play among the great powers: the Arctic. And while China was laying claim to a new aerial front, Russia was holding its grasp on the vast expanse on and below the surface at the top of the world.

Even as the Ukraine war has bogged down and destroyed the bulk of Russian ground forces, Russia's blue-water navy has remained largely unscathed. And in an effort to show it remains a great power able to project its power around the world, Russia has maintained and even expanded its activities in the Arctic.

"Russia wants to demonstrate that it remains a power to be reckoned with," a senior US military official told me. This holds in particular, this official told me, in terms of projecting the power of Russia's nuclear forces—and its submarine force is central to this frightening objective.

In recent years, Russia has been testing new nuclear-capable, nuclear-powered missiles and torpedoes, which travel faster, making them harder for US missile defense systems to track and destroy. As recently as July 2023, Russia carried out one in a series of tests of a new nuclear-powered torpedo. The Poseidon torpedo carries its own nuclear reactor to power its flight. The size of a city bus, it doesn't fit inside conventional torpedo tubes. "They have to build a sub around it, essentially," the senior US military official told me. To date, tests of the Poseidon have largely failed. In the July test, Russia was able to fire the weapon out of its tube, but not much farther. Still, the US is monitoring Russian testing and deployment extremely closely, preparing for the moment when the tests are successful.

Russia is also deploying its newest, most advanced submarines in and around the Arctic. In May 2023, the Borei-class ballistic missile submarine *Generalissimo Suvorov* joined Russia's Northern Fleet, transiting through the Arctic Sea before taking up a position at a more permanent base on Russia's Kamchatka Peninsula. Ballistic missile submarines—"boomers" to submariners—are one central element of Russia's nuclear deterrent, each equipped with sixteen missile tubes that fire Russia's most advanced Bulava submarine-launched ballistic missile, each of which in turn carries six nuclear warheads. This repositioning has now put Russia's two most advanced ballistic missile submarines on opposite sides of the US, within striking distance of the continental US.

Russia has clear advantages over the US in the Arctic. Its Arctic coastline extends some fifteen thousand miles, and along it, over decades, Russia has built and expanded an "arc of steel" comprising army, navy, and submarine bases. The US operates one and sometimes two submarines in the Arctic—along with flights by P-8 Poseidon surveillance aircraft—enough to monitor but not compete with Russia's naval presence. In terms of capabilities, Russian has engineered its submarines—as I document in detail in *The Shadow War*—to run quieter and quieter, making them more difficult for US forces to track. In general, the US must operate two submarines and as many as four P-8 aircraft to reliably and consistently follow a single Russian submarine over a long period of time. That allocation of resources is not sustainable for the US Navy at all times.

China's balloon flights notwithstanding, its activities on and underneath the surface of the Arctic are far more limited. Unlike the US and Russia, China does not operate its submarine forces there. And Moscow has made clear that its "no limits" partnership with Beijing does not extend to the top of the world. This means the "great game" among the great powers in the Arctic is largely, for now, a competition between the US and Russia—and a daunting one.

MEASURING UP CHINA AND RUSSIA

The imbalance in resources between the US and its great power rivals is not confined to the Arctic. Who is winning the intelligence war among the great powers? In the view of intelligence officials, the US and its allies cannot beat China at its own game—its resources are simply too vast. Multiple intelligence officials have described the current environment, in both the number of adversaries and their capabilities, as unparalleled in history. And rivals' aggressiveness is unparalleled as well. What had been red lines in the past were fading or disappearing. For instance, brazen interference in US and western elections has become standard since 2016, and not just by Russia, but also by China, North Korea, and Iran. The only question now, as I explore further in the next chapter, is whether any one of those adversaries will take the step of attempting to interfere in voting systems.

There are gradations, however, of the intel threat. MI6's Moore, the CIA's Burns, and other senior intelligence officials have pointed to the West's recent successes penetrating the highest levels of Russian leadership. In 2019, I was the first to report that the US had maintained a human intelligence source inside Vladimir Putin's inner circle for years. The asset had risen to the most senior levels of the Kremlin with direct access to Putin, providing deeply valuable insight into the Russian leader's planning and thinking. As I reported for CNN at the time, the US extracted this covert source in a previously undisclosed secret mission in 2017.

Western intelligence agencies had logged other successes against Russia as well. Their interception of communications among Russian military commanders discussing military plans in the weeks prior to February 2022 helped form the basis of their assessment—proved correct, of course—that Russia intended to invade Ukraine. Intelligence collection also contributed to the west's assessment that Russia was considering a tactical nuclear strike later that year. The US and its partners had clearly developed a meaningful capability to penetrate Russian communications networks.

Ukraine, Moore told me, was proving a victory for western intelligence. "I think we're winning that," Moore said of the intelligence battle with Russia. "In that we had the intelligence to predict the way in which the Russians would act. And then we were able . . . to shape the international response to it. And also help the Ukrainians to get ahead of it and do some of the stuff they were able to do in those early days in the battle for Kyiv. And then we were able to take out roughly half of all of the Russian intelligence presence [operating] under cover in Europe." This was, western officials told me, through both the expulsion of Russian agents operating under diplomatic cover and the exposure and arrest of other Russian spy networks.

The US was opening and exposing Chinese vulnerabilities as well. Intelligence collection had led western intelligence to believe Xi distrusted his own generals regarding the Chinese military's ability to take Taiwan. And such collection, as I describe later in this chapter, exposed Xi's frustration with his own generals' handling of the balloon incident.

One continuing target for western intelligence is any Chinese provision of weapons to Russia for its war in Ukraine. Such collection efforts had already helped inform the West's assessment that Chinese officials were considering such arms supplies. And Moore made clear to me this his and other western agencies' collection efforts were continuing.

"We are watching that really, really closely, because it's important that China does not open up a full type of resupply to Russia," Moore said. "That will obviously make life for the Ukrainians a lot more difficult. So you can expect us to be looking at that really closely."

Moore assured me that if western intelligence agencies detected any further consideration or movement of arms from China to Russia, they would act. "If we see activity which we feel might grow into a more strategic threat in that space, we'd be intervening early and directly, either to expose it or to intervene directly with the Chinese," he said. "So we're trying to make sure that we can spot that activity."

SPY FLIGHT OVER THE SOUTH CHINA SEA

As I watched the balloon standoff play out, it was easy to discern the circumstances that might escalate it. Chinese officials and propaganda arms were, after all, leveling threats at US surveillance flights close to China, making the path to escalation clear.

The distinction between surveillance inside and outside a nation's airspace would seem to settle the issue. Outside is acceptable, inside unacceptable. Unfortunately, there are several areas on the map where the US and China disagree on whom the airspace belongs to. I found myself in one of those disputed areas aboard a US P-8 Poseidon on a surveillance flight over the South China Sea in May 2015. China claims the islands—and therefore the airspace and seas over and around them—as Chinese territory. The US does not recognize them as such, given these islands are claimed by half a dozen nations, some of them US allies like the Philippines. It regularly conducts so-called freedom of navigation exercises to demonstrate these remain international waters and airspace.

During our flight, the Chinese navy repeatedly warned the P-8 flight crew away, delivering the same message every few minutes in increasingly shrill terms. "This is the Chinese navy. This is the Chinese navy. Please go away quickly." The warnings culminated with a shout: "You go now!"

How would such an encounter near China go next time, more than eight years later, and after that US F-22 had destroyed the Chinese surveillance balloon? P-8s, unlike Chinese surveillance balloons, are crewed. Would China challenge these surveillance flights more aggressively? There had been a worrisome precedent. In 2001, two Chinese fighter jets intercepted a US Navy EP-3E surveillance aircraft, the predecessor to the P-8, seventy miles off China's Hainan Island. One of the Chinese jets came so close that it clipped the wing of the US jet. The Chinese jet crashed and disappeared, its pilot presumed dead. The US aircraft was forced to make an emergency landing on Hainan Island, where China then detained the twenty-four-person crew for eleven days.

Would Beijing follow through on its threat to more aggressively challenge US surveillance flights? And how would the US respond? Escalation is a game of actions and reactions, with increasing levels of risk. There are two halves to the equation: what you can control (your own actions) and what you cannot (your adversary's). The events off the coast of South Carolina were not a video game. They were part of a real-life war game.

OPEN SEASON ON BALLOONS

Within less than a week, the US had already fired its next salvos. Interrupting what might otherwise have been a quiet news cycle over Super Bowl weekend, US warplanes shot down three more "objects" off the northern coast of Alaska, over northern Canada, and then over Lake Huron in Michigan. US officials did not attribute them to China or any other nation. In fact, US officials I spoke with left open the possibility that the objects belonged to private entities. But the events were riling up the public and politicians alike. I received messages from otherwise levelheaded friends asking if this was a prelude to war or, perhaps, evidence of aliens.

In an attempt to tamp down the worst fears and conspiracy theories, the Pentagon sent a memo to lawmakers with rough details on each of the objects, making clear that none of them resembled the large Chinese surveillance balloon in size or capabilities. It described the object shot down over Canada as a "small, metallic balloon with a tethered payload below it," noting that it had crossed near "US sensitive sites" before it was shot down. The memo said that the object shot down over Alaska was the "size of a small car," adding: "We have no further details about the object at this time, including the full scope of its capabilities, its purpose, or its origin." The US military offered fewer details about the object shot down over Lake Huron in Michigan that Sunday, other than to say that it had "subsequently slowly descended" into the water.

The one consistent message was that none of these new objects appeared to be a clear and present danger to the US. "We did not assess it to be a kinetic military threat to anything on the ground, but assess it was a safety flight hazard and a threat due to its potential surveillance capabilities," Pentagon spokesman General Ryder said of the object over Lake Huron. "Our team will now work to recover the object in an effort to learn more."

As events were unfolding, Democratic representative Elissa Slotkin of Michigan tweeted she had received a call from the Pentagon explaining that the US military had "an extremely close eye" on an object above Lake Huron, adding, "We'll know more about what this was in the coming days, but for now, be assured that all parties have been laser-focused on it from the moment it traversed our waters."

Turns out the Pentagon had been speaking literally when it said "close eye." The military based its assessment, in part, on what pilots had been able to see as they darted by. More detailed descriptions would have to wait until they were able to recover debris. "These objects did not closely resemble and were much smaller than the PRC balloon and we will not definitively characterize them until we can recover the debris, which we are working on," a National Security Council spokesperson told CNN.

What had happened in the span of a week? Were there suddenly more surveillance balloons, or was the US simply looking more closely? US officials told me the most likely explanation was almost certainly the latter. NORAD had adjusted from looking solely for fast-moving missiles and aircraft to also watching for slower-moving objects floating in near space. And those sensors were now picking up a swarm of objects.

"We continue to refine detection settings, and that won't stop just because we have identified these smaller objects," a NORAD spokesperson told reporters.

The US military seemed to have jumped from a delayed reaction to a giant surveillance balloon to shooting down virtually anything approaching over the horizon. And the White House denied the president was reacting to criticism following the long transcontinental journey of the Chinese surveillance balloon. "These were decisions based purely and simply on what was in the best interest of the American people," NSC coordinator for strategic communications John Kirby told reporters.

But the administration had decided there needed to be other consequences for China as well. On February 3, Secretary of State Blinken announced he was postponing his upcoming trip to Beijing. "In my call today with Director Wang Yi, I made clear that the presence of this surveillance balloon in US airspace is a clear violation of US sovereignty and international law, that it's an irresponsible act, and that the (People's Republic of China) decision to take this action on the eve of my planned visit is detrimental to the substantive discussions that we were prepared to have," Blinken said.[7] A long-planned meeting, which had been intended to defuse tensions between the great powers, was now off, with tensions boiling further.

China was digging in as well. After initially taking care to characterize the surveillance balloon as purely a scientific research craft, on February 13, China accused the US of "illegally" flying high-altitude surveillance balloons over its own airspace more than ten times since 2022. "Since last year alone, American high-altitude balloons have illegally crossed China's airspace more than ten times without the approval of relevant Chinese authorities," Foreign Ministry spokesperson Wang Wenbin said. The White House immediately denied the claim, stating that no US surveillance aircraft had violated Chinese airspace.

China's statement continued a shift from its initial description of the balloon as a mistake to a more aggressive stance, not only accusing the US of similar spying but also threatening to take military action against US surveillance flights.

On Super Bowl Sunday, as US aircraft were taking down the unidentified object over Lake Huron, authorities in China's coastal Shandong province said they had identified what they called an "unidentified flying object" above the port city of Rizhao. They added they were "preparing to shoot it down," according to the state-run news website the Paper.[8]

Beijing took aim at not just alleged airspace incursions but also US surveillance aircraft operating close to, but not inside, Chinese airspace. By China's count, US ships and aircraft had conducted such close-range surveillance 657 times in 2022 and 64 times over the South China Sea in January 2023 alone. "For the longest time, the US has abused its own technological advantages to carry out large-scale and indiscriminate wiretapping and theft of secrets all over the world, including from its allies," describing the US as "without a doubt the world's largest surveillance habitual offender and surveillance empire."[9]

Regardless of how the US and its allies responded to these first forays into near space, they were now resigned to the emergence of an entirely new front in their standoff with China. Canadian foreign minister Mélanie Joly told me that Canada and the US now needed to view near space as a front in China's assault on the rules-based international order, comparable to existing competition in cyberspace and outer space.

"China is testing the international norms and trying to bend them in their favor," Joly told me. "I think that there are new areas, which either the international norms don't address or which international norms have not been as clear, and the question of near space and space is one. The question of digital and cyber is another.

"And these are the two new landscapes that we will have to address on the diplomatic front and two potential battlefields that we will need to address on the defense front," Joly said.

On the sidelines of the Munich Security Conference later in February, Secretary of State Blinken met his Chinese counterpart, Foreign Minister Wang, for the first time since he'd canceled his planned visit to Beijing. Thinly cloaked in diplomatic language, the two sides' readouts indicated their interaction had been tense.

"The Secretary directly spoke to the unacceptable violation of U.S. sovereignty and international law by the PRC high-altitude surveillance balloon in U.S. territorial airspace, underscoring that this irresponsible act must never again occur," read the State Department's official readout. "The Secretary made clear the United States will not stand for any violation of our sovereignty, and that the PRC's high altitude surveillance balloon program—which has intruded into the air space of over 40 countries across 5 continents—has been exposed to the world."

"Unacceptable" and "irresponsible" are not descriptions of a polite conversation, and a demand that such a flight "must never again occur" left no room for compromise. Briefing reporters on background, a senior State Department official gave further details, saying that Blinken had been "very direct and candid throughout" the hour-long meeting with Wang. The balloon's flight had violated US "sovereignty and territorial integrity," the official recounted. "And the secretary underscored multiple times that something like this must never happen again."

Going further, the official said Blinken had expressed disappointment that China had not accepted US requests for military-to-military dialogue during the Chinese balloon incident. "He stated, candidly stated, our disappointment that in this recent period that our Chinese military counterparts had refused to pick up the phone," said the official. "We think that's unfortunate. And that is not the way that our two sides ought to be conducting business."

The US, on the other hand, would deliberately keep such lines of communication open in order to prevent miscalculation or escalation in the future, said the official, adding "that the primary reason for doing so is to, again, engage in de facto crisis communication so that through those open channels, we reduce the risk of miscalculation and unintended conflict."

China's post-meeting messaging placed the onus for de-escalation entirely on the US side. According to a Chinese Foreign Ministry readout of the meeting, as aired by CGTN, Foreign Minister Wang "asked the US to face up to and resolve the damage caused by the indiscriminate use of force to Sino-US relations." "Indiscriminate use of force" is not the language of a diplomatic confrontation primed for cooling off. China was digging in once again.

Though Blinken had once again raised the possibility of a direct conversation between Biden and Xi, the two sides left Munich with no formal agreement for any further high-level contact. Blinken's Beijing summit was still off, and no new dates had been set or discussed. Xi had not accepted Biden's invitation to speak. And the Chinese military had not committed to reopening military-to-military channels regarding surveillance flights. In fact, a senior State Department official said there had been "no formal agreement" on any kind of means to increase dialogue between the two capitals.

Following the meeting, the NSC's Kirby said he was not surprised by China's tough words in Munich. "We shouldn't be surprised by the

Chinese rhetoric coming out of this and the bluster that they are known to put out there in the information space after a discussion like this," Kirby told *Fox News Sunday*. "Secretary Blinken had a very forthright, very candid exchange with the foreign minister of China and made clear, laid bare our deep concerns about what they did." He added, "Believe me, the message was clearly sent to China that this is unacceptable, it was a violation of our airspace."

As for whether the balloon's long flight over the continental US had been intentional—a deliberate decision by China at the highest levels to test US defenses and resolve—Blinken said, in effect, it didn't matter.

"I can't say dispositively what the original intent was," Blinken told ABC's *This Week*. "But that doesn't matter, because what we saw when it was over the United States was clearly an attempt to surveil very sensitive military sites. The balloon went over many of them. It, in some cases, loitered, and as I said, we took measures to protect that that information. We took measures to get information about the balloon. And I think we'll know more when we when we . . . actually get the remains."

Later, he went further, describing the balloon over the US as part of a much broader intelligence-gathering effort by China in near space. "There's absolutely no doubt in our minds about what the balloon, once over the United States, was attempting to do," Blinken said. "And no doubt in our minds about this surveillance balloon program that China has, and again, has been used over more than forty countries around the world."

US FRIENDLY FIRE

There was a domestic front to the Chinese balloon incident as well. Testifying before the House Armed Services Committee in March

2023, General Glen VanHerck, who commands both NORAD and the US Northern Command (NORTHCOM), told lawmakers how the episode and political finger-pointing demonstrated China's capability "at driving wedges between the American people."

"Candidly, the internal discord this event caused just showed one of the ways our competitors target us each and every day in the information space, and they're becoming increasingly adept at driving wedges between the American people," VenHerck said.[10]

VanHerck also warned that the balloon had exposed the limits of US domain awareness in this new "near space" front of great power competition. "I commit to you that this event has already generated critical lessons for my commands," he said. "And our mission partners and I can guarantee you that both NORAD and NORTHCOM are going to continue to learn and do whatever is necessary to keep our country safe."[11]

CYBER: LAYING GROUNDWORK FOR A "HOT WAR"

Near space is of course not the only high-technology front in renewed great power conflict. In fact, it pales in comparison with the constant battle among the US, Russia, and China—and other middle powers—in cyberspace. As it does in so many domains, the US and its allies view China as the greatest threat.

According to the 2023 *Annual Threat Assessment of the U.S. Intelligence Community*, from the Office of the Director of National Intelligence, "China probably currently represents the broadest, most active, and persistent cyber espionage threat to U.S. Government and private-sector networks. China's cyber pursuits and its industry's export of related technologies increase the threats of aggressive cyber operations against the U.S. homeland, suppression of the free flow of information—such as U.S. web content—in cyberspace that Beijing views as threatening to the CCP's hold on power, and the expansion of technology-driven authoritarianism globally."[12]

US and western officials consistently tell me that Russia, while not a threat on the scale of China, is still daunting, given it is the intelligence community's assessment that Moscow will rely more on cyber capabilities following the routing of its conventional military forces in Ukraine. "Moscow's military forces have suffered losses during the Ukraine conflict that will require years of rebuilding and leave them less capable of posing a conventional military threat to European security, and operating as assertively in Eurasia and on the global stage," reads the *Annual Threat Assessment*. "Moscow will become even more reliant on nuclear, cyber, and space capabilities as it deals with the extensive damage to Russia's ground forces."[13]

As with its conventional forces, however, the Ukraine war also exposed the limits of Russian cyber capabilities. Western intelligence agencies had assessed that Russia's initial invasion of Ukraine would include massive cyber and electronic warfare operations that would likely shut down communication networks inside Ukraine. That assessment is one reason CNN moved some of its broadcast resources to Lviv in Western Ukraine to ensure the network could remain on the air following the invasion. Russia did not, however, make Ukraine go "dark."

Was that a choice or a failure by Russian intelligence? Regardless, in terms of impact on the war, Ukraine was the clear winner.

"The Ukrainian command-and-control remained really strong all the way through from Zelensky down," MI6 chief Richard Moore told me. "If they hadn't had that, and Zelensky hadn't been able to lead as publicly and as well as he did, you've got to believe that the response wouldn't have been quite as amazing and admiring and brilliant as it was. But we're speculating. It's a what-if business."

Still, as the Office of the Director of National Intelligence assessed, western intelligence agencies certainly did not expect Russia to scale back its cyberattacks going forward. "Although its cyber activity surrounding the war fell short of the pace and impact we had expected," according to the 2023 threat assessment, "Russia will remain a top cyber threat as it refines and employs its espionage, influence, and attack capabilities. Russia views cyber disruptions as a foreign policy lever to shape other countries' decisions."[14]

Cyberattacks and intrusions are routine activities of intelligence agencies even in times of peace. A preeminent concern for US leaders, however, is how the great powers are deploying cyberweapons to further disrupt and weaken their adversaries in the event of conflict. Increasingly, all sides were planting or attempting to plant cyberweapons inside critical infrastructure, to be activated if war were to go "hot."

"There is lots of evidence of trying to do stuff that you would then use in a hot war," a western security official told me. "In other words, try and put down attacks on cyber infrastructures, which you can then activate at the time of the conflict in question."

The threat assessment states that "Russia is particularly focused on improving its ability to target critical infrastructure, including underwater cables and industrial control systems, in the United States as well as in allied and partner countries, because compromising such infrastructure improves and demonstrates its ability to damage infrastructure during a crisis."[15] As for China, the Office of the Director of National Intelligence describes similar planning for a "hot war."

"If Beijing feared that a major conflict with the United States were imminent, it almost certainly would consider undertaking aggressive cyber operations against U.S. homeland critical infrastructure and military assets worldwide," says the 2023 threat assessment. "Such a strike would be designed to deter U.S. military action by impeding

U.S. decision-making, inducing societal panic, and interfering with the deployment of U.S. forces." The assessment continues, "China almost certainly is capable of launching cyber-attacks that could disrupt critical infrastructure services within the United States, including against oil and gas pipelines, and rail systems."[16]

The goal of such cyberweapons in the event of conflict would be to bring the war home to an adversary—to disable key military infrastructure and capabilities *and* to inflict pain on the civilian population. It is yet one more frightening prospect in any great power war.

SPACE: A GREAT POWER WILD WEST

The great powers have also increasingly weaponized space. And since I first reported some ten years ago on the growing testing and deployment of space weapons by Russia and China—and by North Korea and Iran to a lesser extent—the space domain has become only more challenging and more complex.

"Space is already an arena of great power competition," Defense Secretary Lloyd Austin told lawmakers during his confirmation hearing in January 2021. He added, "Chinese and Russian space activities present serious and growing threats to U.S. national security interests. While Russia is a key adversary, China is the pacing threat."[17]

Like cyber, space is now one more front in any potential great power war, deeply integrated into the military planning of all the powers, including Russia and China. "As China's and Russia's space and counterspace capabilities increase, both nations are integrating space scenarios into their military exercises. They continue to develop, test, and proliferate sophisticated antisatellite (ASAT) weapons to hold U.S. and allied space assets at risk," noted the Defense Intelligence Agency's 2022 assessment *Challenges to Security in Space*.

One significant factor is the growing commercialization of space. The arrival and expansion of private launch firms, led by SpaceX, have reduced the cost of space launches enormously and greatly increased their frequency. What were once bus-size satellites, costing hundreds of millions of dollars apiece, could now be as small as toasters, easy to launch by the dozen or more, and at a fraction of the cost. Space is getting more crowded. As the DIA's 2022 report *Challenges to Security in Space* noted, "Between 2019 and 2021 the combined operational space fleets of China and Russia have grown by approximately 70 percent," with China making the biggest leap in space assets.

A busier and more crowded space creates more chances for encounters among the great powers, both intentional and unintentional. The low earth orbit is now a busy highway of satellites and space junk. "The probability of collisions of massive derelict objects in low Earth orbit (LEO) is growing and almost certainly will continue through at least 2030 because of rising numbers of space launches—especially those with multiple payloads—and continuing fragmentation from collisions, battery explosions, and further ASAT testing events," the DIA assessed.

While the rapid expansion of space launches creates an increased threat, it also provides increased opportunities to mitigate threats. Nations can now launch multiple satellites in vast constellations to create redundancies and to minimize the damage from the loss of any one of them.

But when it comes to operations, space is only becoming more, not less, of a "wild west." There are still no treaties or laws to govern the weaponization of space assets, or even the simplest interactions among satellites. For instance, there is no law preventing one nation's satellite from parking right next to another nation's, to disrupt its operation or conduct collection.

Taking advantage of the space-age wild west, Chinese satellites have engaged in a host of activities in close proximity to US satellites. In one encounter, space officials described a virtual "dogfight" playing out between Chinese and US satellites. Simulations of the encounter, based on real-life tracking of the satellites' movements, mimicked an aerial battle reminiscent of World War I or II—or in planes over the South China Sea—though playing out many miles above the earth and at immense orbital speeds.

As the great powers compete for dominance in space, the middle powers are—as in other areas of great power competition—playing both sides. Even some US allies are increasingly seeking to partner with China for certain space missions, blurring the dividing lines among the great powers. And back down on earth, the great powers are engaged in another great game of dominance on the earthbound portion of space activities. Satellites don't fly without ground-based control systems and installations. And China, seeking to expand its global reach, has prioritized building ground stations right in the US backyard in Latin America—all as part of its "Belt and Road" strategy for global infrastructure investment.

Officially, China is in favor of the peaceful use of space and is seeking international agreements to govern its use via the United Nations. However, Chinese military doctrine considers space an essential front in any war. As the DIA notes, "The PLA views space superiority, the ability to control the space-enabled information sphere and to deny adversaries their own space-based information gathering and communication capabilities, as a critical component to conduct modern 'informatized warfare.'"

To that end, China has tested and deployed several categories of weapons capable of destroying or disabling adversaries' space assets, including cyberweapons, directed energy weapons, and ground-based anti-satellite missiles. China's space arsenal also includes offensive satellites. In *The Shadow War*, I detail the "kidnapper satellites" China has launched. Officially described as "repair" satellites, they have a grappling arm that could, if ordered, pluck another nation's satellite right out of orbit. The great powers have entered the *Moonraker* age of great power warfare.

AI: "WE'RE THERE ALREADY"

Each great power weapons system—new and old—is increasingly influenced by yet one more new technological realm: artificial intelligence. AI is not part of a future threat environment. It is—intelligence officials emphasize to me—here today.

"We need to tell ourselves we're there already," Moore of MI6 told me. "We have been thinking about this and trying to work through our business model around the threat posed to it by emerging technology for quite a while now."

Moore recounted how he took his team at MI6 to an off-site meeting recently with the intention of sparking a broader conversation about how artificial intelligence would affect the work and mission of intelligence gathering and analysis. Their conclusion: AI is a force multiplier for a whole range of intelligence tools and practices.

"There is now a significant amplifying factor in play here," Moore said. "We don't fully understand the potential. We don't know quite where LLMs (large language models) will end up over the next five, ten years, but we better try and get ahead of that. And for us, therefore, there has to be a focus on making sure we keep in the game."

Like any new technology, despite the most alarmist views, AI has potential uses ranging from the good to the bad to somewhere in between. As chief of one of the world's most feared and respected intelligence agencies, Moore said he and his team looked at how AI could help the UK and its allies, rather than just pose new threats from rival great powers.

"There is a whole kind of positive side of this . . . around targeting, around being able to flag opportunities for us, sure," Moore said. "And then there is the generic issue for us and for every single organization in the world: there are opportunities for optimization and getting operations slicker, releasing resources to focus on the tough end of keeping in 'the human business.'"

Even in a time of enormous technological advances, human intelligence—HUMINT, in intelligencespeak—remains an essential part of intelligence gathering among the great powers, security officials from multiple countries have told me. To emphasize the point, the CIA has launched new efforts to recruit human sources inside Russia, sensing an "unprecedented" opportunity among Russians upset by the war in Ukraine. As CNN reported in May 2023, the effort includes a new channel on the messaging app Telegram, frequently used in Russia, with instructions on how to contact the CIA secretly.[18] There is a reason Moore himself said in rare public comments on a visit to Prague in July 2023, "Our door is always open. We will handle their offers of help with the discretion and professionalism for which my service is famed. Their secrets will always be safe with us."[19]

However, artificial intelligence, as Moore described it to me, is an "amplifying factor" for every aspect of intelligence gathering, human, electronic, and otherwise. And as with human intelligence gathering and recruiting, he believes the UK and its Five Eyes partners maintain the advantage.

"I remain really optimistic. I think we'll do it. I think we have the right sort of mindset, and entrepreneurialism and people to do it," he said.

In Moore's view, AI need not be purely a new field of conflict. "I think it would be a strategic mistake if we approached AI purely in the paradigm of a competition," he said. Like so many fronts of this competition, AI presents both risks and opportunities, including chances for cooperation among the great powers.

DEFLATING THE BALLOON INCIDENT

As the US-China great power relationship continued to wobble because of the balloon incident, western intelligence agencies were hard at work gauging Xi Jinping's thinking. Behind the scenes, US intelligence agencies assessed that the Chinese leader himself was concerned about the rapid escalation of tensions over the balloon. According to a senior US official, the US assessed that Xi was "mortified" by the incident and that while the Chinese leader had been aware of the spy balloon program, he did not expect to see one slowly floating across the continental US. As this senior US official described it, Xi was upset at PLA leadership for allowing the crisis to expand. In late February, Defense Secretary Austin told my colleague Kaitlan Collins that it was possible Xi did not know about the balloon, but he would "let the Chinese speak for themselves."[20] Could Xi's upset provide a path to deflate the balloon standoff?

The US was still concerned that near space remained a new field of competition between the US and China in July 2023, when I asked Alaska senator Dan Sullivan (R) if the US military had by then plugged the holes exposed by the spy balloon. His answer was a firm no.

"The issue of domain awareness for any kind of weapons system that's going to be coming to potentially threaten the US—to Chicago or Aspen or New York or Miami—they traverse over us," he said, speaking of his home state. "That's ballistic missiles. That's hypersonics. That's cruise missiles—these are all threats.

"We've been focused on ballistic missiles but not on hypersonics, not on cruise missile capabilities, and—believe it or not—not on spy balloons," he continued. "So that was a wake-up call with regard to domain awareness. These systems don't just protect Alaska—they protect the whole country. This was a real demonstration of our vulnerabilities."

Still, the US eventually concluded—as I first reported in February—that the Chinese balloon had not gathered intelligence while airborne over the US. The Pentagon assessed that US capabilities had helped disrupt the balloon's collection. "We believe that (the balloon) did not collect while it was transiting the United States or flying over the United States, and certainly the efforts that we made contributed," Pentagon spokesman General Ryder told reporters.[21]

By September, CNN was first to report that China appeared to have suspended the spy balloon program altogether, according to US intelligence assessments, and that the US had not observed any new launches since the incident.[22]

China was ratcheting down its public rhetoric as well. In a statement, Chinese embassy spokesperson Liu Pengyu called the February episode "an unexpected, isolated incident."[23] His description of the event as "unexpected" was consistent with what US intelligence agencies had assessed privately: the Chinese leader did not expect a giant, plodding surveillance balloon to drift across the entire US and send the great powers into a public standoff. What could have been a major new rift between two great powers appeared to be de-escalating.

What worked? Senior US officials told me they credited discipline on both sides. From US intelligence gathering, it became clear that Xi himself was alarmed at the incident—and even berated his generals for not keeping him fully informed of the program. Conscious of this, US officials—after the initial spate of balloon shoot-downs—toggled back military action and rhetoric. In effect, both Beijing and Washington wanted to diffuse the situation and so they did.

ARCTIC TEST

As China and the US appeared to be defusing one crisis, Russia was escalating another. In early October 2023, Russia tested a new nuclear-capable, nuclear-powered cruise missile in the Arctic. Like the Poseidon nuclear-powered torpedo, the "Skyfall" cruise missile (as NATO has code-named it, perhaps with a view to the world of James Bond) carries its own nuclear reactor to power its flight. And also like the Poseidon, it is designed to travel at hypersonic speed to overwhelm and avoid US missile defense systems. US officials believe the fact that Russia chose to test the Skyfall in the Arctic was no accident. As with its ongoing submarine activities, Russia wants to demonstrate to the great powers that it continues to exercise influence in the Arctic—and with new, more powerful weapons, no less.

"We have now virtually finished work on modern types of strategic weaponry about which I have spoken and which I announced a few years ago," Putin said at a nationally televised meeting at the Black Sea resort of Sochi. "A final successful test has been held of Burevestnik, a global-range, nuclear-powered cruise missile."[24]

US military officials I spoke with said the US was not convinced the test was as successful as Putin claimed. And numerous previous tests had been failures. But Russian efforts continued unabated—and the US was watching closely. The Skyfall, together with the Poseidon and Russia's deployment of new, more advanced ballistic missile submarines around the US, was all part of a broader Russian effort to project the power of its nuclear arsenal up to the very top of the world.

Over a tense year, the US and China had precipitated and then diffused a potentially explosive situation in near space, while Russia had escalated another one in the Arctic, providing lessons for the great powers going forward—among them, the immense value of communication. The MI6's Moore touts the value of such direct contacts at all levels, even when the messages aren't friendly.

"Our professional diplomats should never elide the decision between engagement and reward," Moore told me. "It's okay to have a channel, even when you're putting down messages which are pretty blunt."

What will stand in the way of a modern descent into global conflict? That is, what will forestall a twenty-first-century *Guns of August*? In the final chapter, I'll examine remedies for peace amid the new global disorder. But first, there is a geopolitical wild card that could transform the entire US approach to great power competition, and that wild card is Donald Trump.

CHAPTER NINE

TRUMP WILD CARD

"FUNDAMENTALLY A CATASTROPHE"

"A second term with him [Trump]—particularly when he would not be worrying about reelection—it would be fundamentally a catastrophe for us." These aren't the words of a mere outside observer of the former president, but of retired Marine Corps general John Kelly, who served nearly two years in the Trump administration, first as secretary of Homeland Security and then, for the bulk of his time in the White House, as chief of staff to the president, with daily face-to-face encounters with Trump on some of the most sensitive national security issues.

Kelly's view of the former president is not an outlier but one I heard from multiple officials in the US and overseas who based their views on firsthand experience with Trump. A senior US official, who also served under Trump, told me that European leaders he's spoken with are "petrified" that he could be reelected.

At the core of their concern is the former president's character and self-interest—and how they believe that impacts not just his personal decisions but ones affecting US relations with the great powers.

"I just don't think he has enough of a brain to have an articulated view, but because he thinks everything through the prism of 'How does this benefit Donald Trump?'" Ambassador John Bolton, former national security advisor to Trump, told me. "He thinks 'If I've got a good relationship with Xi Jinping, the US and China have a good relationship,' which is obviously not the case."

Bolton is a lifelong Republican who served long stints at senior levels of the Reagan and the two Bush administrations and then as Trump's national security advisor from 2018 to 2019. He and Kelly both fear that the marriage of Trump's self-interest with his ongoing frustration at a loss in the 2020 election he still refuses to accept could make a second Trump term more damaging than the first.

"If you look at the start of a second Trump term as a resumption of where he was when he left the first term, maybe made worse by four years of being pissed off and not being in the White House, I think it just goes downhill from there," Bolton said. "I don't think it necessarily means you fall off the edge of the cliff, although that's possible. But I mean, I think you keep going downhill."

"It would be the first term, only more so, and that is to say incoherent," Bolton told me.

The "incoherence" of Trump's worldview has enhanced relevance in a world increasingly defined by great power competition. A fundamental dividing line among the great powers is between democratic and autocratic governments. In the accounts of former advisors and in his many public statements, Trump has demonstrated no recognition or appreciation of that dividing line. In fact, he has often stated that he personally sees no fundamental difference among the great powers. To that point, his words to Bill O'Reilly in 2017, in his answer to the Fox anchor's statement that Putin is "a killer"—"You think our country's so innocent?"—were an early and revealing expression of his worldview. And so, a Trump return could flip the US response to great power competition on its head.

"HE MISSED THE HOLOCAUST"

How far does Trump's redefinition of US principles extend? As president, according to John Kelly, Trump repeatedly expressed admiration for Adolf Hitler.

"It's pretty hard to believe he missed the Holocaust, though, and pretty hard to understand how he missed the four hundred thousand American GIs that were killed in the European theater," Kelly told me. "But I think it's more, again, the tough-guy thing."

Kelly was a US Marine for four decades, enlisting during the Vietnam War and ultimately rising to the armed forces' highest rank of four-star general. In person, he shares his stories and insight with a deadpan seriousness and accessible affability that might surprise anyone who's only seen him speaking more formally and ramrod straight from behind a podium. With his signature "Bah-ston" accent and no-nonsense style, he is direct and unapologetic.

What specifically about Hitler did Trump praise? "He said, 'Well, but Hitler did some good things.' I said, 'Well, what?' And he said, 'Well, [Hitler] rebuilt the economy.' But what did he do with that rebuilt economy? He turned it against his own people and against the world.

"And I said, 'Sir, you can never say anything good about the guy. Nothing,'" Kelly continued. "I mean, Mussolini was a great guy in comparison."

Trump's admiration for Hitler went further than the German leader's economic policies. Trump also expressed admiration for

Hitler's hold on his senior officers—senior *Nazi* officers, that is. Trump lamented that Hitler, as Kelly recounted, maintained his senior staff's "loyalty," while Trump himself often did not.

"He would ask about the loyalty issues and about how, when I pointed out to him the German generals as a group were not loyal to him, and in fact tried to assassinate him a few times, and he didn't know that," Kelly recalled.

"He truly believed, when he brought us generals in, that we would be loyal—that we would do anything he wanted us to do," Kelly told me.

"HE LIKES THE DICTATORS SO MUCH"

Of course, Trump's affinity for dictators extends beyond the man who ordered the Holocaust and launched the bloodiest war in history. As president and since, he expressed admiration for Vladimir Putin and Xi Jinping, as well as Kim Jong Un. His admiration for the leaders themselves coincided with his belief that those leaders' positions—again, on crucial issues of US national security—were more valid than US positions. US positions such as opposition to the Russian invasion of Ukraine and the US security posture on the Korean peninsula—that is, some of the most defining features of US national security policy.

"He thought Putin was an okay guy and Kim was an okay guy—that we had pushed North Korea into a corner," Kelly recalled. "To him, it was like we were goading these guys. 'If we didn't have NATO, then Putin wouldn't be doing these things.'"

Why does Trump admire dictators? Kelly and others who served under Trump believe he envies their power and believes he should have wielded similar power.

"My theory on why he likes the dictators so much is that's who he is," Kelly said. "Every incoming president is shocked that they actually have so little power without going to the Congress, which is a good thing. It's Civics 101, separation of powers, three equal branches of government.

"But in his case, he was shocked that he didn't have dictatorial-type powers to send US forces places or to move money around within the budget," Kelly continued. "And he looked at Putin and Xi and that nutcase in North Korea as people who were like him in terms of being a tough guy."

Several former members of the Trump administration shared a similar assessment: he sees himself as tough, though, in their experience, did little to back up that self-image. "He's not a tough guy by any means, but in fact quite the opposite," said Kelly. "But that's how he envisions himself."

"He views himself as a big guy," Ambassador Bolton agrees. "He likes dealing with other big guys and big guys like Erdoğan in Turkey get to put people in jail and you don't have to ask anybody's permission. He kind of likes that."

Trump "kind of likes" the idea that foreign leaders can put their opponents in jail. Consider the impact of that in a US as divided as it is today, on the judicial system and as Trump has attacked prosecutions against himself and his allies while often praising those against his opponents.

His former advisors say that Trump most consistently lavished praise on Vladimir Putin. Bolton recalled with alarm a comment from Trump during the 2018 NATO summit, when the then president very nearly pulled the US out of the alliance. Following sometimes tense encounters with several NATO leaders—that is, the leaders of US treaty allies—Trump said that his meeting with Putin, the leader of America's great power adversary "may be the easiest of them all. Who would think?"[1]

"He says to the press as he goes out to the helicopter, 'I think the easiest meeting might be with Vladimir Putin. Who would ever think that?'" recalled Bolton. "There's an answer to that question. Only one person. You. You are the only person who would think that. The shrinks can make of that what they will, but I think it was 'I'm a big guy. They're big guys. I wish I could act like they do.'"

Trump has continued to praise authoritarians into his 2024 presidential campaign. At a town hall organized by Fox News in July 2023, Trump said, "Think of President Xi: central casting, brilliant guy. When I say he's brilliant, everyone says, 'Oh, that's terrible.' He runs 1.4 billion people with an iron fist: smart, brilliant, everything perfect. There is nobody in Hollywood like this guy."

In an interview with Fox that same month, he lavished praise on Putin as well, describing him as smarter than US president Joe Biden. "These are smart people, including Macron of France. I could go through the whole list of people, including Putin. . . . These people are sharp, tough and generally vicious," Trump said. "They're vicious, and they're at the top of their game. We have a man that has no clue what's happening. It's the most dangerous time in the history of our country."[2]

Trump was again praising the leaders of the US's two great power adversaries over the leader of his own country. And inherent in his admiration for them was a generous appraisal of his own personal skills and influence as a leader.

"Trump believed in the power of his personal charisma and diplomacy," recalled Matthew Pottinger, his deputy national security advisor, who was deeply involved in Trump's meetings with North Korean leader Kim and Chinese president Xi. "He had almost unlimited faith in it. That was as true with Kim as it was with Xi—but also with allies too."

GREAT POWER CONUNDRUM

Trump's affinity for authoritarians represents a defining question for the US and its citizens in a great power conflict that pits democracies invested in an international system of laws and treaties against autocratic powers that reject those standards as fundamentally biased in favor of the US and its allies—and that, given the chance, have violated international law and borders to pursue their interests. Russian and Chinese officials—and Trump himself—cite examples of US transgressions against its own standards in Vietnam, Afghanistan, and Iraq. However, if Trump doesn't believe there is a qualitative difference between those wars and a twenty-first-century Russian war to absorb Ukraine, a potential Chinese war to absorb Taiwan, or, for that matter, a twentieth-century war by Nazi Germany to absorb large parts of Europe, his return could bring a fundamental shift in the US vision of itself and its role in the world.

Trump already has a track record as president that fuels those fears looking forward. During his administration, he gave Putin the benefit of the doubt in Helsinki on Russian interference in the 2016 US election, Erdoğan the okay to invade northern Syria (as I detail in *The Madman Theory*), and Kim the historic international recognition of three summits for which the US received no nuclear concessions in return. As Ambassador Bolton described in his book, *The Room Where It Happened*, Trump endorsed Xi's incarceration of more than a million Muslim Uighurs in Xinjiang province. "At the opening dinner of the Osaka G-20 meeting in June 2019, with only interpreters present, Xi had explained to Trump why he was basically building concentration camps in Xinjiang," Bolton wrote. "According to our interpreter, Trump said that Xi should go ahead with building the camps, which Trump thought was exactly the right thing to do." The parallel to Trump's praise of Hitler was alarming. Here was the sitting US president endorsing modern-day concentration camps.

The combination of his lack of a philosophy with a fundamental misunderstanding of great power geopolitics extends to the economic relationship between the US and China as well.

"He has certain things that he thinks he understands more than others," said Bolton. "One of them is trade, because it deals with numbers, but he's got a simple-minded view of the balance of trade, that a surplus is good, and the deficit is bad. He can't make up his mind what kind of deal he wants with China. He wants the biggest trade deal in history, but does he really want to stop them from pirating our intellectual property or does he just want them to buy more agricultural products?"

TRUMP'S NEAR NATO EXIT

Perhaps more consequentially, his track record includes very nearly removing the US from his country's most consequential military alliance—one that protects its members in the midst of tectonic changes in great powers' geopolitics, including its most generous member, the United States.

As Kelly recounts, Trump set the wheels in motion for the US to exit NATO at the alliance's 2018 summit in Brussels. "He was always ranting and raving and jumping up and down, and oftentimes he would spin up in terms of, 'Well, I'm smarter than they are,' and all of this," Kelly said, describing Trump's mindset in Brussels.

Kelly said he found himself sitting across from Trump, trying to explain the importance of NATO to him in terms that the president would understand. Kelly's approach involved a combination of explaining what was actually possible and what might make him look bad. In the case of withdrawing from NATO, Kelly tried to convey to Trump that both applied here.

Remarkably, their discussions did not focus on the nature and severity of threats to US and European security, or the emergence of great power competition with Russia or China, or really any fundamentals of national security. Kelly found what worked with Trump was to focus on how any given decision, including Trump's desire to leave NATO, would make him look with voters—and then *hope* Trump would drop it.

But at the summit, Trump was not dropping it. A former senior US official told me that Trump issued orders to then chairman of the Joint Chiefs of Staff General Mark Milley and then defense secretary Mark Esper for the US to withdraw from NATO. Despite vehemently opposing the move, they considered the president's direction a "lawful order" and drew up plans to execute the withdrawal.

Bolton recalls Trump's near exit from NATO with genuine trepidation. "Honest to God, it was frightening because we didn't know what he was going to do up until the last minute. And I mean, I think, he all but said he was going to get out of NATO and then pulled back on it," said Bolton.

NATO Secretary General Jens Stoltenberg told me he remembers what he described as the "dramatic NATO summit" when NATO leaders found themselves openly questioning whether the US would remain in the alliance.

"I'm glad that United States stayed," Stoltenberg said. "And I think there are strong political forces inside the United States that also helps to ensure that."

In the end, only a last-minute intervention from Trump's most senior advisors averted a US exit.

"In many cases I would say, 'Look, if you do this, you're going to get killed in the press and public opinion. And what's the point of it?' Americans, generally speaking by polling, think that we should be involved in the world," Kelly said. "The small number of people in America that support you, ex-president, that want us out of NATO, they don't represent the majority opinion. And again, you will have a problem in Congress."

His goal—the only one Kelly thought was achievable—was not to convince Trump of the merits of remaining in NATO, but to get him to drop what were often fleeting impulses and move on. "That's oftentimes where I was trying to get him to go"—that is, Kelly said, to get Trump to say: "Fuck it, do what you want."

SHOOT DOWN THAT MISSILE

Trump's impulsivity extended to one of the nation's other primary national security threats: Iran. Kelly recounted an episode in which the US received intelligence that Iran was preparing to carry out a missile test, to which President Trump then suggested the US shoot it down.

"I'd say, 'Okay, well, sir, that's an act of war,'" Kelly recalled. "A country is going to launch a missile from its own territory, for its own airspace, and it's going to impact a thousand miles away in its own territory. A country has a right to do that. There's no imminent threat.

"'They can't hit the United States with the missile,'" Kelly continued to explain to Trump. "'So, yes, if you want to shoot it down, it is an act of war. So you really need to go over to Congress and get at least an authorization to.'

"And he said, 'Well, they'll never go along with it,'" Kelly recalled. "'Well, I know, but that's our system,'" Kelly said he replied.

In Kelly's view, Trump's approach to Iran stood in stark contrast to his approach to other authoritarian states, including Russia, China, and North Korea. While Trump rewarded Putin, Xi, and Kim with praise and warm interactions on the international stage, he consistently directed fire at Iran, even to the extent of risking a war. "He was much more inclined to act against Iran than he was certainly against Russia and China, who were his friends," Kelly said.

Biden's deputy national security advisor Jon Finer described Trump's deference to Russia as without precedent: "I don't know how you want to characterize the Trump-Russia period, because . . . there was a leader-level coziness that was probably almost completely unprecedented in the overall history of the US-Russia relationship."

HOW GOVERNMENT WORKS

At the root of Trump's often impulsive foreign policy decision-making was his fundamental misunderstanding of the office of president.

"I'd go back to explaining to him how the government works. How it's supposed to work," Kelly told me. "'You don't have dictatorial powers. You have to make the case if you want to do this and that. . . . You got to go out and make the case to the American people, and then that brings Congress along. But you just can't unilaterally make these decisions even if you might have the authority to make them,' which, thank God, in most cases, he didn't. But even if you had the authority, you're going to ask yourself, Is this the right thing to do?"

"The whole time I was there, he was one of these guys that just had very little base knowledge about anything but assumed he was an expert on everything, and something would set him off," Kelly recalled. "This is multiple times a day. And he'd read something or see something on TV, and he'd go, 'Why are we in NATO? They're not living up to their two percent,' and all of this kind of thing. And he literally, again, really had no idea what NATO was about, how we got there."

"Trump doesn't have a philosophy," said Bolton. "He doesn't adhere to policies in the sense that that term is understood in Washington. His decisions tend to be ad hoc and not firm or stable."

TRUMP'S NEXT TARGETS

There are other issues of character, according to his former advisors. John Kelly recalled Trump's apparent disgust for wounded veterans, which he witnessed and heard from the then president on multiple occasions. Kelly recalled that Trump, having attended the 2017 Bastille Day parade in Paris, told him to keep wounded veterans out of future military parades.

"The one thing he didn't want—he didn't want any wounded guys," Kelly recalled. "They had two groups of amputees, people in wheelchairs. 'I don't want those. They don't look good,'" Kelly recalled Trump saying to him.

And to Kelly, who lost a son in combat in Afghanistan, Trump would often say, "Why do you people all say that these guys who get wounded or killed are heroes?" Kelly recalled Trump saying. "They're suckers for going in the first place, and they're losers."

"Suckers" and "losers"—a sitting president's description of Americans who had given their lives in military service to their country.

Perhaps that's his mindset around longtime allies. In a second term, his former senior advisors envision Trump undoing a whole host of US security commitments around the globe—and in a more lasting way than he managed in the first term. Moreover, they believe that, in a second term, Trump would stock agencies and departments with loyalists who would better deliver on these decisions, generating a dramatic turn in the US position in the world in the midst of new great power competition.

One immediate target for Trump if he's reelected: formally withdrawing the US from NATO. A senior US official, who served in both the Trump and Biden administrations at a high level, said that in a second term "the US will be out of NATO." "NATO would be in real jeopardy," Bolton agreed. "I think he would try to get out."

Many veterans of the Trump administration have a similar warning for Ukraine. "US support for Ukraine would end," said the senior US official who served under Trump and Biden.

They also see a reelected Trump pressuring Ukraine to make a deal to immediately end the war there, including ceding territory to Russia. Noting Trump's comment at a Fox News town hall in July 2023 claiming, if reelected as president, he could end the war in one day, Bolton said, "If I were Ukraine, I'd be very worried, because if everything is a deal, then 'what's another ten percent of Ukrainian territory if it brings peace?' kind of thing."

Taiwan, they say, should be similarly worried. Bolton recalled a stunt Trump would carry out in the Oval Office. "He would hold up the tip of his Sharpie pen and say, 'That's Taiwan. See this Resolute Desk, that's China.'" His point: that Taiwan is too small to successfully defend itself against a Chinese invasion—and too small for the US to care about.

Bolton recalled, "I mean, if I were in Taiwan, I would be very worried about a Trump administration."

Trump's aversion to US security commitments abroad is one rare, consistent aspect of his worldview, albeit one at odds with decades of bipartisan US foreign policy. Kelly and other current and former US officials fear Trump would end or reduce the US security commitments to South Korea and Japan as well.

"The point is, he saw absolutely no point in NATO," Kelly said. "He was just dead set against having troops in South Korea, again, a deterrent force, or having troops in Japan, a deterrent force."

"If he went back and had another meeting with Kim Jong Un and Kim said, 'Your successor put those war games back in effect,' Trump [would say], 'They're gone. They're gone right now. I'm just telling you; they're gone,'" Bolton said, imagining a second Trump term. "I think it's possible."

A CASE FOR MADMAN THEORY

Matthew Pottinger, Trump's deputy national security advisor, argues that Trump's approach to dictators was not, in practice, always deferential, and may even have yielded benefits.

"The funny thing about the dynamic, as idiosyncratic as Trump's approach was: it did have some benefits and some deterrent effect," Pottinger said.

Pottinger gives the example of Trump's approach to North Korea and Kim Jong Un, noting that during his administration the US tightened sanctions on North Korea at the same time the president was pursuing a personal relationship with Kim.

"It had a funny effect of two things. One, it damaged Kim Jong Un's ability to resource his nuclear and missile programs, because his economy was doing a lot worse and continues to do much worse, thanks to those UN sanctions that we got the go-ahead [for] in 2017," said Pottinger. "Kim was also unwilling to offend Trump because he thought that as long as he kept Trump kind of close, there was always a chance that he might strike a deal that would be favorable to the North Koreans. For the three years, the final three years of the Trump administration, 2018, '19, and '20, Kim stopped testing long-range missiles and he stopped testing nukes."

Pottinger concedes the outcome of Trump's relationship with Putin was mixed. "At the personal level, you had the idiosyncratic flattering diplomacy, and it's possible that Putin would've judged that in a second Trump term, he might have been able to work some kind of a deal that would've given him a more favorable runway over the long term," Pottinger said. "He might have also felt that the weapons that the Trump administration was providing were a sign of resolve, and that Putin, therefore, wasn't as likely to test our resolve, but we'll never know. It's like history doesn't reveal its alternatives, as Edward R. Murrow used to say."

NATO Secretary General Stoltenberg also cited some positive steps for NATO under Trump, though largely driven by bipartisan congressional support for the alliance.

"During the Trump years, we had increased US presence in Europe, and I was invited to speak to a joint session in the US Congress," Stoltenberg said. "And the main reason for that was to demonstrate solidarity with NATO from Republicans and Democrats."

More broadly, he hopes, NATO has proved its usefulness to the US to members of both its parties, who might then resist any new attempts by Trump to leave the alliance.

"Russia, China, they don't have anything like the United States has in NATO," Stoltenberg said. "They hardly have any allies at all. So, of course, that makes the United States stronger and safer."

Like many European leaders I interviewed, though, he conceded that elections can bring surprises, even for the world's oldest defense alliance and even in the midst of the return of great power competition.

"In democracies, there is no guarantee for anything. Voters decide," he said. "But I'm confident that the United States will remain committed to NATO, because it is in the United States' security interests to do so."

And in some ways, NATO supporters were giving it a head start. As the 2024 US presidential election approached and Trump was the Republican front-runner, western leaders began to make moves to firewall certain aspects of the West's strategy for great power competition against a possible second Trump administration. The security guarantees for Ukraine negotiated at the NATO summit in Vilnius were a prime example. As one senior western official said to me, "Having long-term security guarantees makes them bulletproof to future governments that could be elected." It was clear to me that one of the "future governments" this official was referring to was a potential second Trump administration. Call it "Trump insurance."

THE 2024 ELECTION THREAT

The 2024 election already plays a big role in great power strategy. Putin, for instance, appears to be aware of Trump's affinity for him. And in the summer of 2023, CNN reported that Putin planned to hold out in Ukraine at least through the 2024 US presidential election, with the hope that American voters might deliver a more pliant president, less committed to Ukraine's defense. The question for those dedicated to safeguarding the US election from interference is whether Putin would do more than wait out the election and attempt once again to swing it toward Trump. Putin put his thumb on the scale in the 2016 election. Will he attempt to do so again in 2024?

In 2016, the US intelligence community concluded that the Kremlin had a preference for Trump and interfered in the election with the intention to hurt his opponent Hillary Clinton and help Trump: "We assess Russian President Vladimir Putin ordered an influence campaign in 2016 aimed at the US presidential election," read the Intelligence Community Assessment released in January 2017. "Russia's goals were to undermine public faith in the US democratic process, denigrate Secretary Clinton, and harm her electability and potential presidency. We further assess Putin and the Russian Government developed a clear preference for President-elect Trump. We have high confidence in these judgments.

"We also assess Putin and the Russian Government aspired to help President-elect Trump's election chances when possible by discrediting Secretary Clinton and publicly contrasting her unfavorably to him," the assessment continued. "All three agencies agree with this judgment. CIA and FBI have high confidence in this judgment; NSA has moderate confidence."[3]

Now, with his invasion of Ukraine failing in part due to US military support, the Russian leader would seem to have an even greater incentive to interfere to the advantage of Trump or another candidate less likely to defend Ukraine. Chris Krebs, who led US efforts to protect the 2020 election as director of the Cybersecurity and Infrastructure Security Agency at the Department of Homeland Security from 2018 to 2020, sees worrisome signs.

"If you think about motivations," Krebs told me, "I would suspect—as US and Western support keeps Ukraine out of existential risk and Putin faces further pressure at home—that he's going to look at alternative methods to change the dynamic. At a minimum, he would have a preference in the election."

What form would those "alternative methods" take? Krebs and many US officials believe Putin is most likely to stick with further information operations, like those he ordered in 2016, rather than directing Russian intelligence agencies to attack or undermine actual election systems.

"My sense is it will be a continued information operation, with Russia looking for opportunities to undercut Biden and others in the GOP who support Ukraine," said Krebs. "Putin would be thinking deliberately of what he can do below the red line [of actual interference with election systems]."

Many in the US government believe that Putin, despite his brazenness in launching a full-scale invasion of Ukraine, recognizes that an attack on US election systems would be a red line for Washington that even he cannot cross. Still, he has already proved himself willing to undermine US elections in other ways and may be preparing to do the same in 2024.

"I'm sure Putin has the SVR [Russia's foreign intelligence service] and GRU [Russia's military intelligence service] looking at how do we undermine public trust in the system of democracy in the US and the West," said Krebs. "For Putin, there is not a whole lot of downside from where Russia already is. What are you going to do: Sanction more people? Cut them off from the international financial system?"

That does not mean that no one will attempt to attack or undermine US election systems. Iran has attempted to access such systems in the past. And the 2020 election proved that domestic actors, encouraged by Trump, could attempt the same. As some of his own former advisors have said, Trump himself considered seizing election machines. Without the powers of the office, Trump conducting nationwide election tampering is an outlier possibility. But local tampering is possible. This could take the form of attempting to change votes or simply to once again raise questions about the official tallies and therefore lead large segments of the public to doubt or refuse to accept the outcome.

"I'm much more worried about domestic actors taking steps not to actually change the election result but, in a narrow way, to get into some systems to create an outcome which allows them to say we can't trust the system," said Krebs.

Remember: most Republicans still believe Trump's lie that he won the 2020 election. A CNN poll in August 2023 found that an overwhelming 69 percent of Republicans or Republican-leaning voters believe Biden's victory in 2020 was not legitimate.[4] Disinformation works.

Having covered Russian election interference in 2016 and written about it in detail in *The Shadow War* in 2019, one thing that strikes me is that while election interference was then largely a foreign threat, today it is at least equally a domestic one. Americans are some of the most influential actors in this disinformation space, from the former president to state lawmakers to members of the right-wing media, according to the Dominion Voting Systems settlement against Fox News.

Before Fox News agreed to pay a jaw-dropping $787.5 million to settle the suit brought by Dominion (a separate $2.7 billion suit brought by Smartmatic was still pending at the time of this writing), Delaware superior court judge Eric M. Davis took the unusual step of using all caps in his ruling denying Fox's attempt to avert a trial to make clear the stolen election claims were false. "The evidence developed in this civil proceeding demonstrates that is **CRYSTAL** clear that none of the statements relating to Dominion about the 2020 election are true," Davis wrote.[5]

But even crystal clear lies won over a large segment of the US public in 2020. Will they do so again in 2024? And if they do, could they tip the election in favor of a US candidate more friendly not just to Russia but also to other dictators, and less friendly to the entire rules-based order at the center of today's great power competition? Where would US leadership go from there? This is the Trump wild card for 2024 and beyond.

Still, these questions for the US transcend a single candidate and a single election. Isolationism has growing appeal within both political parties. And China and Russia—ruled by leaders for life with no election timetables—have their own decision timelines and their own perceptions of the US's power and place in the world. In fact, one of the ties that bind Putin and Xi is a shared conviction that the US is in a state of perpetual decline, regardless of who leads it. The fault lines among the great powers are deeper and more lasting than Trump. And so, divining the paths away from conflict requires delving deeper into history.

CHAPTER TEN

PATHS TO PEACE

FROM *THE GUNS OF AUGUST* TO THE *TACTICAL NUKES OF 2024?*

The same year the Cuban Missile Crisis unfolded, in 1962, Barbara Tuchman released her chronicle of Europe's inexorable tumble into World War I, *The Guns of August*. President John F. Kennedy had read her book and, as the US and Russia sat on the brink of nuclear war, he was determined to learn from the mistakes of world leaders half a century before him—and to avoid repeating them.

According to Jonathan Glover in his book *Humanity: A Moral History of the Twentieth Century*, Kennedy spoke to his brother Robert F. Kennedy about what he described as the "stupidity, individual idiosyncrasies, misunderstandings, and personal complexes of inferiority and grandeur" of the German, Russian, Austrian, French, and British leaders of 1914.[1]

"I am not going to follow a course which will allow anyone to write a comparable book about this time, *The Missiles of October*," Kennedy said. "If anyone is around to write after this, they are going to understand that we made every effort to give our adversary room to move. I am not going to push the Russians an inch beyond what is necessary."[2]

Tuchman's book, as relevant today as at any other time, had deftly documented the entangling alliances, unpredictable personalities, miscommunications, and miscalculations that had helped propel the great powers of that era into the largest and bloodiest war the world had ever seen. Five decades later, Kennedy was loath to lead his own country into an even more devastating war with the Soviet Union in the nuclear age. Are there lessons for today's leaders to avert someone someday writing a book entitled, say, *The Tactical Nukes of 2024*?

During those thirteen harrowing days, Kennedy and Soviet leader Nikita Khrushchev only very narrowly navigated their nations away from a devastating great power war. Kennedy rejected the recommendation of his senior military leaders to invade or carry out a nuclear strike on Cuba. At the same time, he dispatched his brother Robert to open a secret back channel with the Soviet ambassador to Washington, Anatoly Dobrynin. That back channel helped lead to the compromise that ultimately defused the crisis: the USSR would remove its nuclear missiles from Cuba, and, in return, the US would remove its nuclear missiles from Turkey.

Along the way, however, the two nations endured military encounters that very nearly escalated into full-blown war. Eleven days into the crisis, on October 27, Major Rudolf Anderson's U-2 spy plane was shot down over Cuba, killing the pilot. In part to help avoid escalation, US leaders kept the incident secret until after the crisis was resolved. On the same day, US warships detected a Soviet submarine, the nuclear-armed B-59, off the coast of Cuba. In an attempt to force it to the surface to identify itself, the US ships dropped depth charges. Having been out of contact with home base for days, the sub's captain believed war between the US and USSR had already begun. He issued orders to fire a nuclear-armed torpedo at the US ships. The first nuclear attack since Hiroshima and Nagasaki was averted only because the submarine squadron commander, who was also on board the B-59, rejected the sub captain's order. Details of this near nuclear catastrophe came to light only many years later. Yet, in the end, it made clear that even with efforts to avert war up and down the US and Soviet lines, the world's two nuclear-armed superpowers nearly tumbled into one nonetheless.

"PLAYING WITHOUT A NET"

Today, the return of great power competition has generated a new architecture of relations among powers great and small, with many of the same forces that sparked war in 1914 and 1939, and very nearly did in 1962. There are new forces and fronts too. There are new territorial fronts, in places such as Ukraine, and emerging ones, in places such as Taiwan. There are new technological fronts from cyberspace to outer space to near space, as demonstrated by the Chinese balloon incident, and, increasingly, each front is impacted by artificial intelligence. There are expanding alliances such as NATO, new ones such as the AUKUS agreement, and less formal alliances and cooperative relationships among Russia, China, Iran, and North Korea, as well as among the US and its European and Asian allies. And there are the radiating impacts of the war in Ukraine, affecting readiness and tensions across the globe. All these new forces coalesce into a witches' brew of dangers.

As CIA Director Burns told me in his office at Langley in late 2023, nations are navigating this new and more uncertain world order without many of the guardrails that had been built up in the last Cold War expressly to reduce the risk of a moment like this. As he said, they are "playing without a net."

There are few treaties or even the outlines of treaties to govern the expanding conflict: no cyber arms control treaties and no broad agreement governing the weaponization of space. And there's a continuing erosion of some of the most crucial nuclear arms control treaties between the US and Russia, and no such arms control treaty as yet between the US and China. Crucial communication channels among the great powers have also closed or grown dormant. Today's return of great powers is a startling break from the relative peace and comfort of the post–Cold War period.

"Since the end of the Cold War until now, at least until a few years ago, we had this idea that things have really changed," NATO Secretary General Jens Stoltenberg lamented. "Now we are, I regret to say, back to more of a situation where we have been so many times before."

The prospect of a great power war is real, but senior officials I spoke with believe the great powers can still avoid it. For this chapter, much as I did for the final chapter of *The Shadow War*, I interviewed multiple current and former leaders around the world in order to crystallize a series of potential steps to adjust to this new conflict and reduce the risk of escalation.

What does a new structure look like? To be sure, this new world order requires the US and its allies to adjust economically and militarily for a new global competition—facing not one but two adversaries in Russia and China.

"I think there's a reckoning at the time of this international security crisis that—should there be other crises—we need to be better prepared," Canadian foreign minister Mélanie Joly told me. "And that's why we have to be clear in terms of our diplomatic stance, but also we have to be clear in terms of the resources that we are investing even more."

This time also requires finding ways to balance interests among the great powers to prevent the competition from escalating. World leaders on both sides of the great power divide are attempting to develop new strategies to pursue their national security interests without descending into war. Western officials agree neither China nor Russia want to go to war with the US. Each side appears to be aware that such a war—with all sides awash in not just nuclear warheads but whole new categories of cyber and space weapons, with complementary developments in artificial intelligence—would be devastating for the great powers, and the world.

LESSONS FROM THE CUBAN MISSILE CRISIS

Conscious of the perils of history themselves, current leaders have taken some early steps. From the beginning of the war in Ukraine, the US and NATO have communicated to Moscow that NATO will not be directly involved in the war. More broadly, they have at times declared some weapons systems, including fighter aircraft, as overly risky of provoking Russia—often to the chagrin of their Ukrainian allies and critics in the US and Europe who deride those limits as overly cautious.

During the nuclear scare in late 2022, as I detail in Chapter 7, the US and its allies opened back channels not just with Russia but also with nontraditional partners in China and India to help avert a nuclear crisis.

How, then, to create a broader framework to defuse the next crisis and prevent a drift into great power war? In his book *The Avoidable War,* former Australian prime minister Kevin Rudd outlined some of the "off ramps and guardrails" needed to navigate the new great power competition, particularly in the relationship between the US and China.

Rudd wrote:

Developing a new level of mutual strategic literacy, however, is only the beginning. What follows must be the hard work of constructing a joint strategic framework between Washington and Beijing that is capable of achieving the following three interrelated tasks:

1. Agreeing on principles and procedures for navigating each other's strategic redlines (for example, over Taiwan) that, if inadvertently crossed, would likely result in military escalation.
2. Mutually identifying the areas of nonlethal national security policy—foreign policy, economic policy, technology development (for example, over semiconductors)—and ideology where full-blown strategic competition is accepted as the new normal.
3. Defining those areas where continued strategic cooperation (for example, on climate change) is both recognized and encouraged.[3]

Senior officials around the world I interviewed for this book generally agree on this combination of communicating and respecting red lines, creating rules of the road for strategic competition, and searching for areas of cooperation as integral parts of the way forward. They concede that applying them to the many current and potential flashpoints of great power competition is, of course, the hard part.

A US DIPLOMAT'S VIEW

As America's top diplomat, Secretary of State Antony Blinken focuses today on finding diplomatic paths to de-escalate within the maelstrom of threats and competing interests among the great powers. And, as such, he is reluctant to characterize the return of great powers as inherently hostile.

"One thing I would resist is equations to the Cold War," Blinken told me. "I think while the great power competition is renewed, it's very different."

Blinken moves with an understated and unpretentious style unusual to Washington. He has decades of government service, beginning on the National Security Council in the Clinton White House before moving to the Senate Committee on Foreign Relations, as a senior advisor to then senator Joe Biden, and later becoming deputy national security advisor under President Obama. I first met Blinken in Pakistan in the early days of the US war in Afghanistan, when he was traveling for the Foreign Relations Committee with Senator Biden and Senator John Kerry. As we spoke in a room off the lobby of the Marriott Hotel in Islamabad, they made the case for economic support for Afghanistan in addition to US military forces. "The Taliban begins where the road ends," Biden said to me. Their point was that both military and economic support was necessary to undermine the Taliban and set the country on a path to stability. A few years earlier, Blinken and Biden had also supported the US invasion of Iraq. A consummate diplomat as secretary of state, Blinken was not then—and is not now—opposed to hard power when necessary to pursue and defend US interests. And the return of great powers pits the world's most powerful nations against one another, on a scale far exceeding the US's long wars in Iraq and Afghanistan.

"This is a renewed great power competition, with the added challenge of dealing in a place that we haven't had to before, with an incredibly complex net of interconnected global challenges," Secretary Blinken told me. "And those challenges are also connected to the great power competition. So that's what makes this, I think, a particularly complicated and consequential time."

The world is far different now. For one, he notes, the US and China are deeply interconnected and interdependent economically, a relationship that the US and the USSR never shared in the last Cold War. When I was chief of staff to US ambassador to China Gary Locke from 2011 to 2013, one statistic reliably made it into his speeches: that the US and China have hundreds of times the bilateral trade the US and USSR shared during the Cold War. And even as tensions between Beijing and Washington accelerated, trade continued to grow. According to the Commerce Department, bilateral trade between the US and China set a new record in 2022, totaling some $690 billion.[4]

"In the case of China, we're, of course, far more interconnected, as are countries around the world, with China than any of us were with Soviet Union," Blinken emphasized. "And that creates all sorts of complexities."

Those complexities present both risk and opportunity. Just as China-US trade has grown, so has China's economic might, giving Beijing military and diplomatic clout that Soviet leaders could have only dreamed of.

"That's a very different dynamic," Blinken said. "Two decades ago, China was, like, four percent of world GDP. Now it's close to twenty percent."

Russia, on the other hand, remains a one-export economy—a "gas station masquerading as a country," as the late senator John McCain used to say. Though with the world's largest nuclear arsenal and a conventional military, it has already shown itself ready to unleash to seize territory in Ukraine, Georgia, and beyond. As a result, Russia, though weaker economically, has so far proved more dangerous. Soviet ideology is no longer a driving force of Russian foreign policy.

Putinism, if it is an ideology at all, is simply about the exercise of pure power.

"Russia, the conflict now is not ideological. It's about power and it's about Russian imperial designs. So that's different," Blinken said.

Together, he sees both different trajectories and different end goals for Russia and China.

"[With Russia] you have a declining but extremely dangerous power that is breaking all the norms," said Blinken. "One of the differences between China and Russia is Russia arguably wants and is creating disorder to its advantage. China actually wants a world order, but it wants a profoundly illiberal one, whereas we continue to seek a liberal one. So that's where that challenge lies."

"We've seen this movie of great power competition again and again and again in history," said Admiral James Stavridis. "There's nothing new under the sun. And if we want to learn the lessons of history, we need to think coherently and avoid the massive consequences we saw at the end of World War I and World War II. We need to look at great power rises that did not end in great power war."

FIRST PRINCIPLES

Gleaning clear lessons from history is difficult when there is no shared view of history among the great powers, or even within them. The most consistent principle among western leaders I interviewed is that international rules and agreements—though not perfect—are at least a fundamental part of keeping the peace among the great powers. Chinese and Russian leaders of course reject that view. They see those rules and agreements as forever tilted against them.

Ambassador John Bolton is also a skeptic, though for a different reason. He argues that rules and agreements have never truly kept the peace. Only raw power holds sway. "The whole arms control approach to international affairs ultimately is self-delusional," Bolton told me. "What deters the Russians or the Chinese? Power. Not our treaty limits, but the power that we could bring to bear, which is why ultimately, even in the cyber age, the nuclear deterrent is still the most important thing."

To that point, his service in the Bush administration was dedicated to withdrawing the US from several key treaties, including the Anti-Ballistic Missile Treaty.

"Winston Churchill once said something like the only countries that adhere to their arms control agreements are the countries you don't need arms control agreements with," Bolton said. "And I don't think the disappearance of the arms control agreements has had any measurable negative effect on global stability."

Today's leaders of the US and its allies in the East and West tend to disagree vehemently. Among them is General Mark Milley. Though also a proponent of hard power, he argues that history proves that the systems and rules established after World War II did manage to keep the peace among the great powers through genuinely perilous times.

"This rule set is one of the fundamental contributing factors to preventing a great power war. It's not the only reason, but it's one of the fundamental reasons why there hasn't been a great power war in eight decades, in eighty years," Milley said. "So, if that rule set goes away . . . the world will return to Hobbesian nature, where it's going to be only the strong survive and it's going to be a dog-eat-dog world. And there won't be any rules."

In the recommendations outlined below, you'll see a combination, in effect, of those two positions: rules *plus* power. It is not unlike the combination the US and its allies have pursued since the end of World War II. And it's not a perfect prescription—that combination very nearly failed to prevent a great power war during the Cuban Missile Crisis. But the choice becomes between that option, tailored to new threats and players and technologies, or hard power alone— or, in some of his former advisors' predictions of a second Trump term, a broader US accommodation to authoritarian regimes in Russia, China, and North Korea and the abandonment of key allies and key areas of US influence in Asia and Europe?

These leaders believe the choice is clear: rules plus power. Because power alone pours gas on the fire, and as Estonian prime minister Kaja Kallas warned, accommodate the crocodile, and you become its next meal.

"WE CANNOT LOSE UKRAINE"

As a senior western official told me in the fall of 2023, the US and its allies agree on a simple proposition: "We cannot lose Ukraine." This is, in effect, a red line for the West and its allies. Western powers believe this not only for the sake of Ukraine's sovereignty but also for the survival of an international order. That is, if Russia can take Ukraine by force, China can take Taiwan, and every authoritarian state can grab whatever piece of land it desires. It's a domino theory for the twenty-first century, but one corroborated by recent history from Russia's partial invasion of Georgia in 2008 to its first invasion of Ukraine in 2014 to China's successful seizure and expansion of islands in the South China Sea. Russia and China have proved themselves willing to seize nations or parts of nations by force or intrigue and—many western officials believe—will do so again if left un-checked, threatening the relative peace that has endured among the great powers since the last world war. The lessons of 1939 loom large.

"That's why arming Ukraine is so important, because it shows that authoritarian regimes can't invade their neighbor and not feel the consequences of their actions," said Foreign Minister Joly. "And when it comes to China, we know that China is watching carefully what is happening in Ukraine, and the more we take a strong stance on the question of Ukraine, the more we are sending a message to Beijing as well."

For General Milley, it comes down to core values *and* core interests. That is, sovereignty is not just a noble idea but a practical one to keep the peace.

"[The Ukraine war] is a frontal assault on the rules. And rule one says that large, powerful countries cannot arbitrarily change the international boundaries of smaller, weaker countries through the use of military force," Milley said. "If understanding goes away, then your risk of great power war goes up exponentially. That's what's at stake in Ukraine."

"We need to work with as many countries of the world to make sure that this conflict doesn't grow in scope," Joly agreed. "That's what I think many of the European countries and American population have in mind. This cannot become an international conflict. That's why the work of diplomacy right now is so important."

Joly cited the meeting at Ramstein Air Base in Germany in April 2022, when defense ministers and senior military officials from some forty countries gathered to discuss support for Ukraine. The group encompassed not just NATO allies but also more than a dozen other countries from the Middle East, Africa, and Asia invested in supporting Ukraine and deterring Russian aggression.

"It is not NATO per se," Joly noted, but added that the group "has been extremely effective in cooperating to help support Ukraine."

The West is united in its defense of Ukraine but remains divided over how to define victory. The US and its allies tried to balance giving Ukraine enough to defend itself while avoiding escalating the war into a direct conflict between NATO and Russia. Some fear this may have prevented both a loss and a victory for Ukraine. And in Putin's cynical calculus—under which Russia's immense human losses and international isolation are tolerable—this outcome could amount to a qualified success.

As the two-year mark of the Russian invasion approached—and as Ukraine's counteroffensive stalled—NATO leaders began to describe a split among the allies on exactly how far Ukraine should push before pursuing peace.

"I see a very worrying trend," Estonian prime minister Kallas told me. "And the worrying trend is that the big ones—France, Germany, US—have agreed that we going to do this one final push, but then we are going to pressure Ukraine to say 'Draw the line here.'"

During his visit to Beijing in the summer of 2023, French president Emmanuel Macron spoke of an emerging peace plan, with China playing a key role. The effort worried some of his fellow western leaders.

"I've been talking to [Macron], also [German chancellor] Scholz in particular. They don't really see the threat if Russia wins here," Kallas said. "They hope that this will go away, and they don't really realize that it's here to stay. That's a new normal. And we have to actually prepare."

The US itself has fought two long wars this century that similarly lacked clear objectives. What was victory in Afghanistan? The end of Al Qaeda and the Taliban or just Al Qaeda? Dismantling a haven for terrorists or establishing a functioning modern state? Similarly, in

Iraq, was the goal a modern democratic state or weak one? On that point, twenty years after the invasion, who held more sway in Iraq: the US or Iran?

I covered both wars for years amid dozens of assignments and watched how the answers to each of those questions varied over time, until, ultimately, the US ceded Afghanistan back to the Taliban, and left Iraq in a hazy zone somewhere between functional and dysfunctional government and somewhere between a partner for the US or Iran. Where would the West ultimately lead Ukraine? It appeared that US and western leaders didn't know.

LAND FOR PEACE?

As the war dragged on, even some of Ukraine's staunchest defenders began to privately raise the prospect of land for peace—that is, Ukraine ceding some territory to Russia in exchange for security assurances from the West in order to end the war.

"You have to find the sweet spot by ensuring that Putin doesn't win in an illegal war of aggression. But at the same time, he's not provoked into escalating the war into a war with NATO or the United States," said General Milley.

In this view, as western officials described it to me, Ukraine was now fighting not for the liberation of all Russian-occupied territory but for a negotiating position.

"If that's your political objective, the withdrawal of all Russian forces, and if the Russian political objective is the collapse of the Zelensky government and the conquering of Ukraine, then I would say that it's unlikely, not zero, but unlikely that the Russians will achieve their political objective by military means. I don't see that happening. I don't see them overrunning Ukraine," said Milley. "And I also think it's unlikely that the Ukrainians will achieve their political end state this year. So then the question becomes when and at what cost? And then that leads you to alternative solutions."

So, what would an eventual deal look like? "You've got to give security guarantees to Ukraine that they're not going to be attacked by the Russians. That may involve building up the Ukrainian military so they can be self-sufficient and defend themselves. It may involve—maybe it's not NATO and maybe it's not joining NATO, but it's some other kind of security arrangement."

NATO allies attempted to articulate such an arrangement at the 2023 NATO summit in Vilnius. Many officials I spoke to began referring to "an Israeli-type of arrangement" that would lack a mutual defense commitment equivalent to NATO's Article 5 but still make clear the West would give Ukraine all it needs to defend itself. Foreign Minister Joly was central to these negotiations in Vilnius, where NATO partners sought to formulate a five-year plan to support Ukraine. The driving force, Joly said, was the conviction that "even when war ends, Russia will still be a very dangerous neighbor for Ukraine."

The Vilnius Summit Communiqué, issued at the meeting's conclusion, described the commitment this way: "We reaffirm our unwavering solidarity with the government and people of Ukraine in the heroic defence of their nation, their land, and our shared values," read the joint statement of NATO allies. "We fully support Ukraine's inherent right to self-defence as enshrined in Article 51 of the UN Charter. We remain steadfast in our commitment to further step up political and practical support to Ukraine as it continues to defend its independence, sovereignty, and territorial integrity within its internationally recognised borders, and will continue our support for as long as it takes. We welcome efforts of all Allies and partners engaged in providing support to Ukraine."

It continued, "The security of Ukraine is of great importance to

Allies and the Alliance. To support Ukraine's further integration with NATO, today we have agreed [to] a substantial package of expanded political and practical support."[5] That support meant long-term military assistance to help Ukraine defend itself and financial assistance to help it rebuild.

NATO allies once again expressed their support for Ukraine's eventual admission into the alliance: "We fully support Ukraine's right to choose its own security arrangements. Ukraine's future is in NATO. We reaffirm the commitment we made at the 2008 Summit in Bucharest that Ukraine will become a member of NATO."[6]

However, their declaration fell short of a clear pathway or timeline for Ukraine to join, which had been Zelensky's hope prior to the summit. Western leaders conceded it was the best they could manage while Ukraine remained at war with Russia.

"We believe in it," Joly insisted. "We are making sure Ukraine has the tools to get there."

"UKRAINE IS NOT GOING TO BE PART OF NATO"

Others are not so certain Ukraine's entry into NATO is truly possible. "In order to have a successful negotiation, you have to somehow address both sets of national security insecurities or anxieties. So you have to somehow convince the Russians that NATO is not going to invade, Ukraine is not going to be part of NATO, and that they shouldn't fear invasion from the West, that sort of thing," General Milley told me.

Convince the Russians that Ukraine is not going to be part of NATO? This proposition was notable from the man who was the nation's highest-ranking uniformed military officer and most senior military advisor to the president. The stated US position has consistently been that NATO has an "open door" policy and that Ukraine's path should be its own choice. Milley had said out loud what multiple western officials had been telling me quietly: that NATO membership for Ukraine may prove to be a step too far for the alliance.

"TODAY IS NOT THE DAY" FOR TAIWAN

There is broad agreement that Ukraine's fate is directly tied to Taiwan's. That is, how the world reacts to Russia's aggression in Europe will help determine whether China takes similar action in Asia.

"China is watching very closely," said General Milley. "They're watching closely to see if Putin succeeds or not. And if Putin walks away with something called a win, and he wins, then arguably that is a serious blow, if not the end of the rules-based order."

Estonian prime minister Kaja Kallas agrees. "China is definitely taking notes on how the world reacts to Russia in this case, because they all have their eyes on Taiwan," Kallas told me. "And they want to plan this better, is my estimate."

Secretary of State Blinken says that Taiwan and the world are watching the West's response closely as well. Ukraine and Taiwan together, they say, will set a precedent for territorial aggression in this new age of great powers.

"One of the reasons that so many countries in Asia have been speaking out forcefully and acting in concert with countries in Europe against the Russian aggression is precisely because they see the potential implications, depending on what happens in Ukraine, for Asia and, for that matter, other parts of the world," Blinken told me. "I think there's a strongly held view, among a number of countries, that if Putin's allowed to get away with this aggression with impunity, it potentially opens a Pandora's box where other would-be aggressors say, 'Well, if Russia can do it and get away with it, so can we.' And, of course, one of the countries of concern would be China when it comes to Taiwan."

For Taiwan's defenders, the key to holding the line is to gradually build up deterrence over time. "You want to make sure that every single day, President Xi wakes up and says, 'Today is not that day,' and that that decision never comes," General Milley told the National Press Club in June 2023.[7]

That phrase—"Today is not the day"—encapsulates the US strategy for deterring a Chinese invasion. In other words, the US, Taiwan, and their allies cannot eliminate the possibility Xi orders an invasion. But they can add to his doubts each and every day and—so they hope—push out his timeline for an invasion indefinitely.

For some western officials, this means avoiding a repeat of the mixed signals sent by the West before Russia's full-scale invasion of Ukraine in 2022. Taiwan's allies must, they say, "go big and go early."

"It's a close call, and I don't want us to take the risk of making it a close call," former deputy national security advisor Matthew Pottinger said. "I think that we should provide an overwhelmingly clear deterrent to influence Xi Jinping's calculus, unmistakably, that war is not going to serve his interests."

Since there is no Ukraine option for Taiwan—that is, no ability to arm and supply the island *after* a Chinese invasion—Taiwan's allies must arm it sufficiently in advance and with the right kind of weaponry. Taiwan for years focused on large weapons systems more suited to power projection than the island's defense. Many western officials, and their Taiwanese counterparts, increasingly agree that the focus now must be on asymmetrical warfare.

"Taiwan will never compete one-on-one with the People's Liberation Army," Democratic congressman Ro Khanna (CA) said after returning from a March 2023 congressional visit to the island. "So, to defend itself, it will need to invest more in asymmetric weapons to deter China from invading. We've seen this strategy work successfully in Ukraine thus far, where the smaller military used asymmetric weapons like drones and stinger missiles against a larger and more conventional Russian force. To do this in Taiwan though, America must fast-track providing the $18 billion of Harpoons, Stingers, Javelins, and HIMARS requested of us."

This new focus is already transforming US weapons sales to Taiwan and Taiwan's indigenous defense planning. Taiwan is now arming itself for a "porcupine"-style defense, with a focus on smaller weapons systems and highly mobile fighting units. In early 2023, as Taiwan unveiled several new surveillance and attack drones, a Taiwanese official told my CNN colleague Eric Cheung and other reporters, "In response to the new global war trends, our military has been actively building asymmetric warfare capabilities." "Asymmetry" is now built into both the strategy and language of Taiwan's defense.

There are other developing aspects of Taiwan's defense. The US has deployed a small number of troops to Taiwan in recent years— just twenty to forty, according to US Defense Department data— mostly to provide security for US diplomatic staff stationed there but also to train Taiwanese defense forces. In February 2023, CNN learned that the US planned to markedly increase the size of the deployment. *The Wall Street Journal* reported the number would grow to between one hundred and two hundred.

A senior US military official told me at the time: "Our support for, and defense relationship with, Taiwan remains aligned against the current threat posed by the People's Republic of China. Our commitment to Taiwan is rock-solid and contributes to the maintenance of peace and stability across the Taiwan Strait and within the region."

END OF STRATEGIC AMBIGUITY

The biggest change in planning for Taiwan's defense, however, has come straight from the US president. For decades, the US maintained a policy of so-called strategic ambiguity when it came to its defense commitment to Taiwan. In the simplest terms, the US would not confirm or deny that it would come to the island's defense in the event of a Chinese invasion. China would, in effect, have to guess just how far the US would go, injecting further uncertainty into its calculus.

President Biden, however, turned that policy on its head when he stated explicitly that the US would come to Taiwan's defense in the event of a Chinese invasion.

Matthew Pottinger believes the change is real and deliberate. "I think that President Biden has been unambiguous about his intentions," he said. "If China decides to attack Taiwan, and I've read his comments carefully—he said it four times, very deliberately—he's drawn a red line, and I think that no future president should retreat from that red line.

"If your question is, Is he bluffing or not? I doubt it," he added.

General Milley, the highest-ranking uniformed military commander for most of Biden's term, does not believe Biden is bluffing either.

"It's not my place to opine on presidential declarations or quotes or that kind of thing," Milley said. "But I would just tell you that, going back to declaratory policy of national leaders from whatever country they are, president of the United States or any other country, when a national leader says 'I will do A, B, or C,' it's worthwhile believing them. That's my read of history."

"Typically speaking, these guys do not bluff," Milley continued. "And they say what they mean, typically speaking, and they mean what they say."

Taiwanese leaders aren't so certain. As I discussed earlier, they remain perplexed about what US defense policy is and how lasting. Is Biden's apparent promise to defend Taiwan now formal US policy? If so, will it survive the 2024 US presidential election? Moreover, will Taiwan's policy toward China survive its own presidential election in early 2024?

These are open questions—with as much uncertainty as the questions hanging over Ukraine. The ideal outcome is not to fight and win a war over Taiwan but to deter one. Here, the US and its allies are trying to learn from recent history by setting and communicating red lines—and engaging multiple nations to do so.

"That's . . . just one example of demonstrating to Xi that any kind of military action that risks creating a real crisis on or adjacent to Taiwan would implicate the interest of virtually every country on earth, and making sure that he hears that from them," Blinken continued. "Working with other countries to try to understand and advance what the economic, political, reputational costs would be for China if it actually took military action on Taiwan and communicating that—all of that has been, in a sense, reinforced by what's going on in Ukraine."

"Virtually every country on earth" invested in deterring China—that is the message the US and its allies hope to send Beijing about Taiwan.

EUROPE UNTOUCHABLE

This is the same lesson NATO is trying to put into action regarding its eastern-facing allies. Are they now under threat from Russia? Ask US officials and they tend to say no: Russia fears NATO too much. Ask eastern European officials and they say yes: Putin's Russia rejects not only Ukraine's sovereignty but that of the Baltics and other former Soviet Republics; given the opportunity, Putin will attack.

US military and intelligence officials at the highest levels tell me they take care to listen to Baltic leaders. And what they hear is that NATO must not forget Russia has already proved it is capable of aggression.

"In dictatorships . . . you only care about your power, the cronies around you keeping you in power," Prime Minister Kallas told me. "You care about the army and the police and the power structures being happy, because they keep you in power. And all else, you don't care."

Eastern Europe's viewpoint is gaining purchase with the addition of two new nations to the alliance in Finland and—soon, NATO hoped—Sweden. As Kallas told me, "The center of gravity in NATO is moving towards [the] North."

Even leaders of western-facing NATO allies grant that Russia may attempt to attack a NATO ally in a manner short of a full-scale invasion. Russia's crippling cyberattack on Estonia in 2007 is one example. Without sending a single tank across the border, Moscow successfully shut down the country, which by then was already a ratified member of the alliance. As CIA Director Burns noted to me, there are many options for Russia short of all-out war.

Regardless of their view of the degree of the threat from Russia, the alliance is in agreement that it must bolster its defenses to match the new great power alignment in Europe—and to ensure that Russia never even considers an attack on an alliance member. Moreover, they see NATO membership itself as, perhaps, the most formidable defense.

"Gray zones create conflict," Kallas said. "Why don't we have war here? It's because we are in NATO, not in a gray zone, but in NATO."

That, for now, remains a path open only to European partners such as Finland and Sweden—that is, partners not currently at war with Russia. Still, Kallas and others argue that NATO is the best path forward for countries including Ukraine, speaking from Estonia's shared experience as a former Soviet republic. "When we got our independence back, then the first thing [we said] was that we are never going to be alone again," Kallas told me. "We have experience from our history."

For some in Europe, "never alone again" is simply smart strategy for the return of great powers.

REVIVE NUCLEAR ENGAGEMENT

The nuclear scare of late 2022 reaffirmed to the US and its allies that nuclear engagement is another necessary response to the return of great power conflict. Russian nuclear threats against Ukraine, the dissolution and weakening of existing nuclear treaties between the US and Russia, and the lack of any such treaties between the US and China have led to a new urgency among western leaders to engage with both Russia and China on nuclear weapons.

"You cannot give up the efforts of trying to have some kind of arms control," NATO Secretary General Stoltenberg told me. "Arms control is important because it reduces the number of weapons, but also because it provides transparency. Verification control arrangements are extremely important to increase predictability, to reduce risk of miscalculations and misunderstanding."

"On the question of nuclear threats, we need to engage," Canadian foreign minister Joly told me. "The START Treaty is extremely important between the US and Russia. We need to be able to make sure that there are security exercises to protect this treaty, which is about nuclear surveillance and nuclear treaty enforcement."

THE PROBLEM OF THREE

Today, all three great powers are nuclear powers. Russia and the US remain the two largest by far in terms of number of warheads. Of the world's 12,500 nuclear warheads, as tabulated by the Arms Control Association, the US (with some 5,244) and Russia (with 5,889) possess close to 90 percent. China is a distant third, with just over 400 warheads.[8] However, China is rapidly expanding its arsenal, having doubled its supply of warheads in just two years. Moreover, the Pentagon's *Military and Security Developments Involving the People's Republic of China 2022* estimated that China, at its current pace, would triple its supply of warheads to 1,500 by 2035.[9]

A world with three nuclear-armed great powers requires nuclear engagement among all three. The hopeful view, despite the lack of meaningful dialogue today, is that such engagement is in the interests of all three great powers. For one, nuclear weapons are expensive to manufacture and maintain and the US, Russia, and China are experiencing economic challenges that would seem to incentivize placing mutual limits. Most pressing, however, is that expanding arsenals means expanding risks.

"With more and more nuclear weapons, the risk increases. That was the rationale for the Soviet Union and United States to agree to arms control agreements during the Cold War," said NATO's Stoltenberg. "So it is a rationale for countries, for big powers with nuclear weapons, to also engage in some kind of arms control arrangements. The question is when, and how many, and how much resources would've been spent before we were able to come into a situation where that's possible again."

Unfortunately, the growth of the nuclear threat has occurred as nuclear treaties have dissolved and negotiations have stalled. I asked each official I spoke with if there were any substantive nuclear negotiations among the great powers now underway, and the answer was consistently no.

"Currently, as we speak, there's no meaningful dialogue between NATO and Russia," Stoltenberg told me. "And we are disappointed by Russia's decision to violate and to suspend these treaties."

NATO and China do have a political dialogue, which involves nuclear disarmament, but there are no formal talks among the US and its allies and Beijing on nuclear arms control.

"The big difference is that soon China will have as many strategic long-range weapons as Russia and the United States," said Stoltenberg. "It's difficult to make an agreement with one country, as a United States and the Soviet Union, it's, of course, even more demanding to have three or more countries involved in arms control arrangements."

Canadian foreign minister Joly sees some hope, however, in the collective effort among the US, China, and India to caution Russia away from using a tactical nuclear weapon in Ukraine.

"I think we're being tested right now, and we can step up to the plate," Joly argued. "We were able, the collective West, to at least get from China an agreement that nuclear threat could not be used in the context of the Russia-Ukraine war. So that was a small step in the right direction."

MIDDLE POWERS WANT IN

Beyond the great powers' nuclear arsenals, the US is watching the nuclear aspirations of middle powers such as Iran, Saudi Arabia, and Turkey very closely. As a senior US official told me, "If one country breaks out, like the Iranians, then you're going to reach a nuclear arms race because the Saudis and the Egyptians and the Turks are all going to want to follow suit too. So I don't think it's inevitable that you have that kind of significant proliferation. But it's a real threat."

Further proliferation has reignited discussion of the Treaty on the Non-Proliferation of Nuclear Weapons, commonly known as the Non-Proliferation Treaty, or NPT, an agreement that had taken on a nostalgic quality among some western leaders as more and more non-nuclear powers observed the weakening of the old world order and decided they may need in to the world's nuclear club.

"I think that the question of the nonproliferation treaty cannot be seen as something that is out of fashion, that [it] is much more an issue between the right and the left of the sixties, seventies, eighties, or during the Cold War," Joly said. "Now more than ever it has again become important."

The rationale for nuclear engagement is there, and the rapidly changing reality in this space has made it urgent. Now, leaders tell me, the great powers must put words into action.

TREATIES FOR SPACE, CYBER, AND AI

Nuclear weapons are not the only dangerous front of the new great power competition. All the great and middle powers are increasingly developing their military strategies on weapons in cyberspace, outer space, and near space. And yet no treaties or even discussions about treaties govern these realms. In the midst of this dangerous, rapid technological advancement is another technology with power to influence the wars of the present and future: artificial intelligence. Without international agreement among the great powers on these new technologies—guardrails that would place some limits on their use in emerging conflicts—the world is a fundamentally more dangerous place.

Yet, this issue—while a subject of broad agreement among the US and its allies—lies once again on the dividing line of the great powers. The West may want to talk, but it's not clear its adversaries do.

"I was chairing the first-ever UN Security Council meeting on cybersecurity when we were members of the Security Council two years ago," Estonian prime minister Kallas told me. "And what was interesting about this was that everybody agreed, except for China and Russia, that international rules should also apply in cyberspace. They were against this."

The adversaries in this new and expanding front extend beyond the great and middle powers. These fields of battle are a digital "wild west," composed of state and non-state actors—with non-state actors sometimes working for states and sometimes for themselves. Determining who is doing what and when and for whom—the perennial challenge of what intelligence officials call "attribution"—creates more questions for negotiators.

"You get domains, like space and cyber, which are in many ways infinitely more complicated than nuclear negotiations because governments don't have a monopoly, especially on cyber," said CIA Director Burns. "We have all sorts of non-state players on that. . . . What you can do, and what's smart to try to do, is develop not so much formal treaties but rules of the road. That at least can begin to put some limits or some sensible construct around some of those issues."

So how do the great powers develop such limits? Are there agreements short of formal treaties to, at least, place some limits on some kinds of attacks?

"To some extent . . . it's transparency," said Burns. "It's the kind of confidence-building measures that come from kind of being transparent with one another about what you're developing. It's trying to identify a few things that are off-limits."

Some western officials see the UN Charter as a potential path for negotiations on guardrails on cyber and space weapons. The key, says Kallas, is harnessing the charter to establish hard penalties for attacks outside the lines of any general agreement.

"At the end of the Second World War, the UN was designed for peace in the world," said Kallas. "And the UN Charter is not a bad thing, actually. That has all the elements. We have to agree that it also applies to cyberspace. But the problem with it is that when you have a charter that says that it's not legal to attack another country, there has to be a response if somebody does."

Admiral James Stavridis suggested the UN Convention on the Law of the Sea as a guide. In the simplest terms, the convention establishes basic principles of sovereignty and good behavior for nations to help preserve both freedom of shipping and the preservation of sea life. Could similar basic principles apply to cyberspace?

"Seventy percent of the world is governed by the Law of the Sea treaty," said Stavridis. "It took fifteen years and twenty thousand negotiators. The US still foolishly hasn't signed it, but the US adheres to it. Look to the Law of the Sea treaty and find a zone where we could at least begin negotiations. You need to start small, but you need to start."

As they do with nuclear weapons, the great powers need to be talking—fears of "mutually assured destruction" can certainly extend to the cyber, space, and AI realms—but they are still searching for the outlines and forums to do so. One major challenge is that Russia and China see some of these guardrails as standing in the way of achieving one of their principal goals: undermining the West. The western hope is that a shared interest in avoiding the worst outcomes will drive momentum for new negotiations and new rules.

GREAT POWER COOPERATION

Do the great powers disagree on absolutely everything? No. The potential areas of engagement and cooperation are limited, but they do encompass some of the biggest challenges for the world today.

"You've got other issues—climate, pandemics, food security—which can be a tool of great power competition. But they are also issues where, no matter how intense that competition, none of us can solve let alone manage them on our own," said CIA Director Burns. "So it requires a certain amount of cooperation amidst the intensifying competition too."

The hope is that a shared appreciation of the shared danger of these threats can—at times and on some issues—overcome the dividing lines of great power competition. Cooperation on climate is the most obvious.

"The rivalry can get in the way of cooperation on what are genuinely existential threats like climate," Burns continued. "However intense the competition, how do you manage it so that it doesn't come at the expense of the cooperation that's absolutely essential in an issue like climate?"

Seeking cooperation on issues such as climate does not require relenting on other red lines, including the West's opposition to territorial acquisition by force. Officials believe the great powers can balance areas of necessary agreement and sharp disagreement. It's not either/or, but disagreements and agreements simultaneously.

"We will communicate that we will confront you where we must. We will confront you on the South China Sea. We're not going to concede it because a Chinese admiral sailed through it hundreds of years ago," said Admiral Stavridis, citing one of those areas of forceful territorial acquisition, the South China Sea. "But on climate, if we can't work alongside China, we are doomed to fail."

DON'T FORGET THE GLOBAL SOUTH

The Global South—that giant portion of the globe outside the immediate backyards of the great powers—has both the makings of a new "great game" among the great powers as well as, to some, an area of potential cooperation.

Secretary Blinken and I spoke after he had just returned from the 2023 G20 meeting of foreign ministries, where—even in the depths of the Ukraine war—the topic of economic development in the Global South dominated.

"While we spent some time talking about the Russian aggression against Ukraine, the bulk of what I focused on were the challenges people around the world are facing in their daily lives, that are particularly concerned in the Global South," Blinken told me.

US investments in military assistance to Ukraine may monopolize American headlines here, but, purely measured in dollars, US overseas spending on other international challenges is equal or greater.

"The United States is, by far, the number one contributor to building food security around the world," Blinken said. "We provide over fifty percent of the World Food Programme's budget. We're making major investments, particularly in African countries, to help to not only deal with the immediate crisis, but to build long-term productive capacity in their countries. And I can say the same thing when it comes to climate, when it comes to global health and preventing the next pandemic, et cetera. And these things are mutually reinforcing."

Those investments by the US and its military presence in the region—measured against China's and Russia's increasing economic and military involvement in the Global South—can devolve into a new field of great power competition, or an area where the powers at times work together with a mutual goal in mind.

A promising and frightening case study is the on-again, off-again grain deal to ensure grain exports from Ukraine. Putin's attacks on grain shipments, first in the Black Sea and then on alternative means of export by river, threatened to starve parts of the Global South, with enormous effects on the international food supply and food prices. The eventual agreements to maintain those exports provided some measure of hope.

"VARIABLE GEOMETRY"

Secretary Blinken calls the approach of embracing different partners at different times and with different, often limited goals in mind a "variable geometry" approach to international relations—that is, pursuing tailor-made alliances with different partners for different issues.

"Not every country, not every institution, necessarily has the means or the interest in acting on some of these fronts," Blinken explained. "And so, it makes sense to, as necessary, build coalitions and partnerships of countries that are particularly focused on one aspect or another. And that's exactly what we've done."

These partnerships, he believes, can include not just nations but also private-sector interests and other global organizations. "Creating new partnerships, new arrangements in countries, and beyond countries sometimes, private sector and others, other key stakeholders, is to make sure that we're fit for purpose across the multiplicity of issues that are out there and that are part of the competition," Blinken said.

"I think when some of the dust clears on this period, in the next decade or so, you're actually going to see a new architecture of international relations," he said. "I equate it to variable geometry. It's different coalitions, partnerships of countries, that are focused on individual aspects of the challenges that we're facing."

These areas of cooperation or potential cooperation currently are limited. I asked Admiral Stavridis if the great powers are opening these pathways to cooperation.

"No. Not at all," he said. "Right now, we are at about twenty percent cooperation, eighty percent disagreement with China. But you can try to dial it. You can start small."

GREAT POWER STRATEGY BEGINS AT HOME

Russia's and China's expanding great power ambitions are driven in part by a shared perception of US and western decline. As discussed in Chapter 2, Putin and Xi, even as they face their own severe weaknesses at home, perceive growing weakness in the US and its allies. Moreover, both Beijing and Moscow attempt to worsen those weaknesses by fueling political division in the US and the West and taking advantage of the West's economic dependencies.

ECONOMIC LEVERAGE

Europe took the biggest step to reduce such leverage by, in the remarkable span of a year, nearly ending its dependence on Russian oil and natural gas. US consumers endured periodic increases in gas prices as the economic cost of the Ukraine war, but Europe had to find entirely new energy suppliers within the span of months—and largely succeeded in doing so. Russia did find other buyers for its fossil fuels, including among western allies such as Turkey and Saudi

Arabia, reducing the damage to its economy and adding income to finance its ongoing war in Ukraine. But it could no longer pressure the West by turning off the heat in Europe.

If energy was the great powers' economic pressure point for Europe, microchips could prove similar for Asia and the world. With Taiwan manufacturing more than 80 percent of the world's advanced microchips, a Chinese invasion or blockade could bring the world economy to its knees. American investments such as the bipartisan CHIPS Act, and other agreements with allies, laid the groundwork for diversifying microchip production beyond Taiwan. The difference is that, while it took months for Europe to wean itself from Russian fossil fuels, it will take years for the world to spread production beyond Taiwan in significant ways.

More broadly, many western leaders emphasize that investments at home are essential to projecting power abroad. "One is the investments we're making in ourselves to maximize our own competitiveness across every area of the competition," Secretary Blinken said, "speaking very loudly and clearly to friend and foe alike, and this is what I hear around the world, and making us more fit for purpose of dealing with the competition."

"DOMESTIC COHESION"

Steps such as boosting chip manufacturing are largely questions of economic policy, which enjoy broad agreement among the political parties. The overall US approach to a new era of great power competition, however, is a foreign policy issue that divides the nation. Our allies are watching this domestic split with trepidation, conscious that each new presidential election could bring an entirely different US approach to the world.

"The difference is that domestic politics has become so closely linked with foreign policy," a senior western diplomat told me. "That wasn't the case in the past. So now, the domestic mood really shifts the foreign policy."

There are isolationist wings in both the Democratic and Republican parties. And it was, after all, Democratic presidents who withdrew US forces from Iraq in 2011 and Afghanistan in 2021, even if the America First movement occupies the right wing of the GOP. With each election, though, the US is experiencing a more dramatic pendulum swing on a question America has long debated: globalist or isolationist? America First, or America as a global leader against China and Russia?

"We have the resources. Russia's economy is the size of Spain or something like that," said the senior Western diplomat. "So, I mean, the idea that we can't do this is completely false, but the problem is also economically and physically we have that capability. But then, do we have it politically? It's going to be a different game. But am I concerned? Yes."

But outside the right and left US fringes, there might be a quieter but vast middle. General Milley is a lifelong conservative. But he is disturbed by the Republican Party's shift away from supporting a robust US role in international affairs.

"They'll say, well, that's globalism, that's globalist. There's global baloney and all this other kind of stuff. And they mock that system," Milley said. "Be careful about that, because in so many ways, that's how World War II ended, and that's what we fought for, was a stable international environment where aggression, military aggression, naked aggression, like what happened with Hitler in the 1930s and stuff, is not permitted. That's one of the fundamental rules."

Milley and others I spoke to for this book believe this deep split on the US role in the world weakens the US in the view of its great power competitors Russia and China. Challenging those great powers, Milley argues, is dependent not just on military power and economic strength but on domestic unity.

"We must maintain a degree of domestic cohesion," Milley said. "If you have those three things in combination and the Chinese perceive that you have those things in combination, then the probability is reduced significantly that you'll have any sort of external aggression that could lead to great power war. Then the opposite is true, to the degree that if you don't have those things, your probability of great power war increases. That's my theory of the case."

Today, those fringes are pulling at the thread of domestic cohesion and, arguably, fraying it further.

REJECT 1939 RULES

Those who rationalize as realpolitik the Russian invasion of Ukraine, or a potential Chinese takeover of Taiwan, risk rationalizing the next invasion. As Estonia's Kallas said, evoking Churchill, the hungry crocodile eventually comes for you. For the many officials around the world I interviewed for this book, the simplest lesson—as relevant today as it was in 1939—is that acts of territorial aggression by the great powers cannot succeed without then incentivizing the next acts of aggression.

"We have to totally discredit the tool, policy tool, of aggression," said Kallas. "You can't walk away with more than you had before. Otherwise, it's incitement to aggression."

The essential challenge for powers who reject brute force as the sole deciding factor in conflicts of national interests is not just to communicate that to the world but also to disincentivize aggression—with as diverse a collection of states as possible. The goal is to make the costs exceed the benefits. This was the theory, at least, behind the UN post–World War II. Is there a modern replacement or replacements?

GLOBAL OVER REGIONAL

Given the new great power conflict is global, the US and its allies in the East and West express the need for building new partnerships globally.

"And when we're doing that," Blinken told me, "we really maximize the effectiveness and shape the environment in which Russia or China is acting, in much more powerful ways. And what I've seen over the last two years is much greater alignment among us, Europeans, Asians."

This extends to countries that great powers might have seen as regional players but whose security interests are global. Canadian leaders, for instance, believe they must make Canada a greater player in Asia.

"We need to play a bigger role as a country in the Indo-Pacific. We need to partner even more with countries such as Japan, South Korea, and the US," Joly told me. "When you look at the globe in a different way, looking from the North Pole down, well, our neighbors are Russia and China, and we have a gateway to the Arctic to the East that is protected through NATO, and we have to do more on the western side as the Northern Pacific, which is our neighborhood as the gateway to the Arctic. And China is positioning itself as a near Arctic state."

MILITARY AND NONMILITARY

Relationships across powers of all sizes include both defense and nondefense partnerships—bridging parts of the world that, until now, had rarely seen their national security interests converge. One notable example is the AUKUS defense treaty linking the US, UK, and Australia, intended to challenge Chinese military expansion in Asia.

Such a group of nations can use multiple tools to deter further aggression, not all of them involving military might or formal defensive alliances. Economic sanctions in particular have become a central tool of US foreign policy.

"When it comes to China, the alignment with Europe is much greater than it's been. And while there are some differences, when you look at what's been done over the last couple years, on everything from aligning on investment screening mechanisms, on export controls, on outward-bound investment restrictions, on supply chain diversification and resilience, on dealing with unfair economic practices that China's engaged in, we have greater conversions now than ever," said Secretary Blinken. "And the way that Europeans are expressing the challenge posed by China, it's very coincident with the way we see it. And similarly with key partners in Asia, we're seeing the same thing. So those two things together allow us to create a different kind of environment in which Xi Jinping or anyone else has to make their decisions."

At the root of this approach is, again, the conviction that certain rules are immutable. Great powers cannot change borders by force. Nations have sovereignty and the right to self-determination.

"Basically, what is the fight about?" Prime Minister Kallas asked. "What Russia is worried about is democracy expanding and not territory. They are not afraid that we are actually going to attack them or like, 'Oh, we need buffer zones.' No. They need buffer zones from democracy, really. That's what they are afraid of."

The key complication is that this commitment to rules is not monolithic. Today's world is as rich in accommodationists as the world of the late 1930s.

"You've got a very vocal group that wants to ignore even containment and just engage China and really try to accommodate Beijing and its goals," said Matthew Pottinger. "It's 'Let's go back to the old engagement policy,' which really means 'Let's lie down and let China run the world. We're tired, and we're not worthy morally. As Americans, we're not a worthy society. Maybe it's Beijing's turn with the totalitarian communist vision.' I mean, it's just ridiculous. All these debates that people were having in the Cold War are back en vogue."

The historically volatile combination of a rising power in China and a status quo power in the US makes the next several years particularly uncertain. "I would argue that over the next ten to fifteen years, you're going to have a window of risk that will increase in the years ahead," warned General Milley.

CONSTRAINMENT OVER CONTAINMENT

These principles do not damn the great powers to war. Like Kennedy attempting to learn from World War I as another war loomed with Russia over Cuba, the great powers need a new approach to a new and more complicated world. And what worked in the last Cold War may not work in today's new great power conflict. Or, at least, while some of it may work, newer tactics may need to be applied as well.

"I'm not sure 'containment' is the word I would use," said Pottinger. "What we need is a successor to that strategy. I call it 'constrainment' rather than 'containment,' because 'constrainment' takes into account the interwoven nature of China's economy with the rest of the world. In the case of Vladimir Putin, it's plain old containment, I think, but for China, it's something a little bit different that I would call 'constrainment.'"

Many European leaders see signs of hope in their own intertwined history.

"It is possible to overcome old antagonist relationships, as we have seen in Europe. In the Nordic countries, the Swedes and the Danes and the Norwegians, we used to be at war with each other for centuries, and now we are the best friends," said Stoltenberg. "In continental Europe, you had France, Germany, United Kingdom, fighting each other for centuries and in the last century, two world wars, and now they are the best friends. So, it is possible to overcome these kinds of historical disagreements or conflicts."

"This is an ancient conversation," said Admiral Stavridis. "The question is, Do we use the modern tools we have to avoid conflict?"

And perhaps the fact that there is debate—over paths forward, over lessons to learn from, over increasing communication even as great powers communication slows—itself gives hope. Hope is a consistent refrain among leaders I met while researching this book—from the front lines of Ukraine to the defensive lines of Taiwan, from expanded NATO patrols in the Baltic Sea to planning rooms of the Pentagon, from leaders who have escaped Russian and Chinese domination to those still seeking to rid themselves of it.

"I'm not a hopeless person," said CIA Director Bill Burns. "I think you could revive that hope."

To Burns's point, the great powers do not want great power war. And no one I spoke to for this book believes that other great power leaders are truly irrational actors. But the powers are pushing the limits and sometimes crossing them. And the path to avoiding wider conflict lies at the intersection of clear principles, power, and cooperation.

The goal, as Kennedy described it in the most perilous moments of 1962, is to avoid the prospect of a modern *Guns of August*—when the great powers descend into war not because they chose to do so, but because they could not resist the momentum toward great power conflict.

THE LONG WAR

The Pentagon

Nearly two years after I got that first, early call from a senior military source about Russia's looming invasion of Ukraine, I sat down with the same official to find out where he and his colleagues saw the war going now. Since the war began, I'd regularly encountered both cheerleaders and doomsayers for the Ukrainian war effort among officials, diplomats, and lawmakers directly involved in the West's response. They were reading the same intelligence assessments and speaking to the same commanders on the ground but still often came away with vastly different appraisals of the direction of the war. This official fell into neither category, most often delivering a sober, unemotional view of where the war stood.

Now he saw a mixed picture. Ukraine, of course, had already outperformed initial expectations, largely repelling an invasion by one of the largest militaries in the world and effectively fighting to a draw in the east. However, he had managed expectations for Ukraine's counteroffensive. "Ukraine can make small gains, but the fighting season is ending soon," this official said.

Yet, he was also seeing a concerning shift among the leaders of Ukraine's allies in the West. Secretary of State Blinken was visiting

Kyiv at the time, and he surmised that part of Blinken's message to Ukrainian leaders was that western military support could no longer continue at the same level in the months ahead. "There's just not enough money or political capital to last," he said. White House officials acknowledged as much to me when I pressed them. "There is talk about the budget of course," one official told me. "How could there not be?"

But my source was concerned about something more impactful than a budget discussion: that the West was now raising pressure on Ukraine to find a way to settle with Russia, including the radioactive topic of exchanging land for peace.

"I can't help but assume that part of the message to Ukraine on this trip is to begin to think about how to end the war," he said.

What lesson would the Kremlin take away if its invasion netted at least some territorial gains? Similarly, what would the message be to China regarding Taiwan?

Helsinki, Finland

Nearly two years into the war in Ukraine and two years after we had first discussed the gathering storm over Europe and the world, I sat down again with Finnish ambassador Mikko Hautala.

Then, as Russian forces prepared to invade, Hautala believed that Putin had decided 'I will see where I can get.'"

Now, even though bloodied and embarrassed by a much smaller Ukrainian force, Putin, in his view, was not at all deterred.

"He will not give up," Hautala said. "I am personally completely convinced that he's going to try to outlast everyone."

Hautala is an experienced diplomat who has met the key players— from Putin to Trump to Zelensky—in person, asked them questions, and listened to their answers while looking in their eyes. He and other Finnish leaders had correctly read Putin's intentions before the war. As we sipped coffee at the Finnish embassy—a fittingly sharp and modern cube nestled in a protective blanket of trees just across from the Naval Observatory in Washington, DC—he delivered another sobering assessment of the Russian leader's outlook and way forward.

"Obviously, by now he has concluded that it was more difficult than he expected," he continued. "There's been a lot of surprises in that sense. But I don't see for a minute that he would have somehow modified the original aims he had. So he bets to outlast us."

Finland was now a fully ratified member of NATO, an outcome that seemed far-fetched just a few years ago. Putin had grown, not shrunk, the alliance. And he had succeeded at something consecutive US presidents, including Donald Trump, had failed at: almost universally boosting the defense expenditures of NATO allies. Russia had isolated itself economically and diplomatically from Europe and severed the few remaining ties it had with its European neighbors, chief among them Finland.

However, as Hautala noted, Russia had not collapsed. Its economy, spurred in part by defense spending and manufacturing, chugged along. Hautala compared the Russian nation to an elderly patient who is ill but alive.

"In a way, it's like an old person who is still in relatively good health but is increasingly fragile," he explained. "They can keep breathing. I mean, the basic functions of your body are okay, your heart is pumping, your functions are okay. So it's not that you are going to win the 'World Championship in Economics marathon,' but you can still function, you can go on."

Russia "can go on." As Ukraine's 2023 offensive stalled, Hautala said he believed the war was likely to go on as well.

"As we see it now, Russia seems to have the capabilities to go on like this well beyond, I would say, 2024," he said, concluding, "I don't expect the war to end this year, I don't expect it to end next year."

Hautala's view was not uncommon. Ukraine's counteroffensive showed that Russia—while not capable of suffocating Ukraine—could at least, like that sick patient, survive and attempt to wait out Ukraine and its allies. His concern for the broader alliance was more worrisome.

"We can outlast everyone," he said of NATO, "*if* we have the political will." Hautala, like many western diplomats and officials I spoke to, was closely watching the upcoming US presidential election, conscious of the potential isolationist turn by the US if Trump or DeSantis were to win. Europeans do not hesitate to criticize the US at times, but few claim the alliance would survive without US leadership. Without the US, Hautala said, "eighty years of peace and stability goes away."

"It would be grand-strategy suicide," he said. Devastating for the alliance, but, like so many things in this new great power conflict, no longer unthinkable.

Penghu Islands, Taiwan Strait

Two years into the Ukraine war and five thousand miles away, Taiwan's military commanders were only more convinced they must prepare for war themselves.

Colonel Chang Chi-Ming the commander of Taiwanese ground forces stationed on the Penghu Islands, again evoked *The Art of War*, noting that Sun Tzu warned that those who ignore the prospect of war will suffer.

"Sun Tzu said: 'The art of war is of vital importance to the state.

It is a matter of life and death, a road either to safety or to ruin. Hence it is a subject of inquiry which can on no account be neglected,'" said Chang.

In our conversation, I didn't sense Chang or his colleagues relished the prospect of war with China. Quite the opposite. They knew the war games forecast a devastatingly deadly battle for both sides. His feelings, two years into Ukraine's war and, perhaps, closer to one with China, were of resignation rather than a soldier's bravado.

"Frankly speaking, warfare is a dangerous business," Chang said. "Battles are perilous, and any neglect can yield bitter consequences. In the face of the enemy's threats, the military always upholds the belief that 'preparedness ensures success and unpreparedness spells failure.'"

"In summary, we cannot rely on the enemy's goodwill for peace," Colonel Chang said. "Security must be established based on our own strength."

On board the Taiwanese frigate *Feng-Chia*, Captain Peng Chung-Hsiao was speaking the language of strength and preparedness as well.

"Holding the honorable position of a ship's captain comes with significant responsibilities," Peng told me. "I am committed to continually enhancing my professional skills, holding myself to strict standards, and diligently fulfilling my duties, at the same time taking on challenges and facing responsibilities with courage, leading my entire crew to innovate and achieve breakthroughs."

Captain Peng said that he and his crew try to uphold "the spirit of 'we're all in the same boat,'" noting that their responsibility is nothing short of defending and safeguarding Taiwan.

Two years since the Russian invasion, Lieutenant Colonel Pi Shih-Chuan, commander of the squadron of Taiwanese fighter jets on the Penghus, looked for hope from the performance of Ukrainian forces.

"During the early stages of the Russo-Ukrainian war, some

analysts believed that Russia could rely on the numerical advantage of their military forces to gain control of the battlefield," Pi said. "However, in reality, the outcome of modern warfare hinges on the 'quality' of the military rather than sheer 'quantity.' I now believe that the key elements for gaining an advantage in warfare include 'unwavering determination of the people,' 'the quality of personnel training,' 'accurate intelligence,' and finally, 'equipment excellence.' This realization has deepened my understanding of my own role, and I hope to further elevate the training of the Air Force with my modest contribution."

The focus of Taiwanese commanders has not changed over time. Like they said and felt at the beginning of the Russian invasion, they see their mission today as clear: ensuring the very survival of Taiwan.

"Joining the navy stems from my personal belief and original intent to defend our maritime territory and protect our homeland," said Peng. "It has been over twenty years, and that initial intent has not changed, nor will it change in the future."

Spain

Yana, her husband, and their three children—now five, eight, and thirteen years old—found their way from Bucha, site of some of the worst Russian massacres of the war, all the way to Spain. Nearly two years into the war, they are safe but deeply missing their home.

"Imagine a tree uprooted and carried into the desert by a storm," Yana told me in late 2023. "That's roughly how we feel. There are different rules, laws, and you are like a black sheep."

Initially, her mother, who had given Yana that first early warning in January 2022 of the coming Russian invasion, escaped with her to Spain. However, her mother later decided to return to Ukraine.

"I was very angry with her for that," Yana confessed to me. "I was trying to persuade her not to go. She is sixty years old. She's there alone now. She knew that I would not take the children back to the hell they had experienced in Bucha, but she left anyway."

Now, as in the early stages of the invasion, her mother is back at work in a hospital in Eastern Ukraine, tending to the war's many wounded.

"She cleans, and she helps to care for the sick," Yana said. "When there were battles in Bucha, she witnessed things in the hospital that you would not wish to anyone. There were people dying at the doors to the hospital. There were children among them."

Yana and her young family are lucky to be together. Ukrainian law bans military-age men from leaving the country. But there is an exception for fathers with three children. And anyway, Yana cannot see her husband on the front lines.

"It was not an easy choice for our family. My husband believed that he was more useful in Ukraine," Yana said. "I have a different opinion. He is not a military man. He never held a weapon in his hands. He was a journalist all his life. I believe that he will be more useful in the rear. He will be more useful near his children."

The rhythm of life for Ukrainians who have managed to flee the war is one of surviving the change as best they can while hoping those they left behind are simply surviving the war.

"I'm often afraid to log on to social media, because every day I see a new post about someone I know who died defending us," she said. "There are those with whom you once worked. And there are those whom you know well. You think, what a wonderful person he was and they don't exist now.

"And you read, and you look at the photos, and you are immediately gripped by incredible sadness and incredible rage," she continued. "Young, beautiful, talented people to whom people write 'Rest in peace.' It doesn't have to be that way."

So, what now for her country? As the counteroffensive stalled and western officials began to speak of land for peace, is she losing hope?

"Everything has a beginning and an end," she said. "The war will definitely end. It will end with the victory of Ukraine." She added, "But in my opinion, it will not be soon. It's not a sprint. It's a marathon."

A punishing marathon, extracting the blood, sweat, and tears of millions of Ukrainians. It is just one front of this new great powers era, but a glaring sign of where conflict unabated can lead.

ACKNOWLEDGMENTS

Stories, even in the grand sweep of history, are primarily about people—the people who make decisions that change the world and the people, that is all of us, who live with the consequences of those decisions. And I'm deeply grateful to—and have great admiration for—so many people I met in Ukraine, Taiwan, Estonia, Israel and the occupied territories, and beyond as I reported out this book. They are forced to live their lives every day in the midst of war or on the cusp of it. The stresses and losses are enormous. I've done my best to convey what they face as an essential part of the story. Without their hospitality, honesty, and generosity, I could not have written this book.

My sincere thanks to CNN for providing me so many opportunities to cover the world. Without the collection of those many assignments abroad and the reporting beat to cover national security at home, I wouldn't have been able to see and connect the dots on this new era of great power competition.

Writing a book like this depends on busy people in high positions to be generous with their time and insight—and I'm indebted to several. Secretary of State Antony Blinken, CIA Director Bill Burns,

ACKNOWLEDGMENTS

Joint Chiefs Chairman General Mark Milley, MI6 Chief Richard Moore, Estonian Prime Minister Kaja Kallas, NATO Secretary-General Jens Stoltenberg, Canadian Foreign Minister Melanie Joly, Deputy National Security Advisor Jon Finer, Taiwan Foreign Minister Joseph Wu, former National Security Advisor General John Kelly, former Deputy National Security Advisor Matt Pottinger, former National Security Advisor Ambassador John Bolton, and former Supreme Allied Commander Admiral James Stavridis all shared their accounts, experiences, and analysis in enormous detail and with candor. I could not have attempted to approach the topic of great power competition at the granular and big-picture level without speaking to them.

Vedant Patel at State, Tammy Kupperman at the CIA, Dave Butler at the Pentagon, Alan Merson and Claire Thornton at MI6, Maris Lindmae in the Estonian Prime Minister's office, Sam Heath at the British Embassy, Hazel Castillo at the White House, and Sarah Tinsley in Ambassador Bolton's office helped to make many of those meetings come together.

Reporting out a book like this requires conducting some interviews on background with officials whose identities I keep confidential due to their roles in government, the military, and intelligence agencies. I'm deeply grateful to them for their willingness not only to help me collect and confirm key details of several events described in this book but also for their own informed insight into the significance of those events. I have relied solely on sources with whom I have long, working relationships and whose track record for credibility is based on their contributions to multiple previous stories.

Rear Admiral Thorsten Marx of the German Navy, Finnish Ambassador Mikko Hautala Taiwan's Deputy Minister of Economic Affairs C. C. Chen, Taiwan's Deputy Minister of the Mainland Affairs Council Jan Jyh-horng, and retired Taiwanese Navy Admiral Lee

ACKNOWLEDGMENTS

Hsi-Min provided me with detailed views inside the perspective of America's overseas allies. Representatives Mike Quigley, Jake Auchincloss, and Mike Gallagher opened valuable windows into Ukraine and China from the perspective of the Hill and their own travels to the front lines. Retired General Mark Hertling shared his wise analysis of the military side of the war in Ukraine.

I'd like to extend particular thanks to the crews of the German Navy frigate FGS *Mecklenburg-Vorpommern,* the Portuguese Navy frigate NRP *Bartolomeu Dias,* and the Taiwanese Navy frigate *Feng-Chia* for welcoming me onboard. I'm also grateful to the soldiers, sailors, and airmen serving on the Hen Hill Army Base and Magong Air Base in Penghu, Taiwan. In particular, my thanks to Colonel Chang Chi-Ming, chief of operations on Penghu, Lieutenant Colonel Pi Shih-Chuan of the Coyote squadron, and Captain Peng Chung-Hsiao, commander of the *Feng-Chia.* They are all highly professional and deeply committed to their missions.

Sabina Chang and Longman Chung at the Taipei Economic and Cultural Representative Office in the US helped make my visit to Taiwan a reality and so productive. Oana Lungescu, Matthias Eichenlaub, and Charlotte Banks at NATO headquarters in Brussels were central to making my embark on the VJTF possible and productive.

In Ukraine, I'm grateful to Yana and her three children for staying in touch from the early days of the invasion to today and sharing the experience of their lives rocked by war. Sofiya Harbuziuk helped make those interviews come together and provided translation. Taras Zadorozhnyy helped me see the war from the perspective of Ukrainians.

Thank you, John Parsley, for your enthusiastic endorsement of this book and topic from the very beginning, and wise editing from conception to execution. My thanks to David Larabell at CAA for helping make this book a reality and, I hope, a success. As always, thanks to my copy editor at Dutton and my fact-checker Julie Tate for keeping me on my editorial toes.

Finally and most important of all, my sincere thanks to my family—Gloria, Tristan, Caden, and Sinclair—for indulging me the time, energy, and headaches to report and write yet another book— and for freeing me to run off to the ends of the earth to help tell these stories. This book is part of my work, but I write for you as well, which I hope you know.

NOTES

PROLOGUE

1. "Ukraine Crisis: Don't Create Panic, Zelensky Tells the West," BBC News, January 28, 2022.
2. David Brennan, Tom O'Connor, and Naveed Jamali, "US Accused of Hyping Russia Invasion of Ukraine, Frustrating Kyiv, Moscow," *Newsweek*, February 2, 2022.
3. "Ukraine Crisis: Don't Create Panic, Zelensky Tells the West."
4. Lexi Lonas, "Zelensky Urges Ukrainians Not to Panic," *The Hill*, February 22, 2022.

CHAPTER ONE: GREAT POWER WARFARE

1. David M. Herszenhorn, "US Warns War Could Be 'Imminent' in Ukraine," *Politico*, February 11, 2022.
2. "Ukraine Crisis: Macron Says a Deal to Avoid War Is Within Reach," BBC News, February 6, 2022.
3. "Macron Pushes for Diplomacy, US Warns Russian Invasion of Ukraine Imminent," France 24, February 20, 2022.
4. Luke McGee, "Here's What We Know About the 40-Mile-Long Russian Convoy Outside Ukraine's Capital," CNN, March 3, 2022.
5. Jim Sciutto, "US Intel Assess 'Major' Strategy Shift by Russia as It Moves Some Forces Away from Kyiv," CNN, updated March 31, 2022.
6. Sciutto, "US Intel Assess 'Major' Strategy Shift by Russia."
7. Sciutto, "US Intel Assess 'Major' Strategy Shift by Russia."

8.   Jim Sciutto, "Ukrainian Forces Aim to Retake Kherson by Year's End as Gains Made in South, US and Ukrainian Officials Say," CNN, September 7, 2022.

9.   Katie Bo Lillis and Natasha Bertrand, "US War-Gamed with Ukraine Ahead of Counteroffensive and Encouraged More Limited Mission," CNN, September 1, 2022.

10.   Rob Picheta, Vasco Cotovio, and Olga Voitovych, "As Ukraine Pushes Southern Offensive, It Also Hits Russia in the Northeast," CNN, September 8, 2022.

11.   Picheta, Cotovio, and Voitovych, "As Ukraine Pushes Southern Offensive, It Also Hits Russia in the Northeast."

12.   Nick Paton Walsh, "The Curtain Protecting the Dignity of Russia's Military Has Been Pulled Back," CNN, September 14, 2022.

13.   Jim Sciutto, "Early Stages of Ukrainian Counteroffensive 'Not Meeting Expectations,' Western Officials Tell CNN," CNN, June 23, 2023.

14.   Sciutto, "Early Stages of Ukrainian Counteroffensive 'Not Meeting Expectations.'"

15.   Jim Sciutto, "Western Allies Receive Increasingly 'Sobering' Updates on Ukraine's Counteroffensive: 'This Is the Most Difficult Time of the War,'" CNN, August 8, 2023.

16.   "Fireside Chat with President Zelensky," Aspen Security Forum, transcript, July 21, 2023.

17.   Sciutto, "Western Allies Receive Increasingly 'Sobering' Updates on Ukraine's Counteroffensive."

18.   Sciutto, "Western Allies Receive Increasingly 'Sobering' Updates on Ukraine's Counteroffensive."

19.   "Fireside Chat with President Zelensky," Aspen Security Forum.

20.   "A New Study Finds That 47,000 Russian Combatants Have Died in Ukraine," *The Economist*, July 12, 2023.

21.   Helene Cooper, Thomas Gibbons-Neff, Eric Schmitt, and Julian E. Barnes "Troop Deaths and Injuries in Ukraine War Near 500,000, U.S. Officials Say," *The New York Times*, August 18, 2023.

22.   "Time for a Rethink: Helping Ukraine Win a Long War," *The Economist*, September 23, 2023.

CHAPTER TWO: DIVIDING LINES

1.   Finnish Border Guard.

2.   George Wright, "Finland Starts Construction of Russia Border Fence," BBC News, February 28, 2023.

3.   "NATO 2022 Strategic Concept," NATO, June 29, 2022.

4. "NATO 2022 Strategic Concept," NATO, June 29, 2022.

5. "Vilnius Summit Communiqué," NATO, July 11, 2023.

6. *Annual Threat Assessment of the US Intelligence Community*, Office of the Director of National Intelligence, February 6, 2023.

7. *Annual Threat Assessment of the US Intelligence Community*, February 6, 2023.

8. Francesca Ebel and Lily Kuo, "Xi and Putin Hold Talks in Russia, Trading Compliments, amid War in Ukraine," *The Washington Post*, March 20, 2023.

9. Brian Spegele, "At the China-Russia Border, the Xi-Putin Partnership Shows Signs of Fraying," *The Wall Street Journal*, March 20, 2023.

10. Ann M. Simmons, "Russia-China Summit Showcases Challenge to the West," *The Wall Street Journal*, March 21, 2023.

11. Lidia Kelly, Ronald Popeski, and Nick Starkov, "Xi: China's Proposal on Ukraine Reflects Unity of Global Views," Reuters, March 19, 2023.

12. Zoya Sheftalovich and Nicholas Camut, "Xi Jinping: China's 'Friendship' with Russia 'Growing Day by Day,'" *Politico*, March 20, 2023.

13. "Vladimir Putin's Article for *People's Daily* Newspaper, Russia and China: A Future-Bound Partnership," Office of the President of Russia, March 19, 2023.

14. Kelly, Popeski, and Starkov, "Xi: China's Proposal on Ukraine Reflects Unity of Global Views."

15. "Vladimir Putin's Article for *People's Daily* Newspaper, Russia and China."

16. "Vladimir Putin's Article for *People's Daily* Newspaper, Russia and China."

17. "Vladimir Putin's Article for *People's Daily* Newspaper, Russia and China."

18. https://www.dni.gov/files/ODNI/documents/assessments/ATA-2023 -Unclassified-Report.pdf.

19. "Speech and the Following Discussion at the Munich Conference on Security Policy," Office of the President of Russia, February 10, 2007.

20. "Wolf Warriors," *The Economist*, March 11, 2023.

21. Jim Sciutto, *The Shadow War* (New York: HarperCollins, 2019).

22. "Wolf Warriors."

23. *Annual Threat Assessment of the US Intelligence Community*, Office of the Director of National Intelligence, February 6, 2023.

24. *Face the Nation*, CBS News, transcript, February 19, 2023.

25. *Face the Nation*, February 19, 2023.

26. Natasha Bertrand and Zachary Cohen, "Intelligence Suggests China Is Considering Sending Drones and Ammunition to Russia, Sources Familiar Say," CNN, February 24, 2023.

27. Jim Sciutto, Sam Fossum, Kaitlan Collins, and Kylie Atwood, "Russia Has Requested Military and Economic Assistance from China, US Officials Say," CNN, March 14, 2022.

28. Bertrand and Cohen, "Intelligence Suggests China Is Considering Sending Drones and Ammunition to Russia."

29. Sam Fossum and Paul LeBlanc, "US Ambassador to the UN Says China Would Cross 'Red Line' by Providing Lethal Aid to Russia," CNN, February 19, 2023.

30. Stephen Collinson, "Blinken's New Warning to Beijing Is the Latest Sign of Deteriorating US-China Relations," CNN, February 28, 2023.

31. Sciutto et al., "Russia Has Requested Military and Economic Assistance from China."

32. Haley Britzky, "US Defense Secretary Tells CNN He Hasn't Spoken to Chinese Counterpart for a 'Couple of Months,'" CNN, February 24, 2023.

33. Andrew Erickson and Gabriel B. Collins, "Putin's Ukraine Invasion: Turbocharging Sino-Russian Collaboration in Energy, Maritime Security, and Beyond?," *Naval War College Review* 75, no. 4 (Autumn 2022).

34. Natasha Bertrand, "Iran Helping Russia Build Drone Stockpile That Is Expected to Be 'Orders of Magnitude Larger' Than Previous Arsenal, US Says," CNN, July 25, 2023.

35. "Transcript: CIA Director William Burns on 'Face the Nation,'" CBS News, February 26, 2023.

36. Bertrand, "Iran Helping Russia Build Drone Stockpile."

37. Natasha Bertrand, "Russia Has Been Sending Some US-Provided Weapons Captured in Ukraine to Iran, Sources Say," CNN, March 14, 2023.

38. "Transcript: CIA Director William Burns on 'Face the Nation.'"

39. Bertrand, "Iran Helping Russia Build Drone Stockpile."

40. "Initial US Intelligence Suggests Iran Was Surprised by the Hamas Attack on Israel," CNN, October 11, 2023.

41. "Hamas Leaders Arrive in Moscow as the Kremlin Attempts to Showcase Its Clout," *The New York Times*, October 26, 2023.

42. "Hamas Sent High-Level Delegation to Moscow at Russia's Invitation," *Middle East Monitor*, March 16, 2023.

43. "Israel Has No Right to Defend Itself, Says Russia at UN," *The Jerusalem Post*, November 2, 2023.

44. "US Intel Suggests Syria's Assad Agreed to Send Russian Missile System to Hezbollah with Wagner Group Help," CNN, November 3, 2023.

45. "War in Ukraine Forces Israel into a Delicate Balancing Act," *The New York Times*, February 27, 2022.

46. "Remarks by President Biden on the October 7th Terrorist Attacks and the Resilience of the State of Israel and Its People," The White House, October 18, 2023.

47. Helen Regan, Gawon Bae, Larry Register, Simone McCarthy, Anna Chernova, and Jake Kwon, "Putin Talks Military Cooperation with Kim as North Korean Leader Endorses Russia's War on Ukraine," CNN, September 13, 2023.

48. Reagan et al., "Putin Talks Military Cooperation with Kim."

49. https://www.wsj.com/articles/biden-administration-in-discussion-to-build-first-nuclear-subs-for-australia-in-u-s-11663963244.

CHAPTER THREE: FLASHPOINT

1. H. I. Sutton, "New Evidence Shows Russia Has Deployed Powerful Missiles to Kaliningrad Coast," *Naval News*, June 29, 2022.
2. "Russia Says It Moved Hypersonic Missiles to the Kaliningrad Region," Al Jazeera, August 18, 2022.
3. Oren Liebermann, "Russian Pilots Tried to 'Dogfight' US Jets over Syria, US Central Command Says," CNN, April 29, 2023.
4. Adam Entous, Julian E. Barnes, and Adam Goldman, "Intelligence Suggests Pro-Ukrainian Group Sabotaged Pipelines, US Officials Say," *The New York Times*, March 7, 2023.
5. Christian Mölling, Torben Schütz, and Sophia Backer, *Deterrence and Defense in Times of COVID-19: Europe's Political Choices*, DGAP Policy Brief no. 9, German Council on Foreign Relations, April 9, 2020.
6. "Fireside Chat with Emmanuel Bonne," Aspen Security Forum, July 20, 2023.
7. "Fireside Chat with Emmanuel Bonne."
8. Timo Kirez, "Germans More Likely to Flee War Than Fight: Survey," *Anadolu News*, February 10, 2023.
9. Sarah Gehle, "The German Navy's Long-Distance Vision Gains Clarity," *Military Balance Blog*, International Institute for Strategic Studies, April 21, 2023.

CHAPTER FOUR: RUSSIA'S NEXT TARGETS

1. Richard Milne, "Estonia's PM Says Country Would Be 'Wiped from Map' Under Existing NATO Plans," *Financial Times*, June 22, 2022.
2. Milne, "Estonia's PM Says Country Would Be 'Wiped from Map.'"
3. "Relations with the Republic of Moldova," NATO, updated May 26, 2023.
4. "Zelenskyy: Ukraine Caught Russian Plan to 'Destroy' Moldova," AP, February 9, 2023.
5. Radina Gigova and Rob Picheta, "Moldovan President Accuses Russia of Plotting to Destabilize the Country," CNN, February 14, 2023.
6. Milena Veselinovic and Tara John, "Alleged Russian Agents Convicted for Masterminding Coup Plot in Europe," CNN, May 9, 2019.
7. "Diplomat Blasts Chisinau's Claim of 'Russia Planning to Destabilize Situation in Moldova,'" TASS, February 14, 2023.

8. Victoria Rusica, "The President of the European Parliament Sent a Message of Solidarity: The Place of the Republic of Moldova Is in the European Union," *Radio Moldova*, February 15, 2023.
9. *Face the Nation*, CBS News, February 19, 2023.
10. *Face the Nation*, February 19, 2023.
11. Diana Scorpan, "Zelensky's Warning: The Kremlin Is Searching for Ways of Strangling Moldova," *Moldova Live*, February 17, 2023.
12. Peter Wilke, "Germany U-turns on Commitment to Meet NATO Spending Target Annually," *Politico*, August 16, 2023.

CHAPTER FIVE: TARGET TAIWAN

1. "Statement on Unsafe Maritime Interaction," US Indo-Pacific Command Public Affairs, June 5, 2023.
2. Mark F. Cancian, Matthew Cancian, and Eric Heginbotham, *The First Battle of the Next War: Wargaming a Chinese Invasion of Taiwan*, International Security Program, Center for Strategic and International Studies, January 2023.
3. Cancian, Cancian, and Heginbotham, *The First Battle of the Next War*.
4. Cancian, Cancian, and Heginbotham, *The First Battle of the Next War*.
5. Cancian, Cancian, and Heginbotham, *The First Battle of the Next War*.
6. Haley Britzky and Brad Lendon, "Taiwan War Would Be 'Devastating,' Warns US Defense Secretary Lloyd Austin," CNN, June 3, 2023.
7. Mark Sommer, "The Short Life of the New USS *Little Rock*: Design Flaws, Setbacks Lead to Decommissioning," *Stars and Stripes*, February 4, 2023.
8. Sebastian Roblin, "After $30 Billion Spent, These 5 Military Weapons Were Scrapped," *The National Interest*, August 1, 2021.
9. Huizhong Wu and Johnson Lai, "Taiwan Suspects Chinese Ships Cut Islands' Internet Cables," AP, April 18, 2023.
10. Elizabeth Braw, "China Is Practicing How to Sever Taiwan's Internet," *Foreign Policy*, February 21, 2023.

CHAPTER SIX: TAIWAN'S EXISTENTIAL QUESTIONS

1. Jonathan Kearsley, Eryk Bagshaw, and Anthony Galloway, "'If You Make China the Enemy, China Will Be the Enemy': Beijing's Fresh Threat to Australia," *Sydney Morning Herald*, November 18, 2020; and Lucas Niewenhuis, "The 14 Sins of Australia: Beijing Expands List of Grievances and Digs In for Extended Diplomatic Dispute," The China Project, November 18, 2020.
2. Kearsley, Bagshaw, and Galloway, "'If You Make China the Enemy, China Will Be the Enemy.'"

NOTES

3. Robert Lawrence Kuhn, "Xi Jinping's Chinese Dream," *The New York Times*, June 4, 2013.
4. Kuhn, "Xi Jinping's Chinese Dream."
5. "Full Transcript of ABC News' George Stephanopoulos' Interview with President Joe Biden," ABC News, August 19, 2021.
6. "Remarks by President Biden in a CNN Town Hall with Anderson Cooper," The White House, October 21, 2021.
7. "Remarks by President Biden in a CNN Town Hall with Anderson Cooper."
8. Anthony Kuhn, "President Biden Says the U.S. Will Defend Taiwan If China Invades," NPR, May 23, 2022.
9. "Biden Tells *60 Minutes* U.S. Troops Would Defend Taiwan, but White House Says This Is Not Official U.S. Policy," *60 Minutes Overtime*, CBS News, September 18, 2022.
10. Yishan Chen and Silva Shih, "Taiwan Defense Minister: China Won't Take Taiwan in a Fortnight," *CommonWealth Magazine*, February 20, 2023.

CHAPTER SEVEN: "NO LONGER UNTHINKABLE"

1. Mary Beth D. Nikitin, *Russia's Nuclear Weapons: Doctrine, Forces, and Modernization, Congressional Research Service*, Report R45861, April 21, 2022.
2. Nikitin, *Russia's Nuclear Weapons.*
3. "What Is a 'Dirty Bomb' and Why Is Russia Saying Ukraine Could Use One?," BBC News, October 25, 2022.
4. Julian Borger and Peter Beaumont, "Russia Steps Up Ukraine 'Dirty Bomb' Claim in Letter Delivered to UN," *The Guardian*, October 25, 2022.
5. Aditi Sangal, Maureen Chowdhury, Adrienne Vogt, Meg Wagner, Helen Regan, Travis Caldwell, and Melissa Macaya, "Medvedev Warns Russia Would Bolster Military over Potential Swedish and Finnish NATO Membership," CNN, April 15, 2022.
6. Tim Lister and Nick Paton Walsh, "Putin Is Trying to Raise the Stakes in Ukraine. Here's What It Means," CNN, September 22, 2022.
7. Alys Davies, "Putin: Nuclear Risk Is Rising, but We Are Not Mad," BBC News, December 7, 2022.
8. *The 2022 Nuclear Posture Review: Arms Control Subdued by Military Rivalry*, Federation of American Scientists, October 27, 2022.
9. Amy J. Woolf, "US Nuclear Weapons Policy: Considering 'No First Use,'" Congressional Research Service, Insight IN10553, March 29, 2022.
10. Tim Lister, "Putin Floats Possibility That Russia May Abandon 'No First Use' Nuclear Doctrine," CNN, December 9, 2022.
11. Uliana Pavlova, "Putin Loyalist Dials Up Nuclear Rhetoric as NATO Partners Push for More Weapons for Ukraine," CNN, January 19, 2023.

12. "G7 Statement on Ukraine, 11 October 2022," The White House.

13. Andreas Rinke and Eduardo Baptista, "Xi, Scholz Warn Against 'Irresponsible' Nuclear Threats over Ukraine," Reuters, November 4, 2022.

14. "Update: Xi Meets German Chancellor Olaf Scholz," Xinhua News Agency, November 5, 2022.

15. Sumit Ganguly, "Why Did Modi Push Back on Putin?," *Foreign Policy*, September 22, 2022.

16. Sudhi Ranjan Sen, "Modi to Skip Annual Putin Summit over Ukraine Nuke Threats," Bloomberg, December 9, 2022.

17. "Trajectory of Ukraine Conflict, Nuke Issue Matter of Anxiety: Jaishankar," *Economic Times*, September 23, 2022.

18. Statement by Marion Messmer, senior research fellow, International Security Programme, Chatham House, February 21, 2023.

19. Statement by Marion Messmer, February 21, 2023.

20. Oren Liebermann and Natasha Bertrand, "US Believes Russia Had Failed Intercontinental Ballistic Missile Test Around When Biden Was in Ukraine," CNN, February 22, 2023.

21. Federation Council of the Federal Assembly of the Russian Federation, February 22, 2023.

22. "Strategic Arms Reduction Treaty (START I)," Center for Arms Control and Non-Proliferation, November 1, 2022.

CHAPTER EIGHT: A MULTIFRONT WAR

1. Emma Helfrich, Joseph Trevithick, and Tyler Rogoway, "Why Shooting Down China's Spy Balloon over the US Is More Complicated Than It Seems," *The War Zone*, February 4, 2023.

2. Oren Liebermann, Haley Britzky, Michael Conte, and Nectar Gan, "Pentagon Tracking Suspected Chinese Spy Balloon over the US," CNN, February 3, 2023.

3. "Prominent Republicans Call for US to Shoot Down Suspected Spy Balloon," CNN, February 3, 2023.

4. Liebermann et al., "Pentagon Tracking Suspected Chinese Spy Balloon over the US."

5. Simone McCarthy and Haley Britzky, "Chinese Surveillance Balloon Did Not Collect Information over US, Pentagon Says," CNN, June 30, 2023.

6. Liu Zuanzun and Chen Qingquin, "Chinese Defense Ministry Sternly Protests Against US' Attack on Chinese Civilian Airship," *Global Times*, February 5, 2023.

7. Jennifer Hansler, Kevin Liptak, Jeremy Herb, Kylie Atwood, Jim Sciutto, and Oren Liebermann, "Blinken Postpones Trip to Beijing After Chinese Spy Balloon Spotted over US," CNN, February 3, 2023.

8. Nectar Gan, Wayne Chang, and CNN's Beijing Bureau, "China Accuses US of 'Illegally' Flying Balloons Across Its Airspace," CNN, February 13, 2023.

9. Gan, Chang, and Beijing Bureau, "China Accuses US of 'Illegally' Flying Balloons Across Its Airspace."

10. Haley Britzky, "US Generals Warn China Is Aggressively Expanding Its Influence in South America and the Caribbean," CNN, March 8, 2023.

11. Britzky, "US Generals Warn China Is Aggressively Expanding Its Influence."

12. *Annual Threat Assessment of the US Intelligence Community*, Office of the Director of National Intelligence, February 6, 2023, p. 10.

13. *Annual Threat Assessment of the US Intelligence Community*, February 6, 2023, p. 14.

14. *Annual Threat Assessment of the US Intelligence Community*, February 6, 2023, p. 15.

15. *Annual Threat Assessment of the US Intelligence Community*, February 6, 2023, p. 15.

16. *Annual Threat Assessment of the US Intelligence Community*, February 6, 2023, p. 10.

17. Sandra Erwin, "Biden's Defense Nominee Embraces View of Space as a Domain of War," *Space News*, January 19, 2021.

18. Alex Marquardt, "CIA Launches Video to Recruit Russian Spies," CNN, May 16, 2023.

19. Huw Dylan, David V. Gioe, and Daniela Richterova, "Western Agencies Offer an Open Door for Russian Defectors," *Foreign Policy*, July 26, 2023.

20. Haley Britzky, "US Defense Secretary Tells CNN He Hasn't Spoken to Chinese Counterpart for a 'Couple of Months,'" CNN, February 24, 2023.

21. Simone McCarthy and Haley Britzky, "Chinese Surveillance Balloon Did Not Collect Information over US, Pentagon Says," CNN, June 30, 2023.

22. Katie Bo Lillis and Natasha Bertrand, "China Appears to Have Suspended Spy Balloon Program After February Shootdown, US Intel Believes," CNN, September 15, 2023.

23. Lillis and Bertrand, "China Appears to Have Suspended Spy Balloon Program."

24. Robert Plummer, "Putin Makes Nuclear-Powered Burevestnik Missile Test Claim," BBC News, October 5, 2023.

NOTES

CHAPTER NINE: TRUMP WILD CARD

1. John Bolton, *The Room Where It Happened: A White House Memoir* (Simon & Schuster, 2020), p. 138.
2. Anders Hagstrom, "Trump Describes How He Could Solve Russia-Ukraine Conflict in 24 Hours," Fox News, July 16, 2023.
3. *Intelligence Community Assessment: Assessing Russian Activities and Intentions in Recent US Elections*, Office of the Director of National Intelligence, January 6, 2017.
4. Jennifer Agiesta and Ariel Edwards-Levy, "CNN Poll: Percentage of Republicans Who Think Biden's 2020 Win Was Illegitimate Ticks Back up Near 70%," CNN, August 3, 2023.
5. Jef Feeley, "Fox Judge Says It's 'CRYSTAL Clear' Election Claims Were False," Bloomberg Law, March 31, 2023.

CHAPTER TEN: PATHS TO PEACE

1. Jonathan Glover, *Humanity: A Moral History of the Twentieth Century* (Pimlico, 1999), page 212.
2. Glover, *Humanity*, p. 212.
3. https://asiasociety.org/policy-institute/china-and-us-case-managed-strategic-competition.
4. Doug Palmer, "What Cold War? U.S. Trade with China Hits New High," *Politico*, February 7, 2023.
5. "Vilnius Summit Communiqué," NATO, July 11, 2023.
6. "Vilnius Summit Communiqué," July 11, 2023.
7. "Chinese Army Invasion of Taiwan Not a Given, US General says," VOA News, June 30, 2023.
8. "Nuclear Weapons: Who Has What at a Glance," Arms Control Association, June 2023.
9. Oren Liebermann, "China Could Have 1,500 Nuclear Warheads by 2035: Pentagon Report," CNN, November 29, 2022.

INDEX

Afghanistan
  arguments for support for, 282
  impact of war in, 46, 48
  Russia in, 30, 42
  US withdrawal from, 57, 191–92, 289
AIM-9X Sidewinder air-to-air
    missiles, 228
air defense exercises (ADEX), 103–7
air defense identification zone (ADIZ),
    149, 164, 168
air defense systems, 50, 104
air picture compilation, 105
Akel, Friedrich, 138
Amazon model, 46–49
America First movement, 309
ammunition, 47–48
Anderson, Rudolf, 277
*Annual Threat Assessment of the US
    Intelligence Community*, 64, 73–74,
    244, 245
"anti-access, area-denial" (A2-AD), 189
Anti-Ballistic Missile (ABM) Treaty,
    214, 285
antisatellite (ASAT) weapons, 247, 248
Antonov Airport, 26–27
Arctic, 231–33, 254, 311
Arctic Dolphin, 112
Arms Control Association, 299

arms control treaties, 214–16
Art of War, The (Sun Tzu), 20, 179,
    319–20
artificial intelligence (AI), 250–55,
    301–3
Aspen Security Forum, 34, 36, 48,
    121, 180
asphyxiation scenario, 166
asymmetrical weapons systems, 161–62,
    293–94
attribution, challenge of, 302
Auchincloss, Jake, 165–67
AUKUS agreement, 91–92, 312
Austin, Lloyd, 79–80, 159, 247, 252
Australia
  AUKUS agreement and, 312
  China and, 169, 174–75
  United States and, 91–92
Avoidable War, The (Rudd), 280–81

B-59 submarine, 277–78
Bakhmut, 68
Bal system, 100
ballistic missile submarines,
    232–33
BALTOPs, 113

INDEX

Bartolomeu Dias, NRP, 103–5, 109,
  115, 123
Bash, Dana, 77
Bastille Day parade, 267
Bastion-P, 100
battalion tactical groups (BTGs), 5, 31
Belt and Road strategy, 249
Bennett, Naftali, 88
Berlin Wall, xiii, 221–22
Bertrand, Natasha, 31
Biden, Joe
  Afghanistan and, 191
  Blinken and, 282
  China's spy balloons and, 226–27
  China's support for Russia's invasion
    of Ukraine and, 79
  Israel-Hamas war and, 88–89
  Japan and South Korea and, 93–94
  Moldova and, 136
  New START Treaty and, 216–17
  nuclear threat and, 210
  Russian election interference
    and, 272
  Russia's invasion of Ukraine and,
    4–5, 180
  Taiwan and, 181, 183–85, 295–96
  Trump and, 261
  in Ukraine, 66
  US-China relations and, 242
  Xi and, 171–72
  Zelensky and, 17
Black Sea Fleet, attacks on, 50
Blinken, Anthony
  on China, 74–75, 77, 79, 156, 312
  Chinese surveillance balloons and,
    239, 241–43
  on competitiveness, 308
  on current global status, 281–84
  on global partnerships, 311
  on Global South, 305
  on lack of treaties/agreements, 215
  nuclear threat and, 208
  on Russia, 101, 142
  on Russia's invasion of Ukraine,
    181–82, 316–17
  on Taiwan, 292, 295
  on variable geometry, 306–7

boa constrictor scenario, 166
Bolton, John, 257, 260–61, 262, 264, 267,
  268, 269, 285
Bonne, Emmanuel, 121
Borei-class ballistic missile submarines,
  232–33
Bortnikov, Alexander, 5
Bradley fighting vehicles, 57
Braw, Elizabeth, 165
Brennan, Margaret, 84
British Foreign Office, 8
Brown, Pamela, 79
Bucha, Ukraine, 14–18, 130, 131, 321–22
Budanov, Kyrylo, 30
Burevestnik cruise missiles, 254
Burns, Bill
  on China, 79, 82
  on cooperation, 304
  on current diplomatic status, xi–xiii
  on current global status, 278
  on cybersecurity, 302
  on damage to Russian military, 39
  on hope, 314
  on human intelligence in Russia, 234
  on Iran and Russia, 84, 85
  on Israel-Hamas war, 89
  on "middle power" countries, 83
  nuclear threat and, 210
  outreach by, 11
  on Russia, 82, 297
  Russia's invasion of Ukraine and, 4–5
  Russia's invasion of Ukraine and, 79,
    180–81
Bush, George W., 214

"Camp David Principles," 94
Center for Strategic and International
  Studies (CSIS), 157–59
Challenges to Security in Space (DIA),
  247, 248
Chamberlain, Neville, 128
Chance, Matthew, 26–27
Chang Chi-Ming, 20, 147, 150, 168, 170,
  319–20
Chatham House, 217

Chen, Chern-Chyi "C.C.," 151, 152,
177, 186
Cheung, Eric, 294
China. *See also* People's Liberation
Army (PLA); Xi Jinping
Arctic activities of, 233, 311
assessment of strategy of, 80
AUKUS agreement and, 312
Australia and, 92, 169, 174–75
challenges facing, 73–75
change in status quo and, 155–57
constrainment and, 314
cyberspace/cyber warfare and,
244–45, 246–47, 302, 303
deterrence and, 181–82, 292–96
economy of, 74–75, 174–75, 263
"gray zone" warfare and, 164–67
intelligence resources of, 234
intelligence vulnerabilities of, 235
lack of communication with,
153–55
lessons learned from Ukraine and,
180–82
military capabilities of, 189–90
military decision-making in, 45
NATO and, 61–63
nuclear weapons and, 211, 212, 213–14,
219, 299–300
perceived US decline and, 307
potential for attack on United States
by, 188–89
potential for invasion of Taiwan by,
150–53, 156–59, 319–20
response of to Russia's invasion of
Ukraine, 58, 76–80
Russia and, 61–62, 63–70, 80–82,
84–85, 95
Russia compared to, 284
space weapons and, 247–50
submarine technology and, 80–82
surveillance balloons from, 225–31,
236, 237–44, 252–53
Taiwan and, 6, 94, 149, 165–70, 174,
175–76, 178–79
trade and, 175–76, 263, 283
Ukraine and, 287
underwater operations and, 165

US policy and, 183–87, 188
US threat assessment regarding, 64
US trilateral partnership and, 94
use of near space by, 240–41
Chinese Dream, 177–78
CHIPS Act, 308
Chiu Kuo-Cheng, 193
Chung-Hoon, USS, 154–55
Churchill, Winston, 137, 285, 310
CIA, 8, 251, 272
civilian infrastructure, targeting
of, 116
civilian targets, 117
climate crisis, 304
Clinton, Hillary, 140, 271–72
cluster munitions, 48–49
Collins, Gabriel B., 81
Collins, Kaitlan, 252
combined forces operations, 31, 148
command and control, 42
commercialization of space, 248
communications
absence of, 279
improvements in, 110
intercepted, 202–3, 234
lack of between Taiwan and
mainland China, 153–55
lack of between United States and
China, 242
reduction in military-to-military, xi
"track two," 172–73
value of, 254–55
Xi and, 172–73
Congressional Research Service
(CRS), 200
constrainment, 313–14
Cooper, Anderson, 184
cooperation, 304
Covid pandemic, 169–70, 174, 175,
176, 216
Crimea, 4, 7–8, 14–15, 57, 139–40, 192
Crusader self-propelled howitzer, 163
Cuban Missile Crisis, xii, 276–78,
280–81, 286
Cyber Defense Unit (Estonia), 146
Cybersecurity and Infrastructure
Security Agency, 272

cyberspace/cyber warfare, 140–41, 142–43, 146, 244–47, 249, 297, 301–3

David vs. Goliath strategy, 27, 29
Davis, Eric M., 274
declaratory policy of national leaders, 72, 185–86, 209, 295
Defense Intelligence Agency (DIA), 247, 248, 249
Democratic Progressive Party (Taiwan), 152
denied areas, 8
"de-risking," 95
DeSantis, Ron, 319
deterrence, 111, 130, 181–82
directed energy weapons, 249
dirty bombs, 201–2
disinformation, 166–67, 274
dividing lines, new, 56–57
Đjukanović, Milo, 134
Dobrynin, Anatoly, 277
domain awareness, 252–53
Dominion Voting Systems, 274
drones, 42–44, 45, 50, 106, 115–16, 150, 162, 164, 294. *See also* UAVs (uninhabited aerial vehicles)
Dwight D. Eisenhower, USS, 89
Dynamic Mongoose, 112

Eastern Theater Command, PLA's, 167–68
economic leverage, 307–8
Economist, The, 49
Eenpalu, Kaarel, 138
EKRE (Estonian political party), 126
election interference, 234, 271–75
electronic warfare, 45, 114
energy supply, 4, 58, 66, 73, 75, 119–20, 307–8
EP-3E surveillance aircraft, 236–37
Erdoğan, Recep Tayyip, 260, 262
Erickson, Andrew, 81

Esper, Mark, 264
Estonia
  independence of, 127
  NATO and, 110, 124, 125–26, 127, 128–32, 143–44
  nuclear threat and, 198, 208, 222–23
  Putin's demands regarding, 10
  Russia and, 126–32, 137–39, 142–43, 145–46, 297
  as tripwire, 125, 130–31
Estonian Defense League, 146
European navies, decrease in size of, 120–21
European Union. *See also* NATO; *individual countries*
  Moldova and, 135–36
  Ukraine and, 136

F-16 fighter jets, 57, 106
F-22 Raptor, 228–29
false flag operations, 134–35, 201–3
FBI, 272
Federal Archival Agency (Russia), 12
Federation Council (Russia), 216
Feng-Chia (PFG-1115), 19, 320
financial crisis of 2008, 120
Finer, Jon, 266
Finland
  border between Russia and, 60
  NATO and, 38, 58–60, 61, 204–5, 297, 298, 318
  Putin and, 11–12, 13
  Russia's invasion of Ukraine and, 9–10, 14
First Battle of the Next War, The (CSIS), 157–59
Five Eyes, 231, 251
Fleet and Force Structure 2035+ (Germany), 122
food supply, international, 305–6
Formidable Shield, 112
"14 Grievances," 175
Fox News, Dominion Voting Systems settlement and, 274
France, AUKUS agreement and, 91

freedom of navigation exercises, 236
frozen conflict, 35, 36
FSB, 4, 134–35
Fumio, Kishida, 66
Future Combat Surface System, 123

G7, 210–11
G20, 305
Gallagher, Mike, 166
Gaza, 86–87
Generalissimo Suvorov, 232
Georgia, Russian occupation of parts
    of, 7, 10, 57, 69
Gerald R. Ford, USS, 89
Gerasimov, Valery, 40, 208–9
Gerasimov Doctrine, 40, 208–9
German Council on Foreign
    Relations, 121
Germany
    after World War II, 101, 102
    military personnel and, 121–22
    military preparedness and, 144–45
    Russia and, 119–20
glasnost, 101
Global South, 305–6
Global Times (China), 229–30
Glover, Jonathan, 276
"Goalkeeper," 104
Gold Star parents, 191
"golden billion," 67
Gorbachev, Mikhail, 101, 222
grain deal, Ukraine and, 306
"gray zone" warfare, 164–67
Griner, Brittney, 139
ground-based anti-satellite missiles, 249
GRU (Russia), 273
Guns of August, The (Tuchman), 276–77

Haavisto, Pekka, 56, 59, 61
Hainan Island, 236–37
Haines, Avril, 36
Haley, Nikki, 226–27
Hamas, 86–87

Haniyeh, Ismail, 87
Hanoi Hilton, 176
Harpoon missiles, 110, 161
Hartford, USS, 115
Haspel, Gina, xi–xii
Hautala, Mikko, 10, 11, 12, 13, 14, 40,
    317–19
Hayashi, Yoshimasa, 93
heavy collective defense approach, 49–50
Hen Hill Army Base, 147–48, 168
Hertling, Mark, 33–34, 43, 45–46, 48
Hezbollah, 87–88
high-mobility artillery rocket system
    (HIMARS) launchers, 31, 45, 57,
    131, 132
history, lessons from, 50–54
Hitler, Adolf, 72, 137, 258–59, 263
Hong Kong, 167, 169, 176
Hostomel, Ukraine, 18, 26–27
Houthi rebels, 89
Hu Jintao, 171, 173
Huawei, 175
human intelligence (HUMINT), 251
Humanity (Glover), 276
Hussein, Saddam, 8, 72
hypersonic missiles, 114, 160, 184, 217

ICEX submarine exercises, 115
India, nuclear threat and, 211–12,
    213–14, 300
information warfare, 43–44
infrastructure
    cyber operations and, 246–47
    targeting of, 116
intelligence
    assessment of state of, 233–35
    declassification of, 43, 134–35
    denied areas and, 8
    as imperfect tool, 7–8
    importance of channels for, xiii
    lack of confidence in, 17, 23–24
    Russian communications networks
        and, 24
    Russia's invasion of Ukraine and, 27,
        31, 32

Intelligence and Security Service
(Moldova), 133
InterContinental Hotel, Kyiv, 21–22
intermediate-range missiles, 222
Intermediate-Range Nuclear Forces
(INF) Treaty, 214, 222
International Court of Justice, 87
International Criminal Court, 65
International Institute for Strategic
Studies, 122, 159
international rules and agreements,
importance of, 284–86
Iran
election interference and, 273
as "middle power," 83
nuclear weapons and, 219, 220, 300
response of to Russia's invasion of
Ukraine, 58
Russia and, 80, 84–89
space weapons and, 247
Trump and, 265–66
Iraq
impact of war in, 46, 48
shock-and-awe campaign in, 22
support of invasion of, 282
US forces in, 89, 191
US withdrawal from, 289
WMDs and, 17, 23
Iskander missiles, 100
isolationism, 274
Israel-Hamas war, 86–89
Italy, Global Combat Air Programme
and, 92–93

J-10 fighter jets, 164
J-11 fighter jets, 164
J-16 fighter jets, 164
Jaishankar, Subrahmanyam, 213
jamming technology, 228
Jan Jyh-Horng, 152–53, 154, 155, 167,
171–74, 175–76, 186, 188, 193–94
Japan
Global Combat Air Programme and,
92–93
as "middle power," 83

NATO and, 93
nuclear weapons and, 219
Pearl Harbor and, 189
Russia-China joint military exercises
and, 95
support for Ukraine from, 66
trilateral partnership and, 93–94
Trump and, 268–69
United Kingdom and, 92–93
Japan Self-Defense Forces, 158
Javelin anti-tank missiles, 27, 29, 43,
85, 162
Jiang Zemin, 171, 172–73
Joint Base Elmendorf-Richardson, 226
Joint Operations Command Center,
PLA, 168
Joint Warrior exercises, 106–7, 112, 113
Joly, Mélanie, 220, 240–41, 279, 287–88,
290, 291, 298, 300, 311

Kaliningrad, 99–101, 128
Kallas, Kaja
on accommodationists, 286
on China, 292
on cybersecurity, 302, 303
on loss of Estonia's independence,
137–38
NATO and, 125–28, 129–32, 143–45,
297–98
on Russia, 139, 141, 222–23, 288,
312–13
on territorial aggression, 310
Kara-Murza, Vladimir, 139
Kelly, John, 41–42, 44–45, 47, 52–53,
190–92, 256, 257, 258–60,
263–67, 269
Kelly, Robert, 191
Kendall-Taylor, Andrea, 218
Kennedy, John F., 276–77, 313, 315
Kennedy, Robert F., 276, 277
Kerry, John, 282
Khanna, Ro, 293–94
Kharkiv, 32
Kherson, 31
Khrushchev, Nikita, 277

kidnapper satellites, 250
Kim Il Sung, 72
Kim Jong Un, 90–91, 259, 261, 262, 269
Kirby, John, 239, 242–43
Kishida, Fumio, 94
KMT (Kuomintang), 166–67
Korean War, 52–53, 66
Kosachev, Konstantin, 218
Krebs, Chris, 272–73
Kyiv, defense of, 29–30

land-for-peace formula, 137, 143,
    289–91, 317, 323
Latvia, 10, 125
Lavrov, Sergey, 24–25, 26, 87, 135,
    208, 221
Law of the Sea treaty, 303
Le Drian, Jean-Yves, 26
Le Journal du Dimanche, 25
Lebanon, 88
Ledgett, Richard, 140–41
Lee Hsi-Min, 161–62, 163, 164, 177, 178,
    182, 186, 187, 189–90, 192
Leopard tanks, 57, 144
Liebermann, Oren, 106
Lillis, Katie Bo, 31
Lithuania, 10, 125
"little green men," 4
Littoral Combat Ship, 162–63
Litvinenko, Alexander, 139
Liu Pengyu, 253
LLM (large language models), 250
LNG (liquefied natural gas), 166
Locke, Gary, 283
Long March, 63
low Earth orbit (LEO), 248
Lü Xiang, 229–30
Lvova-Belova, Maria, 65

Macron, Emmanuel, 25–26, 121, 137,
    261, 288
Madman Theory, The (Sciutto), 262
Magong Air Base, 148–49

Mainland Affairs Council (Taiwan),
    152, 153, 167, 171, 186
Mao Zedong, 66, 72
Marx, Thorsten, 60, 100, 101–2, 109, 110,
    111–12, 113–14, 115, 118–20, 123–24
Matsu Islands, 165
McCain, John, 263
Mecklenburg-Vorpommern, FGS, 99,
    103, 104, 109–12, 123
Mediazona, 39
medivnyk, 17
Meduza, 39
Medvedev, Dmitry, 204–5, 206
Mein Kampf (Hitler), 72
Merkel, Angela, 119
Messmer, Marion, 217
Metsola, Roberta, 135
MI6, 231, 250–51
microchips, 308
"middle power" countries, 82–83
MiG-29s, 106
military supply chain, 46–49
Milley, Mark
    arms control and, 285
    on Biden's position on Taiwan, 295
    on China, 178–79, 292, 293
    declaratory policy of national leaders
        and, 72
    on global power, 83
    on historical context, 50–52
    nuclear threat and, 208–9
    on rising risk, 313
    Russia's invasion of Ukraine
        and, 7, 37
    on Taiwan, 185–86
    Trump and, 264
    on Ukraine, 287, 289–90, 291–92
    on US role in international affairs,
        309–10
Modi, Narendra, 212
Moldova, 132–36
Montenegro, 134
Moore, Richard, 83, 231, 234, 235, 245,
    250–52, 255
Morawiecki, Mateusz, 135–36
Morrison, Scott, 175
Moskva, 162, 207–8

Munich Security Conference, 69, 77, 78,
136, 144, 222–23, 241–43
Murrow, Edward R., 270
mutual-defense agreements, 184

Nansha Islands, 71
Naryshkin, Sergey, 210
National Advanced Surface-to-Air
Missile Systems (NASAMS),
131, 132
National Human Rights Museum
(Taiwan), 176–77
National People's Congress (2023),
71–72
National Press Club, 293
National Security Agency (NSA),
140, 272
National Security Council, 198, 199
NATO
2022 summit and, 55–56, 58, 59
acceptance of Finland and Sweden
into, 58–59
arms control and, 214–15, 299
Article Five and, 184
Baltic States and, 131
China and, 61–63
civilian targets and, 117
confrontation between Russia and, 61
Estonia and, 125–26, 127, 128–32,
143–44
expansion of, 58–60, 204–5, 318
increased readiness of, 118
integration as focus of, 118–19
Japan and, 93
Maritime Command of, 118
military supply chain and, 46, 49
nuclear threat and, 207, 211, 221–22,
223–24
Putin and, 5, 10–11, 25, 38, 68–69, 142
response of to Russia's invasion of
Ukraine, 58, 120
rules of engagement and, 107–9
Russia and, 100–113, 115, 117–20,
296–98

"Strategic Concept" document of, 61
support for Ukraine from, 66
training provided by, 44
Trump and, 260–61, 263–65, 266–67,
268–69, 270–71
in Ukraine, 40
Ukraine and, 280, 288, 290–92
US leadership and, 319
Very High Readiness Joint Task
Force of, 60, 99–100, 106–7, 109–13,
117–18, 123–24, 125, 129, 165
Navalny, Alexei, 139
near space, 225–31, 238–39, 240–41, 244,
252, 301–3
Nebenzya, Vasily, 87
Neptune missiles, 162, 207–8
New START Treaty, 215–17
New York Times, 39
Niinistö, Sauli, 11, 13
NKVD, 138
"no limits" partnership, 58, 73, 76, 77,
82, 84–85, 213, 233
no-first-use policy, 200, 205
Non- Proliferation Treaty (NPT), 301
Nord Stream pipelines, 117
North America Air Defense Command
(NORAD), 226, 238–39, 244
North Korea
as "middle power," 83
nuclear weapons and, 219
response of to Russia's invasion of
Ukraine, 58
Russia and, 80, 90–91
space weapons and, 247
Trump and, 269
US trilateral partnership
and, 94
nuclear submarines, 91–92
nuclear weapons. *See also* weapons
systems
Iran and, 85–86
reviving engagement regarding,
298–301
Russia and, 100–101, 197–214,
232–33, 254
treaties regarding, 215–19

Obama, Barack, 71, 79, 282
Office of the Director of National
    Intelligence, 244, 246
One China policy, 183, 184–85, 188
opioid crisis, 53
Opium Wars, 64
O'Reilly, Bill, 257–58
Oren, Michael, 89
Oryx, 32

P-8 Poseidon surveillance aircraft, 99,
    103, 233, 236
Palmerston, Lord, 214
Päts, Konstantin, 138
Pearl Harbor, 189
Pelley, Scott, 185
Pelosi, Nancy, 149, 167
Peng Chung-Hsiao, 19, 320, 321
Penghu Islands, 19–20, 147–48, 149–50,
    167, 168, 170, 319–20
People's Daily (China), 66–67
People's Liberation Army (PLA). *See
    also* China
    capabilities of, 64, 179
    lack of communication with, 154
    lessons learned from Ukraine
        and, 180
    new drills for, 167–68
    space and, 249
    surveillance balloons and, 252
    Taiwan and, 147, 149, 151, 157, 166, 179,
        293–94
perestroika, 101
permanent war, 40
phosphorous weapons, 201
Pi Shih-Chuan, 19, 149, 320–21
Poland, Putin's demands regarding, 10
Pompeo, Mike, xii
"porcupine" strategy, 160–62, 294
Poseidon torpedoes, 232, 254
Pottinger, Matthew
    on accommodationists, 313
    on China, 76, 80, 188–89
    on constrainment, 313–14

on deterrence, 293
on impact of Iraq and Afghanistan
    wars, 48
on nuclear threat, 214
on Putin and NATO, 142
on Putin and Xi, 64, 72–73, 75, 182–83
strategic ambiguity and, 295
on Trump, 261, 269–70
preventive strikes, 205–6
Prigozhin, Yevgeny, 68, 221
proxy wars, 41, 50, 53–54, 65–66
Putin, Vladimir. *See also* Russia
    annexation of territory by, 139–40
    assassination fears of, 5
    assessment of strategy of, 30, 40,
        75–76, 317–18
    Baltic States and, 124, 126–27
    containment and, 314
    demands from, 10–11, 25, 38
    diplomatic "off-ramp" for, 25–26
    Finland and, 11, 13
    frozen conflict and, 35
    grain deal and, 306
    Kim Jong Un and, 90–91
    land-for-peace formula and, 289
    Macron and, 25–26
    manufactured history of, 12–14, 69–70
    Modi and, 212
    NATO and, 59, 115, 120, 142, 143
    New START Treaty and, 215–18
    nuclear weapons and, 198, 199, 200,
        205–6, 208, 210, 212, 214, 215–16,
        223–24, 254
    Prigozhin and, 221
    Russian election interference and,
        271–73
    Russia's invasion of Ukraine and,
        4–5, 8, 9, 21
    Russia's invasion of Ukraine and,
        57, 153
    "true believer" theory regarding, 13
    Trump and, 259, 260–61, 262, 270, 271
    Ukrainian counteroffensives and,
        36, 37
    US human intelligence and, 234
    view of United States of, 275

Putin, Vladimir (*cont.*)
  West's support of Ukraine and, 180
  Xi and, 63–70, 170, 172, 174
"Putin's Ukraine Invasion" (Erickson
  and Collins), 81
Pyatt, Geoffrey, 139–40

Qin Gang, 71–72
Quigley, Mike, 35, 36, 40, 42, 44, 47

RAM (rolling airframe missile), 110
Ramstein Air Base meeting, 287
Reagan, Ronald, 222
Reaper drones, 106
Reciprocal Access Agreement, 93
red lines, 78–79, 155, 281
René (helicopter squadron
  commander), 106, 107–8
Republic of China (ROC) Armed
  Forces, 153
Rodrigues Pedra, José, 105, 113, 115–16
Romania, 121, 132
Room Where It Happened, The
  (Bolton), 262
Rossiyskaya Gazeta, 67
Rubio, Marco, 227
Rudd, Kevin, 280–81
rules of engagement, competing, 107–9
Russia. *See also* Putin, Vladimir
  adaptations by, 45–46
  aggressive aircraft from, 105–7, 109
  annexation of territory by, 7–8, 10
  Arctic activities of, 232–33, 254
  Asia's response to invasion of
    Ukraine by, 94–95
  assessment of strategy of, 42, 75–76
  assessment of war effort and, 316–19
  Baltic States and, 125
  border between Finland and, 60
  challenges facing, 73, 76
  China and, 61–62, 63–70, 76–82,
    84–85, 95, 284
  civilian targets and, 117

  cyberspace/cyber warfare and, 245,
    302, 303
  damage to military forces of, 38–39
  democracy and, 312–13
  denial of invasion plans by, 24–25
  economic decoupling and, 95
  economy of, 76, 263
  election interference and, 271–72
  electronic warfare and, 45
  energy exports and, 307–8
  Estonia and, 126–32, 137–39, 142–43,
    145–46
  false flag operations and, 134–35,
    201–3
  Germany and, 119–20
  hacking by, 140–41
  Hamas and, 86–87
  human intelligence in, 251
  human losses in, 39
  invasion of Ukraine by, 3–6, 8–11,
    14–20, 21–24, 26–28, 55–56, 111, 220
  invasion of Ukraine by in 2014,
    139–40
  Iran and, 84–89
  losses experienced by, 30, 245–46
  military decision-making in, 45
  Moldova and, 132–36
  NATO and, 55–56, 61, 100–113, 115,
    117–20, 204–5, 280, 296–98
  navy of, 113–17
  New START Treaty and, 215–19
  North Korea and, 90–91
  nuclear weapons and, 197–214,
    220–24, 232–33, 254, 299–300
  penetration of communication
    networks of, 24
  perceived US decline and, 307
  Putinism and, 283–84
  retreats by, 32
  rules of engagement and, 107–9
  space weapons and, 247–48
  strategy shift by, 29
  submarine technology and, 80–82
  as threat, 10
  Trump and, 266
  Ukrainian counteroffensives and,
    30–36

unconventional weapons systems
and, 76
underwater operations and, 165
US human intelligence in, 234
US threat assessment regarding,
64–65, 73
weapons systems of, 43
West's response to invasion of
Ukraine by, 57–58
Xi in, 65
Russian Geographical Society, 12
Russian Historical Society, 12
Russian War History Association, 12
Russia's Nuclear Weapons
(CRS report), 200
Ryabkov, Sergei, 218
Ryder, Patrick, 226, 228, 230, 238, 253

SA-22 missile system, 87–88
sabotage operations, 31
Sachsen, FGS, 106
Sandu, Maia, 133–34, 136
SAR-MAT ballistic missiles, 217
"SATAN II" missiles, 217
satellites
commercial, 43–44
intelligence from, 227–28
interference between, 248–49
offensive, 250
Saudi Arabia, 219, 300
Scholz, Olaf, 212, 288
Sea Sparrow missiles, 104
Senate Armed Services Committee,
160–61
Shadow War, The (Sciutto), 71, 81, 114,
116, 139, 164, 179, 233, 250, 274, 279
Shanghai Cooperation Organization
Summit, 212
shock-and-awe campaign, 22
Shoigu, Sergei, 90, 201
shoulder-fired missile systems, 43
Skyfall cruise missiles, 254
Slotkin, Elissa, 238
Smartmatic, 274
social media, war in Ukraine on, 29

South China Sea
construction of islands in, 70–71
as disputed territory, 236
surveillance in, 240
territorial acquisition and, 304
US trilateral partnership and, 94
South Korea
as "middle power," 83
nuclear weapons and, 219
trilateral partnership and, 93–94
Trump and, 268–69
Soviet Union
collapse of, 64, 200
Cuban Missile Crisis and, 276–78
Estonia and, 137–39
Finland and, 9–10
space, 247–50, 301–3
SpaceX, 248
Spain, 321–23
Spratly Islands, 71
Stalin, Joseph, 45, 66, 72, 137
START Treaty, 215–17, 298
State Duma (Russia), 216
State Elders Room (Tallinn, Estonia), 138
Stavridis, James, 41, 42, 43–44, 284,
303, 304, 307, 314
Steinmeier, Frank-Walter, 119
Stinger missiles, 43, 85, 161
Stoltenberg, Jens
on arms control, 214–15, 298, 299, 300
on China, 62–63
on current global status, 279
on end of Cold War, xiii
on investment in defense, 47
on military supply chain, 49
on modern warfare, 28, 41, 44
on nuclear threat, 211
nuclear threat and, 222, 223–24
on overcoming antagonistic
relationships, 314
on Putin, 38
Trump and, 264, 270
Storm Shadow cruise missiles, 57
Strandman, Otto August, 138
strategic ambiguity, 183, 184–85, 295–96
Strategic Arms Reduction Treaty
(START I), 222

Su-30 fighter jets, 164
submarine technology, 80–82, 89,
    91–92, 115, 232–33
submarine warfare, 112, 114, 117
Sukhoi Su-27 fighters, 103, 123
Sullivan, Dan, 252–53
Sullivan, Jake, 48–49, 77–78
Sun Tzu, 20, 179, 319–20
Sunak, Rishi, 93
SVR (Russia), 273
Sweden, NATO and, 38, 58–59, 204–5,
    297, 298
Swedish Air Force, 110
Switchblade drones, 162
Syria, 79, 87, 89

Taiwan
  air defense identification zone and,
    149, 164, 168
  authoritarian past of, 176–77
  China's strategy regarding, 6, 165–70,
    174, 178–79
  deterrence and, 181–82, 292–96
  disruption of supply chain and, 167
  "gray zone" warfare in, 164–67
  lessons learned from Ukraine and,
    150, 159–60, 180–82, 192
  microchips and, 308
  military preparedness and, 147–49
  opposition to Chinese military
    action against, 94
  "porcupine" strategy and, 160–62
  potential for invasion of, 150–53,
    156–59, 319–20
  Russia's invasion of Ukraine and,
    19–20
  self-defense of, 192–93
  trade with China and, 175–76
  Trump and, 268
  United States and, 183–88, 190–92
  Xi Jinping and, 76, 171–72, 193–94
Taiwan Relations Act (TRA; 1979),
    183–84
Taiwan Strait, 147, 154–55, 156, 159
Taliban, 282, 288–89

Tan Kefei, 229
Teemant, Jaan, 138
Telegram, 251
Tenth Corps, Ukrainian Army, 35
theater ballistic missile defense, 117
Thomas-Greenfield, Linda, 79
Thucydides Trap, 51
Tōnisson, Jaan, 138
"track two" communications,
    172–73
Tracy, Lynne, 221
treaties, absence of, 279
Treaty on the Non- Proliferation of
    Nuclear Weapons, 301
trench warfare, 28, 41
tripwire posture, 125, 130–32
Trump, Donald
  admiration of for dictators,
    259–62
  admiration of for Hitler, 258–59, 263
  assessments of, 256–57, 259–61
  disgust for wounded veterans
    from, 267
  election interference and, 273
  expectations of potential second
    term for, 267–68, 270–71, 319
  INF treaty and, 214
  Iran and, 265–66
  lack of understanding of government
    and, 266–67
  NATO and, 260–61, 263–65, 266–67,
    268–69, 270–71, 318
  Russian election interference and,
    271–75
  as wild card, 255
Truss, Liz, 24
Tsai Ing-Wen, 152–53
Tuchman, Barbara, 276–77
Turkey, 59, 300, 307
Twain, Mark, 51

U-2 spy plane, 277
UAVs (uninhabited aerial vehicles), 106,
    115–16, 123. See also drones
Uighurs, detention of, 70, 169, 262–63

Ukraine. *See also* Zelensky, Volodymyr
    adaptations by, 45–46
    ammunition and, 47–48
    Asian support for, 93
    Asia's response to Russia's invasion
      of, 94–95
    assessment of strategy of, 40–42
    assessment of war effort in, 316–17, 319
    China's lessons learned from, 180–82
    China's support for Russia and,
      76–80
    "combined forces" operations
      and, 148
    counteroffensives by, 30–36, 221
    cyber warfare and, 245
    defense capabilities of, 27
    Estonia and, 126
    European Union and, 136
    expanded military of, 39–40
    false flag operations and, 201–2
    grain deal and, 306
    heavy collective defense approach
      and, 49–50
    human losses in, 39
    importance of victory in, 286–92
    innovation of, 44
    intelligence successes regarding,
      234–35
    Iran's support for Russia's invasion
      of, 84
    Israel's response to Russia's invasion
      of, 88
    Japanese prime minister in, 66
    land-for-peace formula and, 289–91
    lead-up to war in, 15–16, 17–18
    NATO and, 38, 40, 115, 120, 271, 280,
      290–92
    North Korea's response to Russia's
      invasion of, 90–91
    nuclear threat and, 198–99, 207, 213
    potential for escalation of war in, 53
    Putin's rewriting of history
      regarding, 12–14
    Russia's 2014 invasion of, 139–40
    Russia's invasion of, 3–6, 8–11, 14–20,
      21–24, 26–28, 55–56, 111, 220
    self-defense of, 187

Taiwan's lessons learned from, 150,
    159–60, 192
    Trump and, 268
    weapons systems of, 42–43
    West's support of, 57–58, 180
Ukrainian Ministry of Foreign
    Affairs, 22
Ukrainian national police, 22
UN Charter, 303
UN Convention on the Law of the
    Sea, 303
UN General Assembly, 212
UN Security Council, 213
unconventional weapons systems, 76
underwater operations, 114, 116–17, 165
unintended conflict, 123–24, 242
United Kingdom
    AUKUS agreement and, 312
    Australia and, 91
    Global Combat Air Programme and,
      92–93
    Japan and, 92–93
    Ministry of Defence of, 8
United States
    ammunition and, 47–48
    AUKUS agreement and, 312
    Australia and, 91–92
    on China's support for Russia's
      invasion of Ukraine, 78–80
    China's surveillance balloons in,
      225–31, 236, 237–44, 252–53
    declassification of intelligence by,
      134–35
    domestic politics in, 308–11
    expansion of NATO and, 59
    Iraq and Afghanistan wars and, 48
    Israel-Hamas war and, 88–89
    Japan and South Korea and, 93–94
    New START Treaty and, 216–19
    nuclear weapons and, 205–8,
      220–21, 299
    One China policy and, 183, 184–85,
      188
    perception of decline of, 307
    potential Chinese attack on, 188–89
    potential for invasion of Taiwan and,
      156–59

United States (*cont.*)
  presidential election in, 140,
    271–75, 319
  Putin's article and, 68
  strategic ambiguity and, 295–96
  Taiwan and, 160–63, 166, 183–88,
    190–92, 295–96
  trade with China and, 263, 283
  trilateral partnership and, 93–94
  Ukraine and, 280
  US troops in, 294
  war in Ukraine and, 31–32, 35, 36
  weapons sales to Taiwan from, 294
  Xi Jinping and, 70–73, 178–79
unmanned technology. *See also* drones;
    UAVs (uninhabited aerial vehicles)
  Black Sea Fleet and, 50
  China's spy balloons, 225–31
  impact of, 42–44
  underwater operations and, 114, 116,
    122–23
US Central Command, 106
US House Armed Services Committee,
    243–44
US House Intelligence Committee, 198
US House Select Committee on China,
    165–66
US Indo-Pacific Command, 155
US Northern Command
    (NORTHCOM), 244

VanHerck, Glen, 244
variable geometry, 306–7
victory gardens, 17
Vietnam War, 52–53, 258
Vilnius Summit Communiqué, 290–91
Vostochny Cosmodrome, 90
voting systems, 234

Wagner Group, 68, 87, 221
Wall Street Journal, The, 92, 294
Walsh, Nick Paton, 32

Wang Wenbin, 78, 240
Wang Yi, 79, 239, 241–43
Watson, Adrienne, 90
weapons of mass destruction (WMD)
    program, 8, 17, 23
weapons systems. *See also* nuclear
    weapons
  adjustments to, 162–63
  asymmetrical, 161–62, 293–94
  of NATO forces, 110
  nonconventional, 201
  of Russia, 43
  of Ukraine, 42–43
  unconventional, 76
"White Terror," 177
Wicker, Roger, 160–61
Wolfsthal, Jon, 218–19
World Food Programme, 305
Wu, Joseph, 151, 186–87

Xi Jinping. *See also* China
  challenges facing, 75
  China's strategy regarding Taiwan
    and, 165–66, 168–72, 174, 193–94
  Chinese Dream and, 177–78
  communications and, 172–73
  consolidation of power by, 74
  deterrence and, 293
  intelligence successes regarding, 235
  lessons learned from Ukraine and,
    180–82
  nuclear threat and, 212
  Putin and, 63–70, 170, 172, 174
  "reunification" and, 6
  in Russia, 65
  South China Sea islands and, 70–71
  surveillance balloons and, 252, 253
  Taiwan and, 152, 155–56, 161, 166
  timeline for, 183
  trade and, 175–76
  Trump and, 259, 261, 262–63
  US view of, 178–79, 275
  US-China relations and, 242
  views of West and, 70–73

Y-8 anti-submarine warplanes, 164
Yana, 14–18, 321–23
Yeltsin, Boris, 63
Yemen, 89
Yoon Suk Yeol, 94

Zakaria, Fareed, 34, 36
Zakharova, Maria, 135
Zelensky, Volodymyr. *See also* Ukraine
    assessment of war in Ukraine by, 36
    European Union and, 136

India and, 212
Israel and, 88
Japanese prime minister
    and, 66
leadership of, 245
lead-up to war and, 16–17, 18, 24
Moldova and, 133, 134
NATO and, 291
on progress of war, 49
Ukrainian counteroffensives and, 32,
    33, 34, 36
zero-Covid policy, 169–70, 176
Zucker, Jeff, 6–7

ABOUT THE AUTHOR

Jim Sciutto is CNN's chief national security correspondent and anchor of *CNN Newsroom*, airing Monday through Friday mornings. He reports and provides analysis across the network's programs and platforms on all aspects of US national security, including foreign policy, the military, the intelligence community, and the State Department. He has reported from more than fifty countries across the globe, including dozens of assignments from inside Iraq, Afghanistan, and Iran. Among the honors Sciutto's work has earned are Emmy Awards, the Edward R. Murrow Award, the George Polk Award, and the White House Correspondents' Association's Merriman Smith Award for excellence in presidential coverage. Sciutto is the bestselling author of *The Shadow War.*